This book is a study of the importance and significance of community identity to a fighting unit in the First World War. In this case the unit in question is primarily 7th King's Regiment and more widely the 55th West Lancashire Division, 1914–18. The book is based upon the author's own PhD thesis "The 1/7th Battalion King's Liverpool Regiment and the Great War – the experience of a Territorial battalion and its Home Towns". It is an analysis of the relevance of the local communities to the battalion and its division and its combat effectiveness; the role played by the army in the local communities' involvement in the War; and the post-War ramifications of this relationship. In focusing on 1/7th Battalion Kings Liverpool Regiment, a Territorial battalion based in Bootle, Southport and the surrounding area of south west Lancashire, the thesis follows a typical Territorial unit and its home towns from recruitment and establishment to demobilisation and beyond. A wide range of primary sources have been examined including local newspapers, local Council records, official War Diaries of the various units, battle reports and private papers of several of the combatants in an extensive compilation of research. New perspectives are presented on several aspects of the First World War including the Lusitania riots; the battles of Festubert, 1915, and Givenchy, 1918; and the role of charities in post-War reconstruction work. It also raises general issues about the role of the Territorial Force and draws attention to several gaps in the social and military historiography of the War. The conclusion of the book is that local and community identity contributed significantly towards the 1/7th Kings' morale, organisation and hence battle effectiveness. This contribution initially stemmed from the local recruits themselves but was actively nurtured and encouraged by commanders at Battalion, Brigade and Divisional level throughout the War. It also establishes that by putting the local Battalion at the centre of its concerns, the rather disparate communities were able to organise, coalesce and maximise their War effort and support. Finally, it demonstrates in the post-War years, that, despite the fluctuations in this mutually important relationship, the local identification with the Battalion was maintained in memorialisation, remembrance and reconstruction.

Adrian Gregson grew up on the Fylde coast in Lancashire and then studied firstly History and then Archives at Leicester and Liverpool Universities. His PhD thesis "The 1/7th Battalion King's Liverpool Regiment and the Great War – the experience of a Territorial battalion and its Home Towns" was awarded in 2004 from the University of Worcester (Coventry). Adrian is also a local politician, twice being elected Leader of Worcester City Council. Adrian has written articles on the 55th West Lancashire Division and also on the British League of Help for Devastated Areas of France. He is currently Archives Policy and Collections Manager for Worcestershire Archive and Archaeology Service, and Worcester Diocesan Archivist, based at the Hive in Worcester. In 2014 he co-authored the book *Worcestershire's War*, with Dr Maggie Andrews and Dr John Peters, Amberley Publishing 2014. Adrian contributed a chapter to the 2015 volume *Courage without Glory: The British Army on the Western Front 1915*, edited by Spencer Jones, Helion 2015. From 2013–2019 Adrian is Project Manager for the Heritage Lottery Funded Project Worcestershire World War One Hundred www.ww1worcestershire.co.uk. This is his first book.

FROM DOCKS AND SAND

Southport and Bootle's Battalion, the 7th King's Liverpool Regiment, in the First World War

---

Adrian Gregson

Helion & Company Limited

Helion & Company Limited
26 Willow Road
Solihull
West Midlands
B91 1UE
England
Tel. 0121 705 3393
Fax 0121 711 4075
Email: info@helion.co.uk
Website: www.helion.co.uk
Twitter: @helionbooks
Visit our blog http://blog.helion.co.uk/

Published by Helion & Company 2018
Designed and typeset by Mach 3 Solutions Ltd (www.mach3solutions.co.uk)
Cover designed by Paul Hewitt, Battlefield Design (www.battlefield-design.co.uk)
Printed by Lightning Source Limited, Milton Keynes, Buckinghamshire

Front cover: A Kingsman outside the Bootle Barracks of 7th Liverpool's.
(Courtesy: Philip Haythornthwaite) Rear cover: Ration party of 1/7th Battalion,
King's Liverpool Regiment in the front line trenches, 15 March 1918. (IWM ref. Q10743)

ISBN 978-1-911512-16-5

British Library Cataloguing-in-Publication Data.
A catalogue record for this book is available from the British Library.

For details of other military history titles published by Helion & Company Limited contact the above address, or visit our website: http://www.helion.co.uk.

We always welcome receiving book proposals from prospective authors.

Contents

List of Illustrations

List of Maps

List of Charts

List of Tables

Acknowledgements

Thanks are due to the following people, in no specific order, for their advice, guidance, assistance and tolerance, through my PhD and into this volume: John Peters, John Wilson, Peter Simkins, Frank Crompton, Joy Squires, Simon Jones of the King's Gallery, Liverpool, Diana Spalton, Pam Hall, Garry Atterton, Pete Threlfall, Eric Greaves, Mr. R Haviland, Mr. J Blakeley, Louise Douglas of the *Southport Visiter*, Janet and Robert Gregson, Richard Halsall, the Earl Derby, Lynne Stanley, Eleanor Ratcliffe, Marion Franklin, Cyril Pearce, Catherine Hemelryk, Mrs. A Teale, Mr. A F Atkinson, Mr. K. Baldwin, Major A S G. Dymond, M Claude Lefebre, M Jean-Luc Gibot, Mr. R Rymer, Jill Baldwin, Jean North, Lucy Balcombe, Paul Griffith, Laurie Gregory, Rachel Hall, Roy Buckland, Peter Fennell, Alan and Adele Coles, the staff at Southport and Crosby Libraries (Sefton Borough Council), and staff at Liverpool Record Office, Lancashire Record Office, the Imperial War Museum, the National Army Museum, the Liddle Collection, the Public Record Office, the British Library at Colindale, John France at Worcestershire Archive Digital Services, Nick Mansfield, Dil Porter, Duncan Rogers and Dr Michael LoCicero at Helion & Company and my grandma, Dorothy Gregson, née Greaves. Their input has made the work richer – what errors remain are, I am afraid, my own.

Foreword

Armies do not exist in a vacuum. They represent and reflect the nature of the society from which they spring. The British army in the First World War was no exception. Some 5,704,000 men and women passed through its ranks, making it the biggest army in the country's history and the largest and most complex single organisation created by the British nation up to that time. However, be they volunteers or conscripts, the vast majority of its members were *not* professional soldiers but basically civilians in uniform, who took with them into the army the attitudes, beliefs and popular culture of their civilian lives. For those serving in the British Expeditionary Force (BEF) in France and Belgium, the continuity of such cultural links was facilitated and ensured by the proximity of the British sector of the Western Front to the Channel Ports and families at home.

Thanks, moreover, to factors such as the increase in regular and frequent postal services, the widening of elementary and secondary education, the rise of mass circulation newspapers and the existence of a powerful local press, the men of the BEF, as well as their families at home, were generally more literate, and therefore better informed, than ever before. Even allowing for the effects of official censorship on both sides of the Channel, there was a constant and prodigious flow of communications and information between the Western Front and the home front, principally – though not exclusively – through letters. The preservation of much of this correspondence in private collections and public archives has left us a rich legacy of evidence which has helped historians, a century later, to piece together a multi-faceted and more accurate than hitherto of what actually made the BEF 'tick', and the extent to which the fighting and the home fronts interacted. There were, of course, major differences between the experiences of those in France and those in the UK. Nevertheless, the widely-accepted and persistent belief that there was an almost unbridgeable gulf between the men at the front and the people at home has recently been seriously questioned by historians such as John Bourne, J G Fuller and Helen McCartney, and is further challenged by Adrian Gregson in this new and fascinating study. Indeed, the trend of recent research has been to bring into sharper focus just how much popular culture imported from Britain – in addition to the receipt of newspapers from home and exchanges of letters – not only enhanced the morale of the BEF but contributed to its remarkable resilience after costly battles and periodic defensive crises.

During the huge and unprecedented expansion of the British army from 1914 to 1916, some 643 out of 994 new infantry battalions formed were initially raised mainly by local effort. Existing Territorial Force (TF) units likewise had strong local links. This meant that many fighting units were closely identified, at least in the beginning, with particular cities and towns, industrial communities or rural recruiting areas at home. It was this that gave the BEF in France, certainly until mid to late 1916, its distinct and highly-localised character. In her important book *Citizen Soldiers*, which looks in depth at the experience of two Territorial battalions – the Liverpool Rifles and Liverpool Scottish – Helen McCartney examines in detail the ties between the troops of these mainly middle-class units and the communities from which they emerged. She contends that, far from being passive victims of the conflict, the officers and men of these battalions largely retained their civilian outlook throughout the war and used it to modify and influence their experiences in the front line. The maintenance of such close personal ties with home buttressed their morale to an appreciable extent. It seems clear that the cumulative effects of battle casualties, conscription and changes in the reserve and drafting system inevitably and progressively eroded this marked local character of units from late 1915 onwards, and McCartney argues persuasively that the authorities consciously strove to preserve at least a strong county or regional identity in these units up to the Armistice. This argument is echoed and reinforced by Adrian Gregson in his work on the 1/7th King's (Liverpool Regiment).

The past three or four decades have seen a proliferation of books on local Pals battalions raised for Kitchener's New Armies in 1914-1915. These include, among others, studies of Pals units from Accrington, Barnsley, Birkenhead, Birmingham, Bradford, Durham, Edinburgh, Halifax, Hull, Kensington, Leeds, Manchester, Oldham, Salford, Sheffield and Tyneside. Local Territorial battalions too have been given their share of attention, as in K W Mitchinson's study of the London Rifle Brigade, Jill Knight's book on the Civil Service Rifles, Alec Weir's work on the 9th Highland Light Infantry and Derek Bird's study of the 6th Seaforth Highlanders. Yet it is the Liverpool-based battalions that have probably the most concentrated scrutiny in recent decades. The publication in 1991 of Graham Maddocks' book on the four Liverpool Pals battalions – the 17th, 18th, 19th and 20th King's (Liverpool Regiment) – was followed in 2005 by Helen McCartney's acclaimed study of the Liverpool Rifles and Liverpool Scottish. Eight years later, in 2013, Joe Devereux produced a detailed analysis of the residential, occupational and social backgrounds of the officers and men of the Liverpool Pals who fell on the Somme on 1 July 1916. Many of the works mentioned above contain an introductory chapter on social, industrial and commercial conditions in the towns and cities where their local Territorial and New Army battalions were raised, but most then devote the bulk of their chapters to the battle experiences of their respective units rather than the interaction of the fighting and home fronts. It is precisely in this latter area that the work by Helen McCartney – and here by Adrian Gregson – has made a particularly distinctive and useful contribution.

It should similarly be re-emphasised that the battalions studied by Maddocks, McCartney and Devereux were predominantly drawn, at least initially, from men of middle class origins, or who worked in the commercial and clerical sectors in civilian life. On the other hand, the 1/7th King's – the battalion examined in detail by Dr Gregson – contained not only lower middle class recruits and artisans from the Southport area but also a substantial working class element from the dockland district of Bootle. This combination gave the unit a character which differed from that of many other Liverpool Territorial and New Army battalions and which makes Dr Gregson's analysis and conclusions all the more fascinating and useful.

A second aspect of Adrian Gregson's book is his examination of how, and to what extent, his case-study battalion was part of, or added to, the identifiable 'learning process' whereby the BEF sought and wrought such improvements in its organisation, logistics, command, technology and tactics as enabled it to play a key role in the ultimate Allied victory. Gregson helpfully assesses the degree to which the 1/7th King's – both as part of the 55th (West Lancashire) Division and as a component of the BEF as a whole – may have had a positive input in that process.

The 55th Division was fortunate to be commanded, from 3 January 1916, by Major-General Hugh Jeudwine, whose tactical ability, thorough planning and insistence on high levels of morale and discipline were all major elements in the division's successes in battle, especially in the outstanding defence of Givenchy during the German Lys offensive of April 1918. While acknowledging and illustrating the GOC's impact on the formation, Gregson shows, in addition, how Jeudwine deliberately cultivated and developed a distinctive Lancashire identity for the division, which was maintained even if the original local character of battalions such as the 1/7th King's were subject to some dilution as the war went on.

An extra strand to be followed in this admirable book is the degree to which, in practice, tactical command devolved downwards to divisional, brigade and even battalion level from late 1916. The fact that Jeudwine was able to exert a considerable personal influence on the division's combat performance, as well as nurturing and maintaining the formation's county and regional identity, appears to support the growing consensus among historians of the BEF that the latter's 'middle management' could, and often did, play a more important part in the learning process, and on the progress towards eventual victory, than might previously have been supposed.

Finally, the author looks at the way in which the effort and sacrifice of the 1/7th King's was remembered and publicly marked – and its community links upheld – in the years after the Armistice. In researching and presenting such a multi-dimensional study of an individual Merseyside battalion, and in setting that battalion's experiences squarely within the story of its parent division, the author has surely made a significant and weighty contribution to our collective knowledge of the British army and society in the Great War.

Professor Peter Simkins
January 2018

Introduction
Why the 7th Battalion King's Liverpool Regiment?

In the hundred years that has passed since 1/7th Battalion King's Liverpool Regiment left the south coast of England bound for France in a ship like a cattle truck we have learned a lot about the Great European, or subsequently, First World War. Research, oral testimonies, publications, articles, volumes have analysed not only the tactics and details of battles but also the War objectives, the planning, the politics; the society, the economy, the involvement of women; the legacies, the memorials, the remembrances, the charities. We have analysed official War Diaries and private letters; scrutinised photographs, calculated casualty figures. We have criticised individuals and units and then revised theories and assertions. And we have tried to apply that education, learning and experience to our current age, how it influenced future conflicts, how even now boundaries drawn with a ruler in a map book have implications for world peace. Undoubtedly the fascination remains. Perhaps because of the last of the veterans' passing, the War has moved into 'proper' history, yet ironically the centennial appears to have provoked much more by way of thought, discussion and debate.

This volume adds to that debate and its relevance can be seen in a number of areas, of more below. But one of the key things that has occurred since the last veteran died, is that the direct link with that age has been nearly entirely severed. Nearly because, statistically, there may be brothers and sisters of soldiers still with us. Nearly because there are children of men and women who fought who may have been told things. Nearly because there is still such a wealth of untapped information out there, in people's attics and cellars, let alone the official records in archives and libraries across the world. And nearly because down most High Streets in the country there is a wreath of red poppies placed every November time which, despite many more battles and deaths, still harks back to that First World War.

Finally, nearly because the breadth of the events, the length of the war and the changes in society that were put in train by it or alongside it mean that everyone can justifiably say they have been touched by it. Even if it is an argument about when the pub you are in should call last orders at the bar.

This volume is based on research which began many years ago simply as something to talk to my Grandma about. Her brother was killed in 1918 when she was just 15. They had been very close but once he had enlisted in August 1914 she saw him only twice more, on home leave. She described her father making him strip in the yard before entering the house with his lousy uniform. And she told me the only time she saw her own father drunk was at the end of the War when Erlam Greaves did not come home and he was shouting "Where's my boy?"

That is an experience shared by many families and is one of those shared memories that we have of the War. It led me into family research but then deeper into where he was when he was killed. When did he join up? Who his mates were – a family story told of one of his friends seeing him killed and spending the rest of his life living close by in the village of Freshfield near Southport. Look through the acknowledgements and dedications of virtually any book about the First World War and the author has a link that started their interest and research. And maybe some of us want to commit that legacy to paper, as part of our own act of remembrance.

Thomas Erlam Greaves was born in 1896 in Kirkdale, north Liverpool. His father, Richard, was a foreman on the railway but after promotion to Inspector the family moved to the more prosperous Freshfield in Formby. His mother died when he was young but he had two sisters – Hilda and Dorothy. Thomas, or Erlam as he was known, got a job on the Gladstone docks working as an insurance clerk and took the train to Bootle every day.

When war came Erlam Greaves enlisted early in August 1914 as Private 2177, later 265482. Comparisons with other regimental numbers and their known dates of enlistment place him alongside some of his friends – Frank Evans, Peter Ackers, Bobby Balshaw, Henry Brooks, Sidney Beardwood. When he died in 1918, his mate Richard Dickinson, 265481, a neighbour in Old Mill Lane, was killed the same day. The War Diary platoon level reports at Givenchy April 1918 give a real opportunity to piece together this band of brothers. In A Company under Captain Leach, were Lovelady and Evans, both contemporaries of Erlam. Captain Cook still led C Company. D Company were in Barnton Trench while A Company were the other front post, at Prince's Island and George Street. Support companies, B and C were at Le Plantin North and South. Erlam was in A Company, right front when he was killed early on 9th April 1918. He and Corporal Lovelady, Richard Dickinson, Beardwood, Mawdesley, Jackson and Sergeant Lowes are all on the Formby War Memorial.

(Thomas) Erlam Greaves, aged 18. (Author's collection)

They lived together, trained together, went away to France, fought, and died together. This volume is a study of what it meant to be in 1/7th King's Liverpool, the Iron Regiment, the crack regiment from the big city down the coast, and the transformation of the Territorial Army into a regular force which eventually won the War.

This battalion, and its sister second line battalion, saw action across the Western Front, once the bulk of the Territorial troops landed in France after the old British Expeditionary Force held on in tatters, through the first winter of the war. The analysis of their social composition and background is followed by a review of their experience in training and then their arrival in France and early engagement in the Battle of Festubert in May 1915. A version of this chapter on Festubert has previously been published in *Courage without Glory: The British Army on the Western Front 1915*. That volume also contains one of only very few analyses of the battle.[1]

In January 1916, this battalion and the other territorials of the West Lancashire area were reunited in what had been their pre-War formation, the 55th Division. When the second lines arrived in France they also formed the second line Division, the 57th. The study reviews their operations through the battles on the Somme, at Ypres, on the defensive at Givenchy in spring 1918, and then in the Final Advance as the Allies secured a victory that November. The study is more than simply a review of their actions but an analysis of tactics and strategies in defence and attack. Key issues of morale and discipline are investigated and in particular the emphasis on the locality and home of the Lancashire Division.

Major General Jeudwine a sceptical Regular Officer who became an ardent supporter of the Territorials during and after the War, placed a lot of emphasis on the importance of the red rose county division he led. He was also a disciplined tactician and we are fortunate that his notes survive in Liverpool City Record Office and the Imperial War Museum, as well as his comments on the drafts of the Official History as it was being written.

Jeudwine was an artilleryman and was a Staff Officer through the South African War and afterwards. He worked under Haig in I Corps in 1914 and was promoted first to V Corps staff, and then to command 41st Brigade. He was appointed to command the newly reformed 55th Division at the start of 1916. At the Armistice he became a Commander of the British Army on the Rhine before being posted back to Ireland until July 1922. He was subsequently made Director General of the Territorial Army and he reportedly used this position to 'do everything possible for the efficiency and well-being of the citizen soldier, for none knew better than he the military value of the Territorial'.[2] On his appointment to the post, he said: 'I revere the Territorial most deeply and I have always found him a thoroughly worthy, creditable and brilliant exponent of all the best principles of the British Army and of the character of the British soldier.'[3]

Other key source material comes from the men of the 1/7th King's itself: four main sets of personal testimony survive relating to the Battalion – Marriott, Critchley, Cook

1 Jones, Spencer (ed.), *Courage Without Glory: The British Army on the Western Front 1915* (Solihull: Helion & Company, 2015).
2 Obituary Lieut. General Sir Hugh Sandham Jeudwine, *The Times*, 3 December 1942, p. 10.
3 Liverpool City Local Studies Library and Record Office (LCRO): 356 COU 1 Jeudwine remarks, November 1923: Council of County Territorial Associations Minutes 1922–1933.

and Fearnhead. The papers of Sydney Marriott consist of letters home to his wife, father, brother and other family members.[4] Marriott started the War as a pre-War Territorial officer, a company commander. By the end of 1915, he was in command of the Battalion and remained until the middle of the battles of the Somme when he was sent home on medical grounds for a rest. When he returned to France it was with the 11th Battalion, Manchester Regiment. His letters provide a unique insight to some of the politics of the Battalion, as well as the action and life on the Front. He was married to Cicely, sister of a brother officer, and was a native of Southport. Copies of his letters are held by the Regimental Museum in Liverpool, but originals and other material including a set of photographs are in the Liddle Collection. Some of his photographs have been published.[5]

Arthur Critchley was interviewed in 1982 and a copy of this interview has also been used as a source.[6] Critchley enlisted as a 17 year old in 1913 because he thought it was a good way into boxing. He was discharged in 1920, having volunteered to join a composite Battalion going to Russia evacuating the British forces from Archangel. He was awarded the Military Medal but was also disciplined on more than one occasion, once for hitting an officer.

Private correspondence, for access to which the author is indebted, has provided important additional source material. Captain James Watson Cook MC and bar, from a solicitors' family in Southport, wrote home of his experiences in 1/7th King's.[7] As Private Cook No. 2388, he served in 8 Platoon, B Company and later in the Lewis Gun Section, until he returned to England for his commission in September 1916.

Private Jack Fearnhead No. 2390 served in A Company.[8] He missed the first draft out to France in March 1915 due to an injury sustained in training at Blackpool. He spent time in 2/7th Battalion and secured his commission with 3/7th before going to France at the end of May 1916 to join 1/7th Battalion. Unfortunately he was killed on 13th August at Guillemont. One of the *Battleground Europe* series on First World War Battlefield sites is dedicated to Fearnhead.[9]

One other publication touches closely on the story and is referenced at length: Tilsley's *Other Ranks* deserves special mention as one of the most relevant of the 'faction' autobiographies which were prevalent in the 1920s and 1930s.[10] Tilsley told the

4 1984.321 War diary of Sydney Marriott 1/7th Battalion King's Liverpool Regiment, King's Regiment Collection, Museum of Liverpool Life, National Galleries on Merseyside: also at the Liddle Collection, Brotherton Library, University of Leeds – hereafter 'Marriott'.

5 Liddle, Peter, *The Worst Ordeal: Britons at Home and Abroad 1914–1918* (London: Leo Cooper, 1994), pp. 49–52.

6 King's Regiment Collection, Museum of Liverpool Life, National Museums and Galleries on Merseyside: 1982.250 Photocopy of diary of Arthur Critchley MM – hereafter 'Critchley'.

7 Access to Cook's letters home was provided by his daughter, Mrs Diana Spalton.

8 Access to Fearnhead's letters home was provided by Pam Hall.

9 Stedman, Michael, *Somme – Guillemont: Battleground Europe Series* (London: Leo Cooper 1998), pp. 5, 26, 27, 82.

10 Tilsley, W.V., *Other ranks* (London: Cobden Sanderson, 1931).

story of his involvement in the 1/4th Battalion Loyal North Lancashire which was in 164th Brigade, 55th Division. Consequently, a lot of his comments, narrative and perspective were common with comrades across the Division, such as 1/7th King's. Mottram's *Spanish Farm Trilogy* is also of some considerable assistance as the Territorial Division at its heart spent a great deal of time in the Lys battlefield area, the 'Spanish Farm' being somewhere close to Hazebrouck and Armentiéres.[11] The little-known diary of the autumn of 1917, *The Winding Road Unfolds*, is surely about life in a Liverpool Battalion in 55th Division, probably 1/10th (Scottish) Battalion, and contains references to the attack on 20th September and also the rout at Cambrai.[12] There are also passing references in the writings of both Graves and Sassoon to their time at Litherland camp and the Formby golf range.[13]

Second Lieutenant Jack Fearnhead. (Courtesy Pam Hall)

There are a number of references to the *Official History* because it is the established narrative of the War, sanctioned and funded as the official record. In relation to the operations of 1/7th King's, however, some of the key aspects of their combat experience have not received much treatment by the official historians. It is also largely accepted that the earlier published volumes have more accuracy than the later ones and it is worth noting that Jeudwine was a personal friend of Sir James Edmonds, the key figure in the process of compiling the 'Official Histories' whom Griffith calls unstable, devious and opinionated.[14] Griffith asserted that Jeudwine and the 55th Division had a good press, despite the Cambrai affair, however, both Travers and Winter refer to the inaccuracies in the Cambrai volume and those covering the Spring Offensive.[15] Jeudwine went to a great deal of trouble to try to secure an accurate version of events at Cambrai.[16] Winter

11 Mottram, R.H., *The Spanish Farm Trilogy 1914–1918* (London: Penguin, 1979 first published 1927).
12 Hope, T.S., *The Winding Road Unfolds* (London: Putnam, 1937).
13 Graves, Robert, *Goodbye to all That* (London: Penguin, 1960, first published 1929) pp. 169–170; Sassoon, Siegfried, *The Complete Memoirs of George Sherston* (London: Faber and Faber, 1972, first published 1937) p. 383.
14 Griffith, P., *Battle Tactics of the Western Front: The British Army's Art of Attack 1916–18* (New Haven: Yale University Press, 1994), p.258
15 Griffith, *Battle Tactics of the Western Front*, pp.80-81; Travers, T. *The Killing Ground: The British Army, the Western Front and the Emergence of Modern Warfare 1900-1918* (Oxford: Routledge, 1992), p.205; Winter, D., *Haig's Command*, (London: Viking, 1991), pp.125-127, 188.
16 LCRO: 356 FIF 44-57 Jeudwine MSS.

perhaps goes too far in calling the Official History 'fraudulent';[17] Griffith was more temperate in calling it 'idiosyncratic'.[18] More recent academic research has, however, countered this view of Edmonds and his work.[19] With reference to the kind of criticism Griffith levelled against Edmonds' critique of Jeudwine's Division, Green believed that despite loyalty to friends and colleagues it was rare for the 'personal pleas of high-ranking officers' to override his intention of maintaining 'literary and academic integrity.'[20]

With such reliance on local newspapers a word must be said about their veracity and motives. Newspapers or perhaps more accurately, reporting, flourished during the First World War, maintaining the link between Home and Front. It has been widely argued that the British public was kept in the dark – increasingly by mutual collaboration between the military and the Press – over what was really happening overseas.[21] Despite this, the newspapers were keen to print practically anything in the early years to report what was happening. Equally, the public had a voracious appetite for news. This was seen most in the local papers, as they followed the progress of local battalions and the sons of the town.[22] Those studied were no exception, although it should be noted that studies of the role of local newspapers have been sparse, notwithstanding local studies which have drawn heavily on local papers for evidence.[23] In contrast, the emphasis of most historians to date has been on propaganda and the role of the War correspondents.[24] According to Finn the study of the local press has been 'long-neglected'. Using the newspapers of the Liverpool area as a case study – including Southport and Great Crosby – Finn was concerned to show that the local and community focus of their reports was crucial to ensuring the reality of the War was not hidden from local people.[25] Until the press was controlled more systematically by the War Office in mid-1915, in terms of what it printed, they were able to secure information and reports from letters home from troops, from the wounded and from some reporters who made it to the frontline.[26] The difference between these first-hand

17 Winter, D., *Haig's Command*, p. 255.
18 Griffith, *Battle Tactics of the Western Front*, p. 259.
19 Green, A.S., *Writing the Great War: Sir James Edmonds and the Official Histories 1915–1948* (London: Frank Cass, 2002).
20 Green, *Writing the Great War*, pp. 224, 287.
21 Haste, Cate, *Keep the Home Fires Burning: Propaganda in the First World War* (London: Allen Lane, 1977); Sanders, M.L. and Taylor, P.M., *British Propaganda during the First World War 1914–18* (London: Macmillan, 1982).
22 Bourne, John M., *Britain and the Great War 1914–1918* (London: Edward Arnold, 1989), p. 206.
23 Pandrich, B.F.J., "Dundee's Flodden, The Battle of Loos: A Sociological Study Through the Written Word" Unpublished MPhil thesis, Dundee University, 1988.
24 Farrar, M.J., *News from the Front: War Correspondents on the Western Front 1914–18* (Stroud: Sutton, 1998), amongst others.
25 Finn, M. "The Realities of War", *History Today* Vol. 52 No. 8 (August 2002), pp. 26–31.
26 Grieves, Keith, "War correspondents and conducting officers on the Western Front from 1915" in Cecil, H. and Liddle P.H. (eds), *Facing Armageddon: The First World War Experienced* (London: Leo Cooper 1996) pp. 719–735; Knightley, P., *The First Casualty:*

reports and the 'Eyewitness' reports passed on by the GHQ official press organisation were vast. The Festubert example was 'Eyewash' of the highest order.

The difference between local and national organs was a significant one. Local papers were much more likely to be able to have letters and first-hand information than the nationals, though they did rely on the nationals for the wider picture. The history of the national press in the War has been chronicled elsewhere, and this study does not add to it.[27] Local papers included many first-hand accounts received in letters from the Front, and their articles as a whole reflected local interest. This became increasingly difficult as the War progressed. The difference between the reports which appeared in local papers in May 1915 and those in September 1915 following Loos are now quite obvious. Letters and reports from men were almost absent by September. As a result, the newspapers prove to be a good source of battle reports predominantly in the first year of the War. Subsequently, they regurgitated manufactured reports, although there continue to be examples of letters from the Front being printed, including those which demonstrated the harshness of the life and death of the soldier in the Front Line. The attempts of local editors to maintain the local interest obviously continued, but soldiers' letters home dwindled, although photographs and short obituaries or biographies did not. The purpose of writing these letters, the choice of which letter to print and the extent to which they were representative of general feeling, needs taking into consideration, but they are nonetheless a valuable source. Editorials criticising the conduct of the War were rare, and not evidenced in Southport or Bootle. Encouragement and motivation for more and more recruits, including the castigation of shirkers, were more prevalent in most editorial comment.

The principal local papers used for this volume have been the *Bootle Times*, the *Waterloo and Crosby Herald and Formby, Bootle and Seaforth Gazette*, the *Formby Times*, the *Southport Guardian*, and the *Southport Visiter*. The *Southport Visiter* was published three times each week, on Tuesday, Thursday and Saturday. The *Southport Guardian* came out every Saturday, as did the *Formby Times* and the *Waterloo and Crosby Herald*. The *Bootle Times* came out once a week, on a Friday. These publication dates clearly influenced the immediacy and extent of some news reports. Some reports and letters appeared in more than one paper. The two Southport papers were divided along political lines, with the *Southport Guardian* favouring the Liberals, and having close connections with the Liberal Councillors, and the *Southport Visiter* holding a more Conservative line. The other local papers were traditionally conservative.

These papers were important sources throughout the conflict for what was happening on the homefront. On average, the *Southport Guardian* devoted two of its twelve pages per edition to War stories, the rest concentrating on local news and events. These local stories also included reports of hospital visitors, troops billeted in the town, meetings

The War Correspondent as Hero, Propagandist and Myth Maker from the Crimea to Vietnam (London: Andre Deutsch, 1975).

27 Haste, *Keep the Home Fires Burning*; Knightley, *The First Casualty*; Sanders & Taylor, *British Propaganda during the First World War*.

and fundraising events, as well as the more usual and predictable local affairs, such as Council meetings and court reports. The *Bootle Times* reduced its pages to eight during the crisis, saving resources. It also had a different approach to War coverage, with a much more integrated style across the whole paper. There were not the same column inches devoted to major actions of the local Battalion as were seen in the Southport papers, though there was not the same level of coverage of the wider War perspective either. The almost verbatim reports of Council meetings, court actions and military tribunals are useful sources and quite different to today's reporting of similar occasions.

This volume is not however solely a military study, but one of the Home Front too. We cannot hope to understand properly the mind and motivations of the men at the Front if we ignore their community at Home and in two regards in particular this community had its own significance. Firstly, it was an area of engineering and munitions, crucially important in the war effort, together with the agricultural flatlands behind Southport and Ormskirk. Secondly, it wrote its own headlines during the Lusitania riots, sparked by the sinking of the Cunard liner in May 1915.

I conclude with a reappraisal of the importance of community identity by looking at the different aspects of military and civilian remembrance in West Lancashire in 1918 and the years beyond, including the particular resonance of the work of the British League of Help, for Givenchy and Festubert. Evidence shows that the community links with the battalion, its soldiers and its experiences were key to the lasting memorialisation both at a military and civilian level.

This is the first study of 7th Battalion, King's Liverpool Regiment in the First World War but there is a canon of other material about the regiment and many of its individual units, dating from 1919 to the twenty-first century. It is surely time to provide a modern bibliography for those histories.[28]

28 Wyrall, E. *The History of the King's Regiment (Liverpool) 1914–19* (3 volumes) (London: Edward Arnold, 1935). Coop, Rev. J.O., *The Story of the 55th (West Lancashire) Division 1916–1919* (Liverpool: *Liverpool Daily Post*, 1919). Tilsley, *Other Ranks*; McCartney, Helen, *Citizen Soldiers: The Liverpool Territorials in the First World War* (Cambridge: Cambridge University Press, 2005). Burke-Gaffney, MC, Lt.Col J.J., *The Story of the King's Regiment 1914–48* (Liverpool: Sharpe and Kellet, 1954); Threlfall, T.R., *The Story of the King's (Liverpool) Regiment, formerly the 8th Foot* (London: *Country Life*, 1916); Wurtzburg, Capt. C.E., *The History of the 2/6th (Rifle) Battalion, the King's (Liverpool) Regiment 1914–19* (Aldershot: Gale & Polden, 1920); McGilchist, A.M., *The Liverpool Scottish 1900–1919 (1/10th and 2/10th King's)* (Liverpool: Henry Young, 1930); Giblin, H., *Bravest of Hearts: The Biography of a Battalion: The Liverpool Scottish in the Great War* (Liverpool: Winordie, 2000); *The Record of the 11th Battalion of the King's (Liverpool) Regiment, August 1914–March 1919* (Liverpool: RE Thomas & Co., 1920); Roberts, E.H.G., *The Study of the 9th King's in France* (Liverpool: Northern, 1922); Bigwood, G., *The Lancashire Fighting Territorials* (London: *Country Life*, 1916); Brown, J.H., "The King's Regiment (Liverpool) – 1 Liverpool's Volunteers and Territorials and their Shako, Helmet and Cap Badges", *The Bulletin of the Military Historical Society* Vol. IV No. 14, November 1953, pp. 23–27; Moore, Lt.Col. (TD) A..,J "The Territorial Battalions of the King's" *Stand To!: The Journal of the Western Front Association* No. 49 (April 1997); Stanley, Brig. Gen. F.C., *History of the 89th Brigade 1914–18* (Liverpool, 1919).

1

Recruitment and War Fever in Southport and Bootle

Society and Economy, Summer 1914

In Lancashire in the summer of 1914 labour, women and Ireland were key areas of tension. Strikes were prevalent in a range of industries which would soon be connected with munitions. As well as women being involved in strike action, suffrage was an issue, particularly in Southport. In sectarian Bootle there was considerable interest in political events in Ireland. However, the declaration of war soon brought those diverse aspects of society into a more cohesive whole. In the first few months from the outbreak of War, the local communities organised recruitment, funds, billetting, nursing and convalescent resources, and developed a sense of belonging which focused from an early stage on the common factor of 7th Battalion.

The 1911 census showing population, occupations and other socio-economic data in this region demonstrates the differences between the areas of Bootle and Litherland which is closer to Liverpool and Southport and Formby around the coast.[1] The 1921 Census figure and mid-year figures from the local Officers for Health also show the fluctuation in population through the war period. From these four tables (Tables 1–4) we can see the differences between the two areas as well as trends in each. Bootle is seen to have been generally working class with high proportions of immigrants, high Infant Mortality Rates (IMR) and considerable overcrowding. Bootle had the highest proportion of Irish immigrants (4,687) and the fourth highest proportion of Scottish immigrants (2,049) in the country. This compared with 723 Scots and 828 Irish in

1 Outside the urban areas, Sefton Rural District included the parishes of Aintree, Croxteth Park, Ford, Ince Blundell, Kirkby, Lunt, Netherton, Sefton, Thornton and West Derby Rural. West Lancashire RDC included the parishes of Altcar, Aughton, Bickerstaffe, Bispham, Downholland, Halsall, Hesketh, Lydiate, Maghull, Melling, North Meols, Rufford, Scarisbrick, Simonswood and Tarleton – Census of England and Wales 1911, 10 Edward 7 and 1 George 5, Ch. 27 – County of Lancaster: Tables extracted from Vols. I–XI of the *Report on the Census of England and Wales 1911* (London: 1914).

Southport.[2] With 2.9 percent of the population being Scottish and 6.7 percent Irish, there was a direct effect, particularly in terms of the religious and political affiliations with which the troops would identify. Liverpool's sectarianism had often spilled over into Bootle and street clashes continued up to 1914 and beyond.[3]

Table 1 Population figures from 1911 Census[4]

Place	Population	Men	Women
Birkdale UDC	18,000	7,286	10,714
Bootle CB	69,876	34,408	35,468
Formby UD&CP	5,947	2,593	3,354
Great Crosby UD&CP	12,273	4,881	7,392
Litherland UD&CP	14,795	7,146	7,649
Little Crosby UD&CP	844	441	403
Southport CB&CP	51,643	21,076	30,567
Waterloo/Seaforth UDC	26,396	11,803	14,593
Sefton RDC	5,953	2,803	3,150
West Lancashire RDC	20,683	10,451	10,232

Table 2 Estimated mid-year population totals

Year	Southport[5]	Bootle[6]
1912	70,640	71,152
1913	71,092	72,186
1914	71,747	73,230
1915	67,700	71,617
1916	67,000	71,135
1917	66,000	68,871
1918	66,000	73,500
1919	70,000	77,000
1921[7]	76,621	76,487

2 1911 Census: Volume IX – Birthplaces Table 2.
3 Neal, F., *Sectarian Violence: the Liverpool Experience 1819–1914. An Aspect of Anglo-Irish History* (Manchester: Manchester University Press, 1988), p. 243.
4 1911 Census Table 5 extracts.
5 Southport Borough Council Medical Officer of Health Reports, 1914–20.
6 Bootle Borough Council Minutes – Medical Officer of Health Vital Statistics 1920.
7 1921 Census Table I extracts.

Table 3 Marital status in 1911 Census[8]

Place	Men			Women		
	Unmarried	Married	Widowed	Unmarried	Married	Widowed
Birkdale	4,159	2,870	257	6,829	3,075	810
Bootle	21,732	11,471	1,205	20,585	12,422	2,464
Formby	1,629	888	76	2,198	918	238
Gt.Crosby	2,859	1,902	120	4,865	2,052	475
Litherland	4,532	2,429	185	4,446	2,720	483
L.Crosby	306	123	12	251	122	30
Southport	15,507	11,777	1,078	25,332	12,330	3,619
Waterloo	7,364	4,093	346	8,741	4,727	1,125
Sefton RD	1,788	919	96	2,030	910	210
West Lancs	6,618	3,427	406	6,099	3,465	668

Table 4 Principal types of employment (Female totals in bold)[9]

	B'dale	Bootle	Formby	Gt.Crosby	L'land	S'port	W'loo
Civic		397				423	
		52				**31**	
Prof./clerical/ medical/ teaching	308	408	130	190	52	995	307
	177	**592**	**56**	**155**	**52**	**839**	**237**
Domestic Service	94	179	26	31	59	503	69
	1,802	**2,244**	**534**	**1,570**	**285**	**4,986**	**1,497**
Rail	256	826	69	49	203	711	317
		4				**5**	
Docks	2	4,167	13	23	322		343
Agric./fishing/ Market gardening	363	110	314	183	74	802	103
	11	**5**	**20**	**11**	**3**	**45**	**3**
Engineering	74	2,714	35	75	236	1,112	321
		30				**32**	
Construction	56	1378	148	354	425	1,677	633
						6	
Chemical/ explosives/ matches	38	86	9	56	203	3	139
	1	**360**	**1**		**155**	**3**	**48**
Tanning etc	11	251	2	17	184	68	26
	1	**49**				**38**	

8 1911 Census Tables 17, 18 extracts.
9 1911 Census Tables 23, 24,25 extracts

	B'dale	Bootle	Formby	Gt.Crosby	L'land	S'port	W'loo
Textiles/jute/bleaching/ dyeing	44 **4**	92 **513**	3 **1**	8 **1**	4 **61**	163 **97**	28 **48**
Dressmaking	125 **346**	340 **1,003**	18 **102**	45 **103**	69 **161**	629 **1,363**	107 **358**
Private means/ unoccupied	1,441	4,013	456	730	881	3,470	1,636

Amongst the overcrowded tenements and courtyard houses or 'slums',[10] Bootle's IMR was one of the highest in the country in the early 1900s.[11] Even by 1915 it was 142 per 1,000 live births while Southport's was 90.[12] Claims for outdoor poor relief in the 1919 Medical Officer's Report for Bootle shows the number claiming relief in 1914 was 1,464 and in 1915 was 1,120.[13] In Southport it had been 334 and 251 respectively, demonstrating a marked difference.[14] The drop in both towns between 1914 and 1915 was probably associated with recruitment to the Army, reflecting Ferguson's view that one factor among many behind volunteering was a man's poverty.[15]

As can be seen in Table Four, work in 1911 in 'Brutal Bootle'[16] was largely dominated by the docks, engineering and construction. The extent of industrialisation in the small area away from the docks was evident from Siegfried Sassoon's account of the industrial area around the Litherland Training Camp with Bryant's match factory and Brotherton's explosives factory a few hundred yards from the Camp.[17] For women, in Bootle and Litherland, outside of domestic service, their main areas of employment were explosives, tanning and textiles. These were large scale factory concerns already employing more women than men. The employment figures in Tables Five and Six emphasise that whole industries were dominated by one gender or the other. When

10 1911 Census Tables 27, 27a, 2.

11 Crosby Library, Sefton Borough Council (CL) B/MO 6: Bootle Borough Council Medical Officer of Health Report 1916.

12 Southport (Atkinson) Library, SBC (SAL): Southport Borough Council Medical Officer of Health Report 1915 CL:B/MO 8 Bootle Borough Council Medical Officer of Health Report 1919. The IMR also fluctuated considerably from ward to ward in Bootle, with one ward, Mersey, having an IMR in 1913 of 199 representing 20% of all children dying in their first year: CL:B/36 Bootle Borough Council Minutes Vol. XXXVII, Medical Officer of Health Report 1919–20.

13 CL: Bootle Borough Council Medical Officer of Health Report 1919.

14 SAL: Southport Borough Council Medical Officer of Health Report 1915.

15 Ferguson, N., *The Pity of War* (London: Allen Lane, 1998), p. 206; Morris, P., 'Leeds and the amateur military tradition: the Leeds Rifle and their antecedents 1859–1918' (Unpublished PhD thesis, Leeds University, 1983), p. 314.

16 Waller, P. J., *Democracy and Sectarianism: A Political and Social History of Liverpool 1869–1939* (Liverpool: Liverpool University Press, 1981), p. 94.

17 Sassoon, S., *The Complete Memoirs of George Sherston*, p. 381.

the number of working men available was reduced by the call to arms, this had an important effect on those male-dominated industries.

Table 5 Southport employment in last week of August, 1914[18]

Building trade	493
Engineers	666
Food retail	512
Other retail	650
Hotels and restaurants	606
Laundries	394
Gardeners	45
Railway workers	426
Taxis	204
Dairymen	32

Table 6 Bootle employment distribution, 1913[19]

Men		Women	
Merchant service	2,383	Teaching	340
Dock labour	3,278	Clerical	291
General labourer	691	Domestic Service	1,495
Coal heaver	252	Charwoman	258
Boiler maker	265	Laundry	380
Matchworkers	86	Matchworkers	360
Tanners	203	Jute Manufacture	240
		Bleaching/dying	273
		Dressmaking	562

Southport, Waterloo, Formby and Great Crosby were more affluent areas than those around Bootle described above. This is partly indicated by the imbalance of women over men, and particularly the higher numbers of unmarried and independent women. (See Table Three). Employment figures show that there were a large number of female domestic servants in these areas. It is also clear from the statistics that Southport had a disproportionate number of middle aged and older people whereas in Bootle age groups were more evenly distributed.[20] The most immediate adverse

18 SAL: Southport Borough Council National Aid Committee Report, 2 September 1914.
19 CL: B/30 Bootle Borough Council Minutes Vol. XXI Medical Officer of Health Annual Report 1913–14.
20 1911 Census Tables 5, 17,18, 23, 24, 25.

effects of the Declaration of War on employment were felt in occupations such as confectionery, domestic service and dressmaking. Table Four shows these as the main sources of employment from Southport's women, where the high number of women in service reflected not just the affluence of families but also the number of hydropathic centres, hotels and private boarding houses. The enthusiasm for billeting troops was not unconnected to this drop in employment in these areas.

For men, Southport's main areas of employment were in professional/medical/teaching, agriculture, engineering and construction, though the latter were small or family concerns compared with the large factory employment in Bootle. A report to the Southport Education Committee in 1914, from the Schools Medical Officer, listed the occupations of pupils' parents including 339 labourers, 156 gardeners, 132 painter and decorators, 110 joiners, 90 bricklayers, 89 charwomen, 73 tailors, 68 cabdrivers, 67 clerks, 42 farmers, 30 farm labourers, 50 working in the railways, 53 fishermen or shrimpers, 36 engineers and 46 mechanics. Table Five, which comes from a report to show the impact of the war on various industries, echoes those areas of work.[21]

There is some evidence of the physical health of Southport's potential volunteers to the Battalion. Details from the Southport Education Committee extracted in Table Seven show the average physiques of male fifteen year olds between 1908 and 1912.[22] These boys would have been the volunteers of 1914, a twenty-one year old showing up as being fifteen in the table for 1908. The statistics for the boys who were fifteen in 1912 and volunteering as seventeen and eighteen year olds in 1914 showed their physique was above the national averages.[23] Therefore the men who volunteered from Southport are likely to have come from a cohort who were of reasonable health, fitting Winter's theory that well paid manual workers and non-manual workers were the most likely to be healthy and therefore most likely to be accepted as volunteers for enlistment.[24]

21 SAL: Southport Borough Council Education Committee, 17 March 1915; Southport Borough Council National Aid Committee Report, 2 September 1914.

22 SAL: Southport Borough Council Education Committee Annual Reports, Table E, 1911–15.

23 For instance, a 14 year old boy who would be 18 in 1914, was 4 ft 11 in and 6 st 6 lbs in 1910, when a national standards table had a similar child at 4 ft 9 in and 6 st, suggesting that Southport children were above the national indicative standards – SAL: Southport Borough Council Education Committee Minutes Annual Report 1911.

24 Winter, J., *The Great War and the British People* (London: Macmillan, 1984), p. 50.

Table 7 Average height and weight of potential recruits (Southport)[25]

	Height @ age 15	Weight @ age 15	Year age 15
Age 21 in 1914	5ft 5in	8st 10lb	1908
Age 20 in 1914	5ft 2in	7st 8lb	1909
Age 19 in 1914	4ft 11in	6st 3lb	1910
Age 18 in 1914	5ft 3in	7st 1lb	1911
Age 17 in 1914	5ft 4in	8st 3lb	1912

With little sign of the co-operation which was to come, this pre-War society was also marked by conflict within the communities, primarily of an industrial nature. The Southport Water Carnival in July 1914 sparked an apprentice boys' strike at the Vulcan Motor Works when over 150 boys missed work to attend the opening of the bathing lake and were told they would have their indentures revoked. The apprentices returned to work after a week[26] but lost their bonuses as a result and these were not re-instated until September, perhaps as an inducement not to join the flood of recruits to the Army.[27]

In a more serious strike, further indicating tension right up until the beginning of the War, thousands of men downed tools on the docks on 13 July in a demand for a standard wage rate. The *Bootle Times* reported that initially two-thirds of the 3,000 Union members had answered the strike call, but that many returned to work either that first day or over the week.[28] Two weeks into the strike, the dockers marched through Liverpool as the Strike Committee pledged to win and 'damn the consequences' but, like others across the country, the strike faded into insignificance in the face of the European War and was ended within a fortnight.[29]

Southport's tradition of a forthright liberal and reforming middle class coupled with a high population of single women meant there were branches of the two main suffrage organisations, the Women's Social and Political Union (WSPU) and the National Union of Women's Suffrage Societies (NUWSS). Their activities had ranged from open air meetings in parks or on the sands to a number of violent incidents including disruption of Churchill's visit to Southport in 1910 and the burning of a shelter on the pier to mark the visit of the King and Queen in 1913.[30] Women showed that they were also industrially militant when a strike of laundry girls started on Thursday 16 July 1914 across Bootle, Blundellsands, Waterloo and Seaforth, in

25 SAL: Southport Borough Council Education Committee Reports Table E 1911–15.
26 *Southport Visiter*, 25 July 1914, p. 7.
27 *Southport Guardian*, 16 September 1914, p. 3.
28 *Bootle Times*, 17 July 1914, p. 11.
29 *Bootle Times*, 31 July 1914, pp. 5 and 6; 7 August 1914, p. 5 and 14 August 1914, p. 5.
30 *Votes for Women: The Events on Merseyside 1870–1928* (Liverpool: National Museums and Galleries on Merseyside, 1992), pp. 57–59.

a campaign for shorter hours, higher pay and a half day on Saturdays. Up to 1,200 marched from the Custom House in Liverpool to Blundellsands and were able to stop girls working along the route through Bootle.[31] Earlier in July a tanners' strike over pay, which began in Warrington, spread to the Bootle district where, despite work continuing at the Liverpool Tanning Company and Walkers' – both in Litherland – 300 workers were reckoned by the local Trades Council to be on strike.[32]

Despite what today looks like the proximity of the War, the *Southport Visiter* did not consider the European situation worthy of comment until the end of July.[33] What was of interest, however, was the Irish Question. The *Southport Visiter* attacked the 'criminal' failure of the Prime Minister, Asquith, to deal with the issue. The newspaper's readers' support for the 'prosperous and enterprising community in the north-east of Ireland' who had been 'treated with contempt' by the Government, was apparently unstinting.[34] These arguments with the Government's policy were soon to be curtailed in the wider interest of the War effort.

In Bootle, the Irish debate was less theoretical and more concerned with actual division between Catholic and Protestant. Sunday 21 June 1914 had seen 4,000 Bootle Catholics take part in the annual procession through the town, though this was not as many as in previous years due to inclement weather.[35] Only a few weeks later the Orange Lodges held their annual 12 July demonstration at the Everton football ground, a huge event.[36] The paper followed events in Ireland and the Commons debate, but rarely ventured into Editorial comment on the matter whereas the leading article of the *Southport Visiter* was keen to place Ireland in context: 'We may be in fact on the brink of the great war, the European Armageddon… We have the Irish problem on our hands. Whatever happens now the Government have created a rebellious Ireland which will be a source of incalculable danger in case of an international war.'[37]

Despite a series of industrial conflicts and other tensions within the local communities, there soon emerged a joint commitment by the communities of Southport and of Bootle to the War effort. Both areas exhibited a coming together of their community which began to focus on the volunteers to the local Battalion who would represent them at the Front. While Bootle and Southport did not have any real sense of belonging to each other, they did develop a shared sense of identity and ownership with the same Territorial unit.

When the holiday atmosphere was broken by the enthusiastic, frenetic and disorganised preparations for War which went on in the autumn of 1914, there were

31 *Bootle Times*, 17 July 1914, p. 11.
32 *Bootle Times*, 3 July 1914, p. 11.
33 *Southport Visiter*, 28 July 1914, p. 8.
34 *Southport Visiter*, 18 July 1914, p. 8.
35 *Bootle Times*, 26 June 1914, p. 10.
36 *Bootle Times*, 17 July 1914, p. 7.
37 *Southport Visiter*, 28 July 1914, p. 8. Note this early use of the phrase 'Great War'.

signs of what previous commentators have highlighted as chaos, hysteria and confusion.[38] Ferguson's analysis injected anxiety and panic into this equation and sought to qualify the impression of mass enthusiasm.[39] The evidence from local newspapers offers limited support for this view. Voices in opposition were raised and reported but the overwhelming impression was one of excitement and expectation. Local agencies and community leaders took up the call for recruits, assistance and organisation. Politicians and churches joined with the general public in an attempt to take steps toward a coherent support mechanism.

By Friday 7 August Bootle Council had put provisions in place to support wives and families of recruited men. In a sign of the importance of the Territorials to local culture, prominent ratepayers in Waterloo founded a movement to encourage Territorial recruiting and Lord Derby called for men for the West Lancashire Terriers.[40] Southport's Liberal Association briefly declared themselves for neutrality, but offered full support to the Government three days later.[41] Crosby Hall, was opened up as a Red Cross collecting centre by the end of the week, as food prices started to rise in Southport.[42] The dock strike was settled within ten days as the Mersey Docks and Harbour Board withdrew notices and agreement was reached on overtime work to build and arm ships and to give a boost to local employment.[43] Ten days on and the national appeal for Territorials and for Kitchener men was underway, just as local papers reported that men in 7th Battalion were volunteering for active service.[44] Reactions ranged from the trivial to the practical. The Hesketh golf championships and Bootle Carnival were cancelled, but golf at Southport and Ainsdale went ahead.[45] In Southport committees sprang up to raise money: the Mayoress' Auxiliary Ladies Committee, the Women's Liberal Association, the Birkdale Ladies Conservative Committee. In Bootle a sewing ladies network guild emerged.[46] Crosby's Relief Committee was founded, recruiting centres established, first aid classes begun and a Voluntary Aid Detachment set up.[47] Southport Trades Union Council held a march

38 Osborne, J.M., 'The Voluntary Recruiting Movement in Britain 1914–16', *Modern British History* Vol. 5; Stansky, P. and Hume, L. (eds), (London: Garland Publishing, 1982); Reader, W.J., *'At Duty's call': Study in Obsolete Patriotism* (Manchester: Manchester University Press, 1988).
39 Ferguson, *The Pity of War*, p. 177.
40 *Bootle Times*, 7 August 1914, p. 7.
41 *Southport Guardian*, 5 August 1914, p. 9; 8 August 1914, p. 6.
42 *Bootle Times*, 7 August 1914, p. 7; *Southport Guardian*, 8 August 1914, p. 8.
43 *Bootle Times*, 7 August 1914, p. 7 and 14 August 1914, p. 5.
44 *Bootle Times*, 14 August 1914, p. 5.
45 *Bootle Times*, 7 August 1914, p. 7; *Southport Guardian*, 19 August 1914, p. 5.
46 *Southport Guardian*, 19 August 1914, pp. 4 and 6; *Bootle Times*, 14 August 1914, p. 5.
47 *Bootle Times*, 7 August 1914, p. 7; 21 August 1914, p. 5 and 14 August 1914 p. 5.

and rally and briefly declared it a 'class war'. The colours of the Bootle Battalion were lodged at the Town Hall as the BEF landed in France.[48]

Behind this frantic and apparently disparate activity was a lot of hard work and quick decision-making, led primarily by the local Councils. As men volunteered, Councils agreed to pay allowances to dependents and to hold their positions open for the duration of the War, with a return with no loss of position 'if still capable of performing his duties'.[49] When the Government put Army pay into place, Councils simply began to agree to make up the difference between the salary currently commanded and service pay.[50] This willingness to pay was based on the notion that the War would be of limited duration. The shipping company, Cunard, followed suit, paying one full month's pay and half pay for three years, or for the remainder of the War, whichever was shorter. Employees other than clerical staff were treated slightly differently, with dependents being paid a weekly allowance of five shillings instead.[51]

Committees were set up creating local versions of the national Prince of Wales Relief Fund, as well as local Civic Distress Committees.[52] Crucially, these committees brought together different elements of the community, including representatives from the local Councils and also individuals who were already experienced in dealing with distress from amongst local residents, philanthropists, the Local Education Authority, Boards of Guardians, employers and ladies organisations.

In just one example, the Formby Guild for War Service was established under the chairmanship of the local Congregational Minister, Revd. Wicks. Over the course of the war they boasted over 100 members who produced more than 25,000 items, from bandages, slings, bed jackets and swabs to splints, ward screens, bed rests, picture puzzles and crutch pads. These were distributed locally amongst Southport and Liverpool hospitals, local ambulances depots and the Formby Camp, as well as to individual soldiers.[53]

48 *Southport Guardian*, 12 August 1914, p. 3; *Bootle Times*, 21 August 1914, p. 5; *Southport Guardian*, 19 August 1914, p. 7.

49 CL: Bootle Council Minutes Vol.XXXI 1913–14: Health Committee, 10 August; Parks and Baths Committee, 19 August; Electric Power and Lighting Committee; 14 August, Sanitation Committee; 18 August, Council, 7 October 1914.

50 CL: Bootle Council Minutes Vol.XXXI 1913–14: Council, 7 October 1914; CL: Waterloo and Seaforth Urban District Council Minutes Vol. 20 1914–15: Council 14 September 1914.

51 Liverpool University Archives (LUA): B4/44 Cunard Board Executive Committee Minutes, 3 and 9 September 1914.

52 CL: Bootle Council Minutes Vol. XXXI 1913–14: Council 2 September 1914; SAL: Southport Council Minutes 1913–14: General Purposes Committee, 6 August 1914;CL: Litherland Urban District Council Minutes, 7 September 1914; Waterloo and Seaforth Urban District Council Minutes, 12 August 1914; Lancashire Record Office (LRO) UDFo 2/4/3 Formby Urban District Council Minutes, 13 August 1914; *Bootle Times*, 21 August 1914, p. 5.

53 A Souvenir of the Formby Guild for War Service (British Red Cross District Committee) 1915–1919.

A key element in the reaction of the community was that of the trade unions and labour movement. Initial opposition was noted by Ferguson but it was to little effect.[54] Local evidence shows that representatives of the Left were anxious to be involved in the organisation of the home community from an early stage. The majority of organisations – the Councils, the clubs, the churches, the suffragists, the politicians – who all came to the fore with their views on the War and their efforts in aiding the effort were a cross-section of the voluntary and community minded middle class. With the sole exception of the trade union movement, the key organisations were drawn from the leaders of the local communities, perhaps unsurprisingly. Waites points to the rapid inclusion of representatives of the trade and labour movement in the organisation supporting the War as evidence of the social cohesion and political accommodation of the working class in society.[55] This was certainly the pattern in Southport, once the Trades Union Council had reversed its initial opposition to the War.

Southport Trades Union Council secured representations on what was to become the National Aid Committee, along with a long list of other local organisations including the Board of Guardians, the Insurance Committee, the Employers' and Traders' Association, the Company Housekeepers' Association, the Ladies Auxiliary, the Soldiers' and Sailors' Families Association, the magistrates, the clergy, the Salvation Army and the press. They joined the Council's representatives of the Mayor, Mayoress, Deputy Mayor, Town Clerk, Borough Treasurer and Aldermen. Although the list of organisations was broad, representatives of labour and the 'ladies' were kept away from the more significant sub-committees dealing with finance and policy. They were involved on the Employment and Ladies' Auxiliary sub-committees, the latter being responsible for organising supplies and comforts for the troops, ambulance classes and nursing arrangements, and for investigating individual cases and reporting to and from the Case Committee.[56]

There was a Joint Committee on Women's Employment but the Trades Council only had two seats on the Employment Committee and they complained in vain at the low representation which labour was afforded on the Food Aid Committee and on the National Emergency Committee.[57] At the Trades Council's Annual Meeting in February 1916, the Secretary reported on the previous year's activities and noted that representatives were on the National Aid Committee, 'but, of course, our representatives were elected onto committees which are of little importance.'[58]

The changing circumstances of the War saw consolidation and co-operation as the disparate elements of the community came together to start to develop the Home

54 Ferguson, *The Pity of War*, p. 178.
55 Waites, B., *A Class Society at War: England 1914–1918* (Leamington Spa: Berg Publishers, 1987), pp. 186–187.
56 SAL: Southport National Aid Committee, Volume 1, Minutes: 10, 12, 13 August 1914.
57 *Southport Guardian*, 5 September 1914, p. 9; SAL, Southport National Aid Committee Volume 1 Minutes, 14 August 1914.
58 *Southport Guardian*, 5 February 1916, p. 9.

Front. That coming together was, at first, somewhat random and unchannelled but in a very short time measures and agencies were in place to provide a more co-ordinated and coherent response. This was achieved despite the recent difficulties and differences within and between elements of the local community and it came to focus the War support on the efforts of the local volunteers who joined a range of service units, but predominantly the local 'Bootle/Southport Battalion.'

Battalion Social Composition

In the absence of attestation records an accurate assessment of the Battalion's composition is not possible without an in-depth study of all available service records of indiviual soldiers. However, it is possible to work towards an understanding – or what Morris calls 'an impression'[59] – of the social composition of the Battalion of pre-draft volunteers in three ways. Firstly, the geographic roots of the men can be established, leading to certain assumptions about their social position. Secondly, there is a range of anecdotal evidence and comment about the nature of the recruits, which give a further indication of the Battalion's composition. Thirdly, there are numerous references to men's trades, commonly in short obituaries in the local newspapers. These all suggest that recruitment from Bootle was from across the working class but with many labourers and semi-skilled men whilst that from Southport was more mixed including more artisans and lower middle class recruits.

Recruiting centres were set up across the area so that nowhere was overlooked. Ferguson established five motives in recruitment – successful recruiting techniques, female pressure, peer group pressure, economic motivation, and impulse.[60] Successful technique, peer pressure in the form of newspapers' rallying cries, and the best recruiting sergeant in Lord Derby, all meant that the battalions in and around Liverpool and south west Lancashire were well supported.[61] Liverpool was one of the recruiting centres set up by the Government for all units,[62] but Southport, and Bootle with the Battalion Headquarters in Park Street, were associated directly with the Territorial Force. When Arthur Critchley arrived at Park Street, Bootle, 'everyone' was already there and they had to sleep on the floor of the nearby Balliol

59 McCartney, H., *Citizen Soldiers: The Liverpool Territorials in the First World War* (Cambridge University Press, 2005), p. 58. In 'The Leeds Rifles' p. 323, Morris built a similar thesis regarding social composition in the Leeds Territorials based primarily on the occupation list of one company and other impressionistic indicators. McCartney relied on a draft book and Casualty Books for her study of 1/10th and 1/6th King'a Liverpool Regiment respectively – 'Citizen Soldiers'.

60 Ferguson, *Pity of War*, pp. 205–7.

61 Grieves, K., *The Politics of Manpower 1914–18* (Manchester: Manchester University Press, 1988).

62 Osborne, 'The Voluntary Recruiting Movement'.

A Kingsman outside the Bootle Barracks of 7th Liverpool's. (Courtesy: Philip Haythornthwaite)

Road School.[63] Southport Council agreed to the use of the old Education offices in the Cambridge Arcade for a recruiting office[64] while Waterloo set up a Recruiting Committee of the Council.[65]

63 Critchley.
64 SAL: Southport Borough Council Minute Book 1913–14, Council Minutes, 11 August 1914.
65 CL: Waterloo with Seaforth Urban District Council Minutes Vol. 20 1914–15, Council Minutes, 6 August 1914.

The 7th Battalion already had companies based in different towns. The pre-War Force had eight companies, lettered A-H, which were merged on mobilisation to conform to the Regular pattern of A-D. Companies A-C were based in Liverpool, D and E in Bootle and F, G and H respectively in Formby, Crosby and Southport.[66] Evidence of casualties from the first attacks at Festubert, which were led by A and B Companies, suggests they were the Southport/Formby group, while the C and D Companies appear to have been more from Bootle, although there is sufficient intermingling to believe that companies were not exclusive in this respect.[67]

An analysis of 7th King's records in *Soldiers Died*[68] shows that more men from Bootle were killed than from Southport – 156:107.[69] Large numbers of deaths from Litherland, Waterloo, Formby, Great Crosby and Birkdale were also recorded. This ratio of deaths from the two main centres of 60 percent to 40 percent compares directly with the total male populations in 1911 of 25,958 (Bootle) and 17,228 (Southport).[70] This would indicate that, in terms solely of this Battalion, both communites suffered losses proportionate to their population and therefore in all probability a similar proportion of men volunteered from both communities for the three Line Battalions.[71]

The number of commissioned and non-commissioned officers (NCOs) appears to further indicate the social differences between the two communities as the figures are not in the same proportions as the population figures.[72] Indeed, Southport and Bootle had similar numbers of Corporals, Lance Corporals and Sergeants. If taken in conjunction with the 60:40 split between Southport and Bootle, this would suggest that slightly more NCOs proportionately came from Southport. This might be a reflection of the balance of classes between the communities, with Southport's more

66 Richards, W., *His Majesty's Territorial Army: A Descriptive Account of the Yeomanry, Artillery, Engineers and Infantry with the Army Service and Medical Corps, comprising 'The King's Imperial Army of the Second Line'* Vol. 2 (London: Virtue & Co, c.1910).

67 Details of the battle of Festubert can be found in a subsequent chapter, but there is no evidence at any stage that A and B Companies were chosen for the night attack because of any superior or inferior ability when compared with C and D Companies. Morris believed the Leeds Rifles were reorganised on the basis of the seniority of the existing Company commanders: Morris "The Leeds Rifles" pp. 378–379.

68 *Soldiers Died in the Great War 1914–19: Part 13 – The King's (Liverpool Regiment)* (Polstead: J.B. Hayward & Son, 1989), pp. 48–58.

69 Beckett used *Soldiers Died* for a similar analysis looking at dilution of Territorial Battalions in 'The Territorial Force' in Beckett, I.F.W. and Simpson, K. (eds.) *A Nation in Arms: A Social Study of the British Army in the First World War* (London: Tom Donovan Publishing, 1990), p. 147.

70 Census 1911.

71 Volunteers from these geographical areas also joined other battalions, including other local regiments, the Territorial artillery and Transport Columns, and for other regiments around the country. This was widely reflected in the names and Units recorded later on War memorials.

72 *Soldiers Died*, pp. 48–58.

affluent community providing more artisans and lower middle class recruits, the groups most likely to provide NCOs, than Bootle.

A number of writers have noted that the predominant group of men in the Territorial Force were lower middle and respectable working class.[73] This describes many of the men from Southport and McCartney confirmed that 5th, 7th and 9th King's Battalions all attracted these artisans.[74] Bootle's population was predominantly working or lower working class so recruitment from there could be expected to be overwhelmingly working class but it is unclear if recruits came from the full range of working and under class including the casual workers and unemployed. The *Bootle Times* stressed the huge level of commitment shown by the 'working classes' already to the War effort, though the unionised workers referred to were more likely to be upper working class. According to the newspaper, Merseyside had contributed 18,000 men for active service, with 6,000 from the National Union of Dock Labourers and Riverside Workers and 5,000 from the Sailors and Firemen's Unions. If the stewards on Atlantic transports were added, this figure rose to 25,000.[75]

There is some anecdotal evidence of the socio-economic position of recruits in the Battalion. After the War the West Lancashire Territorial and Auxiliary Force (WLTAF) discussed reductions to the number of Battalions it could sustain and a strong case was made for keeping the 6th Battalion as it attracted the 'best sort of fellows' and had a history as a 'class battalion'. The minute went on to report that a similar standard of men were attracted from Crosby and Southport to the 7th Battalion, 'but in Bootle they got the ordinary sort of Territorial'.[76] Their own Commanding Officer, Lieutenant-Colonel Marriott, wrote home in early 1916, reflecting on the men of the Battalion coming from the 'slums of Bootle'.[77]

The Battalion also appears to have reflected the immigrant population of Bootle in particular. A relatively casual study of *Soldiers Died* on the basis of Celtic surnames suggests up to 10 percent of the Battalion were Irish, Scots or Welsh, though it is not clear if they were first or second generation migrants. Census figures for Bootle quoted earlier had shown levels of 2.9 percent Scots and 6.7 percent Irish. The higher levels of recruitment implied by surnames, especially in the context of the attraction of Liverpool's ethnic Battalions – the 8th Irish and 10th Scottish – could suggest a more fervent commitment to the War than amongst the English. In the light of Ferguson's

73 Beckett, 'The Territorial Force', p. 145; Sheffield, G., *Leadership in the Trenches: Officer-man Relation, Morale and Discipline in the British Army in the Era of the First World War* (London: Macmillan, 2000), p. 14; Mitchinson, K.W., *Gentlemen and Officers: The Impact and Experience of War on a Territorial Regiment* (London Rifles), (London: Imperial War Museum, 1995), p.21.

74 McCartney, *Citizen Soldiers*, p. 27.

75 *Bootle Times*, 30 October 1914, p. 5.

76 LCRO: 356WES/1 1/1(1) WLTAF Minutes, 7 June 1921.

77 Liddle Collection, Brotherton Library, Leeds University (Marriott): GS – Marriott, SC correspondence, 20 April 1916.

comment noted earlier, it was more likely that these were economic migrants who had the least to leave behind in their casual dockland employment.

In addition to geographic and anecdotal references there is evidence of the men's occupations and backgrounds, albeit inconsistent and unscientific. An analysis of newspaper obituaries for men from Southport has revealed information about the occupations of 54 Other Ranks.[78] This shows that the men joining 7th King's in Southport were drawn from the artisans, upper working class and lower middle classes of occupations found in the Census and other occupational tables referred to earlier. There were shop assistants, bank clerks, printing workers, Council staff, builders, insurance agents, railway workers, plasterers, gardeners, painters and decorators, porters, cabinet makers, postal workers, tailors, teachers, employees from Vulcan engineering works, florists, butchers and the odd footballer. A further eleven volunteers were listed as drivers or conductors from the Borough's Tramways Department.[79] The Officers were graduates, solicitors, architects and in one case the director of the family business. The analysis is patchy as the potted biographies that accompanied grainy photographs of the volunteers did not always refer to their occupations. Indeed, some were still too young to be called anything at all.

Study of casualties reported in the *Bootle Times* in 1915 gives occupations for 60 men. These have included workers on the Lancashire and Yorkshire Railway, the Diamond Match Works, the White Star Line, Harland and Wolff, the police, Bootle Corporation, plumbers, engineers, a number of apprentices, and forty men from the Liverpool Tanning Company in Litherland.[80] The *Bootle Times* reported that many men had joined the Battalion from the Bootle Tanning Works too.[81] Cunard noted that a large number of clerical workers had joined the local Territorial Battalions.[82] Random checks of newspaper reports on casualties from both communities throughout the War have not revealed any discrepancy with the above findings. Study of selected Soldiers' Documents at the National Archives has revealed that some forms recorded occupations while others did not.[83]

However, the main occupational group found in Bootle according to the Census of 1911, but not highly represented in available records, were the dockyard workers. They do seem to have been amongst the ranks for Divisional General Jeudwine later

78 Bannister, V., (ed.), *Southport's Splendid Hearts: A Tribute to the Men of Southport Who Gave Their Lives in the Great War* (Southport: Watkinson & Bond Ltd, 2002).

79 *Southport Guardian*, 28 April 1915, p. 9.

80 *Bootle Times, 28 May* 1915, p. 7; 4 June 1915, p. 5, 6 and 7; 11 June 1915, p. 5; 18 June 1915, p. 6 and 10; 26 June 1915, p. 7; 2 July 1915, p. 7; 31 December 1915, p. 3.

81 *Bootle Times*, 7 December 1917, p. 3.

82 LUA: PLOC 4.321 LIVKR 1995.1.3 Cunard Clerical Staff Record [c. 1915].

83 The National Archives (TNA) WO363: Service Records. For example, 2107 Private Lappin was a clerk from Kirkdale and 2087 Sergeant Beveridge was a wireworker from Bootle; but 4461 Private Abbot and 6111 Private Ackers, from Formby and Birkdale respectively, had no occupation noted.

wrote that his troops were recruited from the 'warehouse, office and docklands of our town'.[84] These particular workers may have joined other units in the area but reports of casualties from other units similarly do not list dock labourers amongst their number. Possibly the families of workers on the docks, from the slums of the dockfront, did not engage with the local newspapers to give the extensive information which was collated for other classes. It is also clear from the newspapers' reports of casualties that large numbers of men were reported killed or wounded but no reference to their occupational status was given, for whatever reason.

Although much of the Battalion was recruited from the local community in the weeks following the Declaration of War, a reasonable number of men were pre-War Territorials. They had been at the annual camp in Westmorland when War was declared and local newspapers reported their activities, demonstrating the attachment between the Battalion and the community. The *Bootle Times* noted that it was expected that 'all ranks [would] uphold the good name of the battalion as in previous years by working with zeal and being exemplary in conduct in and out of the camp'.[85] The *Southport Visiter*, reporting on the 72 men of the Southport and Formby companies, recorded names of men which recur over the subsequent four years of war: Lieutenants Tweedale, Pittendrigh, Shaw and Roper, along with Sergeant-Instructor Carr, Sergeants Lee and Groves, Machine Gun Sergeant Hines and Corporal Hunt.[86]

Based on pre-War recruitment figures and known numbers of between 651 in 6th King's Battalion and 700 in 10th King's, the indications are that 1/7th Battalion complement on the eve of the War was no more than 700 men.[87] Despite the contract of a Territorial for Home defence, the crisis called for men to go overseas. On 11 August the Battalion at Bootle was asked for volunteers for 'foreign service', with the undecided allowed leave to discuss it with their families. The whole of the Southport contingent, bar one, had volunteered, according to the *Southport Visiter*.[88] It was reported on 29 August that all officers and 850 men had volunteered for foreign service, and a further 200 were now needed to make up a full Battalion.[89] The Bootle paper reported that the 'Bootle Battalion' (sic) had all similarly volunteered.[90] By 10 September, applications for foreign service had been closed and recruits were being taken on for a Second Line Battalion. Advertisements were printed every day calling for men for this 2/7th Battalion, as well as for Kitchener's Battalion, for all branches of

84 LCRO 356 FIF/45: Letter from Jeudwine to Derby, 28 August 1918 Jeudwine MSS.
85 *Bootle Times*, 24 July 1914, p. 7.
86 *Southport Visiter*, 4 August 1914, p. 6.
87 LCRO: 356 WES/56 WLTAF Recruiting and Discharge Committee Minutes, 26 June 1912; 5 March 1913; 27 May 1914; 356 WES56/4/1(21) WLTAF Clothing Committee Minutes, 25 February 1913.
88 *Southport Visiter*, 13 August 1914, p. 6.
89 *Southport Guardian*, 29 August 1914, p. 6; 2 September 1914, p. 3.
90 *Bootle Times*, 14 August 1914, p. 4.

the Army, for the Special Reserve and for Special Constables.[91] Undoubtedly numbers of recruits were high for a considerable time, urged on by the competitive figures given in the press, but it is a little difficult to accept the reports that crowds of youths were reporting to join Kitchener's Army at a rate of forty or fifty per day.[92]

Kitchener's concern about the limited fighting potential of the Territorials is well documented and can perhaps be summed up in Beckett's words as 'an instinctive one for a regular soldier'.[93] There is no evidence that the use of some Territorial units as early as the autumn meant his view had changed but it did not take long for him to have to use the organisation to assist with recruiting his New Armies and to appeal directly to the Territorials to enlist for foreign service.[94] The Territorial Force also made its own appeals, with direct personal calls from Lord Derby himself. As a key figure in national recruiting Derby was also instrumental in the establishment of the Pals movement in Liverpool, and men of the town were reported to be flocking to join this 11th (Service) Battalion of the King's Regiment, encouraged by calls from the mayor of Southport.[95] Such duplication of effort could have been damaging – as Beckett suggests[96] – but appears not to have been too problematic in the case of 7th Battalion, which raised three lines despite competition from so many other locally-based units.

Keen to encourage recruitment in the local Battalion, the Southport papers were full of pictures and reports of men who had volunteered. They were, perhaps, unfortunately over-eager when several from the same family joined up, fathers and sons, uncles, as well as brothers in arms. The creation of a Roll of Honour in the *Southport Guardian* was further encouragement, along with lists of men from the same work-place or sports club.[97] This was some time before the term 'Roll of Honour' acquired the definition we know it by today, and was simply a roll of those who had volunteered to take up arms.[98] When the Roll was updated in the New Year the editor wrote: 'Never before in the history of the country has a war come home so closely to the people. The effect of the Territorial Force being embodied in the Regular Army is to find almost every household represented in the ranks.'[99]

The *Formby Times* was also an enthusiastic recruiter, printing names and photographs, and helping to forge a community spirit. The *Bootle Times* did not print the

91 *Bootle Times*, 28 August and 11 September 1914.
92 *Southport Guardian*, 2 September 1914, p. 6 and 5 September 1914, p. 6.
93 Beckett, 'The Territorial Force', p. 131.
94 *Bootle Times*, 14 August 1914, p. 3.
95 *Bootle Times*, 7 August 1914, p. 7; *Southport Guardian*, 19 August, p. 4; 26 August, p. 6; 5 September 1914, p. 7.
96 Beckett, 'The Territorial Force', p. 132.
97 A Roll of Honour of Southport's Rugby Union Football Club appeared in the *Southport Guardian*, 23 January 1915, p. 2.
98 *Southport Guardian*, 29 August 1914, p. 11.
99 *Southport Guardian*, 9 January 1915, p. 4.

lists of men or the local names and pages dotted with photographs which appear elsewhere. This does not seem to have unduly affected the figures for recruiting in Bootle or the south of the area in question but there was a noticeable difference in approach. On 21 August, the *Bootle Times* reported that 180 men had volunteered at Bootle, although a number had been rejected due to bad teeth.[100] By the end of August, however, it seemed not everyone was rushing to join as perhaps they should. Reference was made to people who would join up, were it not for the meagre allowances paid to dependants and calling on the Government to increase the separation allowance.[101] The *Bootle Times* also urged recruitment from all sections of the community, noting: 'If a clerk is as good a man as a docker let them fight side by side… this is no time for class distinction'.[102]

After another push for volunteers for 2/7th Battalion numbers rose at Headquarters. In the week ending 4 September 325 men attested at Seaforth Barracks, but the following week 95 turned up on Monday alone. This was followed by 45 on Tuesday, 36 Wednesday, 36 Thursday, 17 Friday and 11 on Saturday, indicating a drop in enthusiasm, although the paper had previously pointed out that a number were joining the Pals. To try to limit the huge numbers of recruits, physical requirements were increased a little to a 35 inch chest and 5ft 6ins in height, though it was expected that these would be slackened shortly. In a further sign that dockworkers were amongst the ranks, a sub-recruiting office was also opened at the Canada Dock.[103]

The experience of women

While the Battalion recruited and trained men, local women were cast in the role of of non-combatants. However, their level of commitment most clearly demonstrates the extent of community identity shared with the troops at home and later abroad. Although women could be seen as a single group of the community, studies have also shown that they too consisted of a range of different identities and experiences within that broad gender grouping.[104] It is evident that in 1914 and 1915 on Merseyside there were three main aspects to their role. Firstly, their involvement in organising material, financial and emotional support for the services; secondly, their position as dependants of men who had marched away; thirdly the developing employment of women in traditional and non-traditional areas of work as a direct result of the War. Women experienced changes in status and employment almost from the start of the War. However, with Southport's history of temperance and Bootle's notorious dependence

100 *Bootle Times*, 21 August 1914 p. 8.
101 *Bootle Times*, 28 August 1914, p. 4.
102 *Bootle Times*, 28 August 1914, p. 4.
103 *Bootle Times*, 18 September 1914, p. 5; 11 September 1914, p. 5.
104 Woollacott, A., *On Her Their Lives Depend: Munition Workers in the Great War* (Berkley: University of California Press, 1994), p. 2.

on liquor in the docklands, there was also an undercurrent of concern in relation to sexual behaviour and drinking.

Local branches of the women's suffrage organisations followed the national lead in supporting the patriotic cause of the War. As Marwick noted, it was the suffragettes who 'outshone all others'.[105] The NUWSS deferred their suffrage campaign, and the WSPU, reflecting its increasingly Conservative membership,[106] became what Marwick called 'fervid' nationalists.[107] The Bootle Branch of the NUWSS agreed to give time, money and energy into co-operating with the relief societies, while the Conservative and Unionist Franchise Association and the National League for Opposing Women's Suffrage agreed to suspend their political activities and work with the Soldiers and Sailors' Families Association.[108] The Church League for Women's Suffrage and the Free Church League for Women's Suffrage agreed to co-operate in organising a Women's Emergency Corps, along with the Women's Freedom League and the National Aid Corps.[109] In March 1915, the local Annual Meeting of the National Union of Women Workers (NUWW) reported that so little activity had gone on in the last year due to their members working for other agencies in the War effort, that they could not formally align themselves with the Central Committee and had to set up an independent committee of NUWW instead.[110]

In concentrating their efforts on comforts for the troops, women identified themselves or were encouraged to identify themselves with the troops, at first generally but very soon in terms of local men and the local Battalion. In this period of depoliticisation, the *Bootle Times* called on women to knit socks and weave body belts, as well as sending money, in the belief that such work by women of means would also assist in lifting other women out of impoverishment.[111] Traditional women's activities were called on in the mass campaign to clothe the troops. Sewing circles and networks were set up by political and religious groups: North Meols Women's Liberal Association, the Southport and Birkdale Women's Unionists League, the Duke Street United Methodists Sewing Meeting – all keen and busy to do something.[112] The War could not completely dampen the enthusiasm of the fashion editors who were of the opinion that this season's colours would be 'dreadnought grey, khaki and dark navy blue,' and who could hardly betray their glee that 'the War has put an end for ever to tango… so

105 Marwick, A., *The Deluge: British Society and the First World War* (London: Macmillan, 1991, first published 1965), p. 127.
106 Smith, H.L., *The British Women's Suffrage Campaign 1866–1928* (London: Longman, 1998), p. 43.
107 Marwick, *The Deluge,* p. 127.
108 *Bootle Times*, 28 August 1914, p. 5; *Southport Guardian*, 26 August 1914, p. 8; *Bootle Times*, 4 September 1914, p. 8.
109 *Bootle Times*, 4 September 1914, p. 8.
110 *Southport Guardian*, 27 March 1915, p. 9.
111 *Bootle Times*, 16 October 1914, p. 4.
112 *Southport Guardian*, 2 September 1914, p. 3.

much the rage last year.'[113] They failed to consider that the most prevalent colour of the seasons to come might be black.

Women were part of the drive for recruits, urging their men to fight, although this could be taken too far. At the annual meeting of the Southport Division of the Women's Liberal Association, the President castigated women who handed out white feathers to men in the street as a 'contemptible' act.[114] The other main role for women was in raising funds – the Women's Liberal Branch was to the fore in a savings campaign in Southport.[115] Flag days were also predominantly organised by and involved women, building on the already popular and effective Alexandra Rose Days. The question of wider participation was not so popular. When the Bootle Education Committee referred to legislation which established the Central Committee on Women's Employment as 'grandmotherly' they provoked a storm of protest from the local suffragists wondering what would have been called 'grandfatherly'? – 'Probably nothing! We are so accustomed to ineffective legislation that effective direct action is called grandmotherly'![116] Depoliticisation did not mean that all tensions had evaporated.

By mid-December, Southport's Ladies' Auxiliary Committee was successfully running five sub-committees. Most significantly, the Sewing Committee had sent nearly 21,000 garments to local men in the 7th Battalion, as well as to local Kitchener men. The Ambulance and Nursing Sub-Committee was holding classes and the Sub-Committees on Civil Distress and the Soldiers' and Sailors' Families Association had raised money for local people.[117]

Female employment, in part to relieve distress, but also to fill gaps left by men, was soon an important issue for the local communities. Southport had a high number of dressmakers, milliners and confectioners and it was these industries, according to De Groot, which faced the most immediate redundancies as a result of the War crisis.[118] Braybon, too, identified areas for which Southport was well provided – domestic service, fish handling – as the first victims of unemployment.[119] It is unsurprising then that the Southport National Aid Committee did recognise the need to provide female employment to try and resolve some of these issues.

During September a joint sub-committee of the Employment Committee and the Ladies' Auxiliary Committee drafted proposals to treat women and girls who had been thrown out of employment due to a downturn in the economy and a Women's

113 *Southport Guardian*, 2 September 1914, p. 2.
114 *Southport Guardian*, 18 November 1914, p. 3.
115 Braham, M., *Southport Liberal Association: The First 100 Years* (Southport: M. Braham, 1985), p. 33.
116 *Bootle Times*, 16 October 1914, p. 7.
117 SAL: Southport National Aid Committee, Vol. 1 Minutes, 18 December 1914.
118 De Groot, G., *Blighty: British Society in the Era of the Great War* (London: Longmans, 1996), p. 126.
119 Braybon, G., *Women Workers in the First World War* (London: Routledge, 1989), p. 44.

Employment Scheme was finally approved at the start of October.[120] The Scheme was not unlike the Queen's Work for Women Fund which ran in and around London for the female unemployed, replacing luxury goods that had become unavailable and the gap created by cutting off the German toy industry.[121] The Southport Scheme and the establishment of the Women's Employment Bureau proved very successful with up to thirty-nine women working in one week, principally making over 3,000 toys, and the Committee was able to report that there was scarcely any unemployment among women in the town as a result.[122]

Involvement in the range of 'nursing' services allowed women to participate actively in the War. They also participated directly through work in the munitions factories. This process represented as meaningful an identification with the War as could be expected by the civilian half of the community. The WLTAF had set up a Voluntary Aid Committee in January 1910,[123] and there was also a Nursing Services Committee run largely by women, albeit well-connected ones, including the Countess Derby and Mrs. Harvey Gibson. They had only recently enrolled 120 new nurses, although predictably the senior medical and military figures were men – (Professor) Lt. Colonel Harvey Gibson, Dr. Caton (Colonel), Lt. Colonel Burns Gemmell.[124] The nursing side was one area perceived as a clear role for women, both in providing the service and in running it. By mid-December 1914, a total of 3,785 cases had been admitted in the Western Command area.[125]

Increasing numbers of wounded put pressure on beds and though 2,000 extra beds were being created as more hospitals were requisitioned, most were without nurses and equipment.[126] The recruitment of more untrained nurses and VADs allowed trained nurses to go to the newer branch hospitals such as the several institutions in

120 SAL: Southport National Aid Committee Vol.1 Minutes, 1 October 1914.

121 Thom, D., *Nice Girls and Rude Girls: Women Workers in World War I* (London: I.B. Tauris, 1998), pp. 30, 86.

122 SAL: Southport National Aid Committee Vol.1 Minutes, 15 December 1914.

123 The newly-established Committee included as Chairman, Lord Derby, then President of the St. John's Ambulance Association (West Lancashire), and Chairman of the West Lancashire Territorial and Auxiliary Force Association, and Countess Derby, President of the Red Cross Society of West Lancashire – LCRO: 356 WES 24/1 (64), West Lancashire Voluntary Aid Committee Minutes, 27 January 1910.

124 LCRO: 356 WES 16/1 (48) WLTAF Nursing Services Committee Minutes, 5 August 1914. Preparations for action had included practising transfering wounded men in and out of railway wagons but the government-issue stretchers had to be abandoned because they would not fit through the doors of an ordinary railway carriage – LCRO: 356 WES 24/1 (64) West Lancashire Voluntary Aid Committee Minutes, 7 January and 4 December 1911, and 2 December 1913.

125 LCRO: 356 WES 16/1 (48) WLTAF Nursing Services Committee Minutes, 16 December 1914.

126 LCRO: 356 WES 16/1 (48) WLTAF Nursing Services Committee Minutes, 21 October, 11 November 1914, and 24 February 1915.

Southport.[127] By August 1915 the Committee reported that the VADs were fulfilling their roles in the hospitals satisfactorily and allowing trained nurses to be used more effectively.[128]

By early 1915 women were therefore involved across a range of employment activities as well as working on comforts and support. In March 1915 the Southport NUWSS had one member nursing at the Grange, three in Women's Patrols, two teaching women on the Unemployment Scheme and one at the Front.[129] In June 1915 Litherland Council established a sub-committee to look at the provision of training in nursing for young women.[130] In April an appeal was made for women to register for work in munitions, clothing factories, agriculture, shop and clerical work[131] and it was reported that they were already being widely used in agriculture in the south west Lancashire area.[132]

This increased involvement in wider society caused some concerns in certain quarters, primarily in terms of drinking and sexual behaviour. In relation to the campaign to blame the shell shortage on slack production caused by drink amongst the working classes, women were often the focus of attention more than men.[133] The editor of the *Southport Guardian* called drunkenness amongst women a 'social menace'. His main concern was the leniency shown by magistrates in discharging seventeen of the forty-five women brought before the Bench in 1915. [134] Correspondents to the paper often blamed the problem on money being available all at once for work that had been done over a matter of weeks, although the drinking was only amongst 'a certain class' of Southport's women.[135] However, in his defence, the Chairman of the Magistrates said that total figures were down owing to the fact that many men had left the town.[136]

In another example of double standards on gender issues, Southport saw debate about the behaviour of its young women when large numbers of troops were billetted in the town. The existing imbalance between the sexes was compounded by the recruitment drive and the influx of new troops. Local suffragist organisations called for patrols to safeguard girls and young women and to restrain their behaviour in these 'abnormal conditions'.[137] This demonstrated that middle-class women did as much

127 LCRO: 356 WES 16/1 (48) WLTAF Nursing Services Commitee Minutes, 24 March, 14 and 28 April 1915; *Southport Guardian*, 2 January 1915 p. 8: these included the Hydropathic, the Homeopathic and the Isolation Hospitals.
128 LCRO: 356 WES 16/1 (48) WLTAF Nursing Services Committee Minutes, 11 August 1915.
129 *Southport Guardian*, 24 March 1915, p. 6.
130 CL: LUD 7 Litherland Urban District Council Minutes, 7 June 1915.
131 *Southport Guardian*, 17 April 1915, p. 9.
132 *Southport Guardian*, 21 April 1915, p. 6.
133 De Groot, *Blighty*, p. 75.
134 *Southport Guardian*, 5 February 1916, p. 6.
135 *Southport Guardian*, 7 November 1914, p. 3.
136 *Southport Guardian*, 5 February 1916, p. 8.
137 National circular of the NUWW, *Southport Guardian*, 17 October 1914, p. 7.

as anyone to promote the fear of so-called 'khaki fever', the result of which was to encourage the establishment of patrols carried out by women to monitor other, usually younger and more working-class, women.[138] Requests for patrols were rejected by the local Watch Committee in November and December, and did not re-surface until spring 1915.[139]

It was assumed that the women, rather than the men of the Army, would be badly behaved and immoral. One letter to the newspaper from a serving Officer called on the ladies who were supposed to uphold moral order, 'to turn their attention to knitting comforts'.[140] The military establishment saw the women as blameworthy and were keen to prevent the outbreak of problems which were associated with sexual immorality and which could weaken the men's army as a result – illegitimate babies and venereal disease being the prime concerns.[141]

By late November the Southport League of Honour – a euphemism for women's patrols – could boast a membership of 900 with twenty enrolling officers,[142] but the reaction of the Watch Committee in refusing to sanction the Patrols in 1914 had not altered by the end of 1915.[143] Whilst it is clear that patrolling was going on in Southport, the local establishment refused to alter its traditionally liberal position and to endorse such a 'moral crusade'. The local newspapers maintained an evenly balanced argument, but the overriding concern of the Police Force and the Watch Committee was to maintain control through the traditional methods and not by employing women in male occupations. There was, however, a more sinister side to the debate too. Simkins quotes Charles Cain, of the 2/5th Manchesters, billetted in Southport, as an example: 'The men I was with were rough with women, boasted of their conquests, many of whom were actually raped, but there were no prosecutions to my knowledge.' Cain also referred to a woman and her three teenage daughters who, putting up ten soldiers, all ended up 'in the family way'.[144]

The evidence demonstrates that the woman's experience of the first nine months of the war was, inevitably, mixed. Women's organisations were running campaigns and women were represented on the many committees of organisations which were doing

138 Woollacott, A., '"Khaki Fever" and its Control: Gender, Class, Age and Sexual Morality on the British Homefront in the First World War', *Journal of Contemporary History* Vol. 29, (1994), pp. 325–347; Levine, P., '"Walking the Streets in a Way no Decent Woman Should": Women Police in World War One', *Journal of Modern History*, Vol. 66 No. 1, (1994), pp. 34–78.
139 SAL: Southport Borough Council Watch Committee Vol. 1911–14 Minutes, 13 November and 31 December 1914.
140 *Southport Guardian*, 24 October 1914, p. 7.
141 De Groot, *Blighty*, pp. 232–5.
142 *Southport Guardian*, 28 November, 1914 p. 3.
143 SAL Southport Borough Council Watch Committee Vol. 2 Minutes, 23 December 1915.
144 Simkins, P., *Kitchener's Army: The Raising of the New Armies 1914–16* (Manchester: Manchester University Press, 1988), p. 175 quoting CA Cain, 'The Footsloggers', unpublished account (1967), Imperial War Museum PP/MCR/48.

similar work. Not only is this significant in the context of the political mood of the time and the eventual, legislation on the extension of women's suffrage from municipal elections to national elections, but also in terms of the actual involvement of women, by choice, in the mechanism of war. Although direct employment for women did not rise perceptibly in the area until into 1916, women were to the forefront of the support campaign for troops, in terms of both money and materials.[145] The one thing which it was agreed women could not do, as the President of the Southport Women's Liberals had pointed out, was actually fight. The consensus that this was (and of course predominantly remains) culturally unacceptable lay behind the desire to be close to the men in khaki who represented the war directly in their vicinity. The question of a more direct involvement in the war, however, was already being answered as the female workforce in industries directly supplying the armaments grew. Furthermore, the need for some form of direct action by women was a contributory element in the rioting after the sinking of the Lusitania.[146]

Unfairly, women were the subject of criticism. If there were any truth in the concern that drinking was having an effect on the munitions industry it was on the dockfront and in the factories where a reduction was most needed. Instead, the press campaign chose easy targets – women in particular – and as a result there is little evidence of any immediate or radical changes to behaviour. The answer to low production lay not in abstinence but in an increase in the labour force which could only come as more attention was paid to the introduction of women to the workforce in crucial industries. It is striking that both in relation to sexual behaviour and to drunkenness, it was women who were identified as being at prime fault. They were supposed to be the moral backbone of society and it was more shocking when they were found not to be complying with their gender role.

The growth of local munitions work

As the War went on, the industrial area of Liverpool and its close environs concentrated on the making and supply of munitions. Clearly a key element in this industry was the growth in the number of women employed in armaments production.

In total, the Liverpool War Munitions Committee ran six national shell factories: Cunard's on Rimrose Road; the National Gauge Factory, in Clyde Street, Bootle; Lambeth Road, Liverpool; Edge Lane, Liverpool; North Haymarket, Liverpool; and Chester. Additionally there was No.2 National Filling Factory near Aintree station, Sefton, the No.3 National Aeroplane factory at Aintree, and HM Explosives Factory

145 There were already high numbers of women employed in particular industries, such as matchmaking, which began to turn their attention to war-related production, including explosives and munitions, as shown by the 1911 Census.

146 *Southport Guardian*, 18 November 1914, p. 3.

at Litherland. By March 1918, 807 people were employed at Litherland, 33 percent of whom were women. The Aeroplane Factory employed 1,054 women (40.5 percent) out of a total 2,634 employees in September 1918. The Filling Factory employed 10,837 at its peak in March 1917, 10,340 of whom were women, although by August 1918 total employees were down to 8,599, of whom 87.1 percent were women.[147] While this was a huge number, the complete site covered 175 acres and included an amatol unit extension which in June 1918 had 2,219 workers.[148] The Clyde Street Gauge Factory employed just 52 skilled tool makers, although twenty-one of these were trained women. Finally, the Cunard Shell Factory employed 1,110 employees in October 1918 with 73.8 percent of them being women.[149] The significance of these figures was that in the southern part of the area, a total of 15,440 people were engaged in munitions work, of whom 12,500 (80 percent) were women.

Women workers were certainly a key element in the Cunard shell works. According to the 'Record of work' of the Liverpool Munitions Committee, 85 percent of labour was female. The manufacture of the heavier 6" and 8" shells was significant enough for the Ministry to send representatives from other factories to see what could be achieved by women workers. [150] In a history of Cunard during the War, the Rimrose Road factory was described as 'the pioneer in the employment of women on shells of large calibre.'[151]

A matron had been appointed in December 1915[152] and later the dining room had to be extended, together with matron's offices, cloakrooms and toilet facilities.[153] The percentage of female labour at Rimrose Road claimed by the 'Record of Work' was 85 percent of the total workforce of 1,053 in January 1918 i.e. 796; by October 1918 this had reduced to 73.8 percent in an increased workforce of 1,110 i.e. 819.[154]

According to the Liverpool Committee record, the women workers at the National Shell factory were 'mostly drawn from middle class homes…not previously engaged in factory work.'[155] If so, this seems to contradict Marwick's view that it was mainly working class women who went into munitions, although he did accept that they

147 *History of the Ministry of Munitions* (London: HMSO, 1923), Vol. VIII, Part II, pp. 64, 65, 108–111, 169, 170, 202–203.
148 WM: MUN 26/7 Report on the National Amatol Factory, Aintree 12 July 1918. The Leeds Filling Factory employed 12,150 women out of a total workforce of 13,315: *History of the Ministry of Munitions* Vol. VIII, Part II, p. 169.
149 *History of the Ministry of Munitions,* Vol. VIII, Part II, pp 109, 110.
150 LCRO: Liverpool Munitions – Record of Work, p. 27.
151 Hurd, A., *A Merchant Fleet at War* (London: Cassel & Co. Ltd, 1920), p. 72.
152 LUA: B4/44 Cunard Executive Board Minutes, 22 December 1915 – Miss De'Ath; also a Lady Superintendent and three assistants – LCRO: Liverpool Munitions – Record of Work, p. 24.
153 LUA: B4/47 Cunard Executive Board Minutes, 26 July 1916.
154 *History of the Ministry of Munitions* Vol. VIII, Part II, p. 109; LCRO: Liverpool Munitions – Record of Work, p. 52.
155 LCRO: Liverpool Munitions – Record of Work, p. 23.

Cunard Shell Works, Rimrose Road, Bootle, 1916. (National Monuments Record Centre, Bedford Lechmere Collection BL24001–96)

were joined by increasing numbers of the middle classes.[156] At the Aintree Filling factory, however, they were the 'city type – undersized, badly developed, with very bad teeth and often anaemic'.[157] The examination for workers at the factories was fairly similar to that carried out on volunteers for the Services. The superintendents were keen to ensure that the workers were fit enough to work in factory conditions and their regular inspections demonstrated concern for the women's welfare. They were also keen to ensure that worries about poisoning or explosions were minimised. According to the report on Aintree, there were only nine cases of toxic jaundice dealt with by the Medical Officer, and they all had septic teeth.[158] Three of these workers died.[159]

156 Marwick, *The Deluge*, p. 130.
157 IWM: MUN 26.4 Report on the National Amatol Factory, Aintree, 12 July 1918.
158 IWM: MUN 26.4 Report on the National Amatol Factory, Aintree, 12 July 1918.
159 Three women were listed from the Merseyside area as having died from poisoning, although the source material is limited in scope: Sarah Cooper, Wavertree; Agnes Deane, Everton; and Elizabeth Walsh, Bootle: IWM MUN 34.2/16 and 17: 'Names and addresses of workers who died of poisoning during war work'.

This was the one aspect of the sacrifice made by the Home communities. Death could be slow, through septic poisoning or maybe sudden as a casualty in one of several explosions. The explosion of a 6" shell at the filling factory in Sefton on 23 July 1918 killed 3 people,[160] and there had been a small explosion and fire at the Litherland HM Explosives Factory on Friday 22 September 1916.[161] It was Brotherton's HM Explosives Factory near Litherland army camp that caused the most persistent problems, described by Sassoon as 'a hissing and throbbing inferno, which incessantly concocted the form of high explosive known as TNT; when the wind was in the east the camp got the benefit of the fumes.' The fumes were a literary device for Sassoon – '[the factory] flared and seethed and reeked with poisonous vapour'[162] – for the local inhabitants they were a constant nuisance.

In spring 1916, Litherland and Bootle Councils started raising concerns about noxious fumes from the factory and the discharged effluent being pumped into the local sewers.[163] Nearby St. Philip's Church joined the fray and Litherland Council sought support from neighbouring Councils in Liverpool, Bootle, Waterloo and Great Crosby. An expert was called in to investigate the effects on the sewers at Bridge Road 'with a view to making a claim against the Ministry of Munitions'. By December, the Home Office and Arthur Stanley MP had also become embroiled and, following another evasive reply from the Ministry, the Council wrote again to complain.[164] Bootle Council had already been moved to action and a visit by the Medical Officer had found that 'fumes escape from nearly every joint in the pipes. There were greenish yellow clouds of nitric acid over the roofs' [of nearby houses].[165]

The continuation of work in the factories was important to the local economy. The local factory superintendent wrote to Litherland UDC claiming that the level of emissions received constant attention and they were likely to reduce considerably in the coming months anyway. Shortly afterwards, in an exhibition of compliant assimilation by the Council, the key players from Brotherton's, Bryant and May and North West Rubber, were appointed to the local National Service Committee. In June 1917 Litherland Council accepted the company's assurance that everything possible was

160 *History of the Ministry of Munitions* Vol. VIII, Part II, p. 170. The 'History' only listed three deaths from an explosion in the Liverpool factories, but six names appear in a list of women casualties who came from the Merseyside area – Margaret Bradshaw, Kirkdale; S. Payne, Liverpool; Agnes Brown, Garston; Mary Taylor and Sarah Wilshaw, both from Liverpool; Charlotte Massey, Seacombe – IWM: MUN 34.2/14 'List of workers to whom fatal accidents occurred' and IWM: MUN 34.2/15 'Names and addresses of workers who met with fatal accidents'.

161 CL: LUD 7 Litherland Urban District Council Minutes, 2 October 1916.

162 Sassoon, *The Complete Memoirs of George Sherston,* pp. 235, 381.

163 CL: LUD 7 Litherland UDC Minutes, 1 May 1916; B/MO5 Bootle Borough Council Medical Officer of Health Report, 29 May 1916; In his further report of 26 June 1916, the Medical Officer also recorded complaints about the Cunard works.

164 CL: LUD 7 Litherland UDC Minutes, 4 September 1916 and 4 December 1916.

165 CL: B/MO5 Bootle Borough Council Medical Officer of Health report, 24 July 1916.

Munitions workers at Vulcan Engineering, Southport, 1916, Jennie Gregson centre. (Author's private collection)

being done about the fumes, but still wrote to the Ministry demanding, perhaps rather naively, that the local factory stop manufacturing explosives. All this was to little avail. The report into the discharges into the sewer proved that the fumes from the factory were a severe danger to the local inhabitants. Unfortunately, this proof came from the inquest verdict on the surveyor and his colleague who had died accidentally, 'by being asphyxiated by gas which came from HM factory', while attempting to carry out their investigation.[166] Fire alarms were introduced under new regulations to try and control the fumes however the factory was eventually closed in April 1918.[167]

166 CL: LUD 7 Litherland UDC Minutes, 5 March, 7 May, 4 June, 2 July, 27 July, 8 August 1917, and 4 March 1918.
167 *History of the Ministry of Munitions*, Vol. VIII, Part II, p. 65.

Conclusion

In nursing, knitting and manufacturing bombs, women played a significant part in not just supporting the War but actively promoting and being engaged in it. The diverse aspects to women's work in south-west Lancashire reflected the inherent diversity in the area's social and economic profile. This diversity was similarly reflected at the Front, where the 7th Battalion's young recruits gradually experienced the increasing challenges and horrors of the war.

2

The 7th Battalion King's Liverpool Regiment

Formation & Recruitment

The recruiting ground for 7th Battalion King's Liverpoool Regiment was clearly defined, as were all the areas for the West Lancashire Territorial Division, being the land between Southport and Bootle along the Lancashire and Yorkshire Railway.[1] This consisted of the coastal swathe from Bootle up to North Meols, going inland only as far as the canal and main road. In theory, Ormskirk was outside the boundary. Away from the bounds of Liverpool, this area was, and is, particularly rural and of key importance to the supply of food.[2] It was also subject to the pervading influence of the local landowner, Lord Derby.[3] Implications for the recruitment of men from this area were that they would be healthier and fitter than their comrades from the factories. However, it also raised the question of the balance between the need for farm work and the need for men for the Front Line. Southport also had its share of light engineering companies, some of which were devoted to munitions work, while at the other end of the region Bootle was the main part of the Liverpool northern docks.[4]

Since volunteers came from across the whole area there was great diversity amongst the recruits with the potential for difficulties in moulding a successful and coherent combat effective Unit. Social, economic, religious and political differences could adversely affect the morale and discipline of the Battalion. The recruiting area contained two towns of quite diverse character both, to some extent, communities divided by politics, class, religion and economics but both feeling they owned and

1 LCRO: 356 WES/56 WLTAF Recruiting and Discharge Committee minutes 2 July 1913.
2 Phillips, C.B. and Smith, J.H., *Lancashire and Cheshire from AD1540* (London: Longman, 1994), pp. 237–240.
3 Walton, J., *Lancashire: A Social History 1558–1939* (Manchester: Manchester University Press 1987), pp. 221–224.
4 Crosby, A., *A History of Lancashire* (Chichester: Phillimore, 1998), pp. 71 – 98; Hyde, F.E., *Liverpool and the Mersey: The Development of a Port 1700–1970* (Newton Abbot: 1971).

were represented by the Battalion.[5] Referring to the creation of 'service' battalions in county regiments, Grieves has commented that there was a 'remarkable symbiosis of voluntary recruiting and pride in the locality'.[6] This description should be extended to include the recruitment within already constituted Territorial Battalions, such as 7th King's.

Earlier writers have shown the importance of the social cohesion of army units in relation to their battle effectiveness.[7] However, the 7th King's provide an interesting example of cohesion and effectiveness despite, or because of, this background of diversity. An important aspect to this collectiveness was the community identity which the Battalion felt which overcame any social or other differences which in other circumstances would have hampered such cohesion. The activities on the Home Front in 1914 and beyond, similarly demonstrated the shift towards an acceptance of 'total war' and the forging of a more holistic 'wartime identity' even in places which had hitherto been extremely diverse.

The traditional view of British society in 1914 has been of a divided country coming together with the onset of War, only for a gradually widening gulf to appear between the War and Home Fronts.[8] This became what Hynes called the myth of the War, an unbridgeable gap between the two wartime worlds. This became an unassailable construct by the thirties, in writing and culture, and has endured to our own time.[9] As Mitchinson commented, this myth can be found in learned studies and in poetry and prose alike.[10] The perspective has been tempered by Bourne, who felt that soldiers in France and Flanders were 'never entirely severed from civilian society',[11] and by McCartney who recognised the broad regional homogeneity in other Liverpool territorial battalions.[12]

The men who formed the early ranks of 1/7th Battalion King's Liverpool Regiment were predominantly from Southport, Bootle and the several towns and villages

5 Walton, *Lancashire*, pp. 219, 226, 295–296.
6 Grieves, K., '"There are times when we would all prefer the factory life": Letters from the trenches to the Shippam Works in Chichester during the First World War', *Family and Community History Journal of the Family and Community Historical Research Society* Vol. 6, No. 1, (May 1993), p. 59.
7 Baynes, J., *Morale: A Study of Men and Courage – The Second Scottish Rifles at the Battle of Neuve Chapelle 1915* (London: Leo Cooper, 1967), pp. 103–104; Fuller, J.G., *Popular Culture and Troop Morale in the British and Dominion Forces 1914–1918* (Oxford: Clarendon, 1991), p. 160; Griffith, P., *Battle Tactics of the Western Front*, pp. 51–52.
8 Tawney, R.H., *The Nation,* 21 October 1916; Fuller, *Popular Culture,* pp. 157–158. De Groot expands this theme to identify divisions between men and women, economic winners and losers; De Groot, *Blighty*, pp. 70–73.
9 Hynes, S., *A War imagined: The First World War and English Culture* (New York: Bodley Head, 1990), pp. ix, 116, 459.
10 Mitchinson, *Gentlemen and officers*, p. vi.
11 Bourne, J.M., 'The British Working Man in Arms' in Cecil and Liddle (eds.), *Facing Armageddon*, p. 339.
12 McCartney, H., *Citizen Soldiers,* p. 58.

around that area. It is clear that recruitment to 7th King's was of a generalised nature. It was not an ethnic-based battalion like the Liverpool Irish, nor one based on a certain proficiency such as the Rifles, nor was it made up of men solely from the same factory or company. It was a Battalion which recruited primarily from a geographical perspective and the evidence shows that in terms of numbers, it was almost 100% rooted in Southport and Bootle. Its closest comparison is with the locally raised Pals units and there is evidence of local identity being the most significant expression of their make-up.

It is also possible to demonstrate that the Battalion reflected the social and economic structure of the area to a considerable degree, although there is a doubt about the extent of its engagement with Bootle's working and under class community. There is sufficient evidence to show that even at Company level, men were alongside men from quite different backgrounds and experiences. However, the nature of training of this disparate group was to be criticised later by Regular Army commanders and therefore their effectiveness as a combat unit in France would appear to rely on those diverse experiences and abilities almost as much as the development of a drilled disciplinary outfit.

Although the transition from civilian volunteer to uniformed soldier on the other side of the Channel was a gradual one taking some eight months, the division between the experiences of the troops and the non-combatants had already begun. There are dangers in relying on this notion of a division, a gulf, too far. Without wishing to further perpetuate the concept of division between Home and Front it is important to assess some of the historical contributions which have established the military and the community contexts for this debate. The division continues to be reflected in the work of historians and in the media.[13] While this is understandable to some extent, given the scale of the War and its myriad topics, it is still disappointing that so many writers perpetuate this emphasis on either the military or the social aspect at the expense of the other.

Military histories were very common throughout the 1920s and 1930s. Primarily these were accounts of particular units and 'their War'. Many were commissioned as a memorial to the men who had been lost and they have a largely uncritical style being particularly strong in heroic deeds, the steadfastness of the men and, especially, the commanding abilities of leading officers. Many were also written by people who had

13 Sheffield, G., *The Somme* (London: Cassell, 2003); Hart, P., *The Somme* (London: Weidenfeld and Nicolson, 2005); Beckett, I.F.W., *The Great War 1914–1918* (London: Pearson Education Ltd, 2001); De Groot, *Blighty* and *The First World War* (London: Palgrave, 2001); BBC 'War Walks' series and accompanying series volume by Richard Holmes, *War Walks* (London: BBC Books, 1996) and *The Western Front* (London: BBC Books, 1999)and the Channel Four series accompanied by Strachan, H., *The First World War* (London: Simon & Schuster, 2003).

either been directly involved in the conflict – or were in contact with those who had.[14] Some individual writers were prolific in their production of such volumes. Colonel H C Wylly, in addition to those listed below, wrote the first two volumes of the history of the King's Own Yorkshire Light Infantry, a history of two battalions of the Leicestershires and one on the Green Howards, all published between 1923 and 1932.[15] The principal skill required in writing these histories or accounts was an ability to make War Diaries more readable.

Their proliferation reinforced the emphasis on the need to identify with the regiment or division as a key element in sustaining the morale of the men. They were frequently commissioned by the regiment as an act of memorialisation. In this sense they could have provided a useful social work function in gradually assisting men back into civilian society after the trauma of war, giving them something to grasp in a period of great uncertainty. In the event, they were unlikely to have been widely available to ordinary soldiers, while the evidence collected for their production by the authors came from the officers, not the men. Nonetheless, those involved in ex-comrades associations may have had wider access to them. Some histories were of a division, others the regiment or just individual units. As a result, some Territorial Battalions had histories of their own. There appears no external logic to which units may or may not have had their deeds written up.

Although no study of 7th Battalion King's Liverpool Regiment exists, there are a number of studies of closely connected units. Wyrall's overall history of the Regiment during the War remains the definitive version.[16] The difficulty with Wyrall's account, worthy and comprehensive as it is, is that it tends to be incoherent, jumping from the narrative of one Battalion to that of another. In nurturing the honours and traditions of the Regiment, it was not able to take a strategic view of particular events as there were, inevitably, many other Battalions involved from other Regiments. The

14 Examples include: Hodgkinson, Capt. A., *The King's Own Territorial Forces – Being a Record of the 1/5th Battalion of the King's Own (Royal Lancaster) Regiment in the European War 1914–18* (Manchester: Lewis Press, 1921); Latter, Maj. Gen J.C., *A History of the Lancashire Fusiliers 1914–18* Vol. 1 (Aldershot: Gale and Polden, 1949); Wadham, Lt. Col W.F.A. and Crossley, Capt. J., *The Fourth Battalion The King's Own (Royal Lancaster) Regiment and the Great War* (London: Crowther and Goodman, 1935); Wylly, Col. H.C., *The Loyal (North Lancashire) Regiment* (London: Royal United Services Institute, 1932); Col HC Wylly *The History of the Manchester Regiment (Late 63rd and 96th Foot)* Vols. 1 & 2, (London: Forster, Groom and Co. 1923–25); Wylly, Col. H.C., *The York and Lancaster Regiment 1758–1919* Vols. 1 & 2, (Richmond: Butler and Tanner Ltd, 1930); Anon., *War History of the 1st/4th Battalion The Royal North Lancashire Regiment Now the Loyal Regiment 1914–18* (Preston: George Toulmin and Sons Ltd, 1921).

15 Bond, R.C., *History of the King's Own Yorkshire Light Infantry* Vols. 1–3 (Bradford: Percy Lund, Humphries and Co, 1930) [Vol. 1 & 2 by Wylly]; Wylly, Col. H.C., *The Green Howards in the Great War 1914–19* (Richmond: Butler and Tanner Ltd, 1926); Wylly, Col. H.C., *The History of the 1st and 2nd Battalions The Leicestershire Regiment in the Great War* (Aldershot: Gale and Polden, 1928).

16 Wyrall, *The History of the King's Regiment.*

Regimental historian rarely dealt with a solitary fighting unit. As a history of the most consistent and significant Army unit, the division, Coop's narrative of 55th Division, commissioned by the West Lancashire Territorial and Auxiliary Force Association in 1919, is therefore potentially a much more relevant account.[17] The advantage of the Regimental history, however, was the attention paid to the individual Battalions, particularly useful if the original source material has been lost or destroyed. Coop's work only focused on particular units if they were key to a specific action or to a point he wished to make. The 1/7th King's fought most closely with 1/5th, 1/6th and 1/9th Battalions of the King's Regiment, even prior to the reforming of the 165th (Liverpool) Brigade in the West Lancashire Division in 1916. Tilsley's oft-quoted *Other Ranks* was based on a sister brigade, 164th, and McCartney's thesis on 1/6th King's and the Liverpool Scottish has covered related ground to this book.[18] There are also a number of other accounts of Liverpool Territorial Battalions relevant to this study.[19]

While unit histories were both specific and unconnected with each other, the Government sanctioned a comprehensive record of the War in the *Official History*.[20] Though the later volumes have sometimes been discredited, at the start of the project, the *Official History* was going to be the definitive work on the War, based on as many interviews and contributions as possible. This, in part, explains the lack of tactical or strategic discussion in the unit histories, although the main purpose of these histories was rarely intended to be analytical. As a result, some events in the unit histories may now appear to have more significance than when the same event was recorded in the *Official History*.

Any analysis of the Territorial Force during the War has tended to be part of a wider study. There has been no real attempt to study their wider military contribution in depth, or in isolation. Studies of particular battles or campaigns have tended to analyse the contribution of all units involved and, where relevant, this has included Territorial units.[21] Recent re-evaluations of the Somme and the events of 1918 by

17 Coop, *The Story of the 55th Division.*

18 Tilsley, *Other Ranks*; McCartney, *Citizen Soldiers.*

19 Wurtzburg, *The History of the 2/6th (Rifle) Battalion, the King's (Liverpool) Regiment 1914-19*; McGilchrist, *The Liverpool Scottish 1900-1919*; Roberts, *The Study of the 9th King's in France*; Moore, 'The Territorial Battalions of the King's'.

20 Volumes of *The Official History* that are most relevant: Edmonds, J.E. and Wynne, G.C., *1915, December 1914–May 1915* (London, 1927); Edmonds, J.E. and Wynne, G.C., *1915, Aubers, Festubert and Loos* (London, 1928); Edmonds, J.E., *1916 to July 1* (London, 1932); Edmonds, J.E., *1916, July 2 to End of Somme Battles* (London, 1938); Edmonds, J.E., *1917, Messines and Passchendaele* (London, 1949); Miles, W., *1917, The Battle of Cambrai* (London, 1949); Edmonds, J.E., *1918, March-April* (London, 1937); Edmonds, J.E., *1918, May-July* (London, 1939); Edmonds, J.E., *1918, August 8–September 26* (London, 1947); Edmonds, J.E., *1918, September 26–November 11* (London, 1949).

21 Clark, A., *The Donkeys* (London: Pimlico, 1991, first published 1965); Passingham, I., *Pillars of Fire: The Battle of Messines Ridge June 1917* (Stroud: Sutton, 1998); Steel, N., and

Gary Sheffield, have attempted to provide interpretations of particular events within a more holistic appraisal of the strategic developments of the War, drawing attention to Territorial units where appropriate.[22] Griffith's more general study of tactics and strategy referred to the Territorials within the context of the overall study of the BEF and he did not consider the Territorials separately in terms of tactics, except to try and point to a hierarchy of divisions in which Regular units were to the fore.[23] In his time-limited review of the Hundred Days, Simkins, in contrast, suggested that New Army divisions were the more prominent divisions.[24]

Although work on the Pals battalions as a whole has also been limited, there are many extant accounts of individual Pals battalions, including the series which has attempted to cover some of the more well-known units.[25] These recent studies have built on the romantic and tragic histories but have sought to examine the community as a whole. Although the Liverpool Regiment is famous for its Pals battalions due to Lord Derby launching the idea in Liverpool, it also had a high number of Territorial battalions. Derby's role in establishing the Pals as a notion, and an entity, primarily though not exclusively in the North of England, has never been fully explored. Lord Derby was and remained hugely committed to the Territorial Force, yet at times appeared to give more attention as Kitchener's recruiting sergeant to the new Service battalions. These new units, especially the locally raised units (Pals) were, ironically, built on the notions of local community pride and identity, not dissimilar to that forged within the existing Territorial Force.

Regardless of the abilities of the battalion as a combat unit, or of the platoon or the division, success depended to a great extent on the tactics handed down from GHQ and the overall strategy within which the operations were occurring. From the *Official History* onward, there has been a plethora of studies of tactics and strategy in the Great War, particularly on the extent of blame which can be apportioned to Haig and his commanders. Some, including attempts to present a wider biography in the context of the First World War, have focused on Haig's own role.[26] However, more recent

Hart, P., *Passchendaele: the Sacrificial Ground* (London: Cassell & Co, 2000).

22 For example, in relation to 46th (Midland) Division (TF): Sheffield, G., *Forgotten Victory – The First World War: Myths and Realities* (London: Headline Book Publishing, 2001), p. 251; Sheffield, *The Somme*, pp. 41–47.

23 Griffith, *Battle Tactics of the Western Front*, pp. 80–81

24 Simkins, P., 'Co-Stars or Supporting Cast? British Divisions in the "Hundred Days", 1918', in *British Fighting Methods in the Great War* (ed.) Griffith, P.. (London: Frank Cass, 1996) p. 64.

25 Pen & Sword series publications: in addition to Liverpool, volumes include Birmingham, Accrington, Leeds, Barnsley, Sheffield, Salford, Hull, Newcastle and Manchester.

26 Terraine, J., *Douglas Haig: The Educated Soldier* (London: Cassell & Co, 1963); de Groot, G., *Douglas Haig, 1861–1928* (London, 1988); Hussey, J., 'A contemporary record or post-war fabrication? The authenticity of the Haig diaries for 1914', in *Stand To!; The Journal of the Western Front Association* No. 42, (January 1995); Laffin, J., *Butchers and Bunglers of World War I* (Stroud: Alan Sutton, 1988); Travers, *The Killing Ground.*

works have tried to address the military rather than the personal issues.[27] Sheffield and Bourne have returned to the personal angle in an attempt to revise the popular picture of what Winter called the 'fiction' of 'Haig's Command.'[28] The relevance to 7th King's of these studies has been limited and while general appraisals of events which the Battalion experienced are useful, such as on the Somme, at Passchendaele and in the initial 1918 Spring Offensive,[29] some key experiences in the Battalion's War – Festubert and the German offensive in April 1918 – have barely received any historical assessment.[30]

Griffith's analysis of the development of training and the emphasis on all-arms tactics as important elements in the effectiveness of a Division was reflected in the evidence relating to 7th Liverpools which shows this progression over the four years of the War.[31] Despite the Pyrrhic victory at Passchendaele, it was clear from Lee's brief analysis that by late 1917 there was no doubting the abilities of Territorial Divisions,[32] a fact acknowledged by Griffith.[33] Both Coop's enthusiastic appraisal of the Division's

27 Travers, T., *How the War was Won: Command and Technology in the British Army on the Western Front 1917–18* (London: Routledge, 1992); Prior, R. and Wilson, T., *Command on the Western Front* (Oxford: Blackwell, 1992); Ashworth, T., *Trench warfare 1914–18: The Live and Let Live System* (London: Macmillan, 1980); Terraine, J., *The Smoke and the Fire* (London: Sidgwick and Jackson, 1980); Griffith, *Battle Tactics on the Western Front*; Griffith (ed.), *British Fighting Methods in the Great War*; Sheffield, *Forgotten Victory.*

28 Sheffield, G. and Bourne, J., *The Haig Diaries: The Diaries of Field Marshal Sir Douglas Haig* (Weidenfeld & Nicholson, 2005); Winter, D., *Haig's Command*, p. 225.

29 Middlebrook, M., *The First day on the Somme, 1 July 1916* (London: Penguin, 1984, first published 1971); Liddle, P.H., *The 1916 battle of the Somme: A Reappraisal* (London: Leo Cooper, 1992); Prior, T. and Wilson, T., *Passchendaele: The Untold Story* (New Haven: Yale University Press, 1996); Liddle, P.H. (ed), *Passchendaele in Perspective; The Third Battle of Ypres* (London: Leo Cooper, 1997); Middlebrook, M., *The Kaiser's battle* (London: Penguin, 1983); Pitt, B., *1918 The Last Act* (London: Papermac, 1984, first published 1962)

30 Some of the few to even mention these events include: Samuels, M., *Command or Control? Command, training and tactics in the British and German Armies, 1888–1918* (London: Frank Cass, 1995); Holmes, R., *Fatal Avenue* (London: Pimlico, 1993); Taylor, A.J.P., *The First World War* (London: Penguin, 1963); Gilbert, M., *First World War* (London: Weidenfeld & Nicolson, 1994). Clarke's *The Donkeys* studied Neuve Chapelle and Aubers Ridge, but did not consider the continuation of that sequence, at Festubert, before moving on to Loos. A few accounts for these actions do exist from the perspective of other units: Andrews, W.L., (re.1/4th Black Watch) *Haunting Years: the Commentaries of a War Territorial* (London: Hutchinson, 1930); Rogerson, S., (re. 2nd West Yorkshire) *The Last of the Ebb* (York: Arthur Barker, 1937); Messenger, C., *Terriers in the Trenches: The Post Office Rifles at War 1914–1918* (Chippenham: Picton, 1982). An honourable recent exception is GD Blades 'The battles of the Lys: The British Army on the defensive in April 1918', M.Phil thesis, King's College London, 1999.

31 Griffith, *Battle Tactics on the Western Front,* p. 200.

32 Lee, J., 'The British Divisions at Third Ypres', Liddle (ed,), *Passchendaele in Perspective: The Third Battle of Ypres,* pp. 224–225.

33 Griffith, *Battle Tactics on the Western Front,* pp. 80–83.

performance and Tilsley's sometimes rose-coloured[34] view of his 164th Brigade could be read with some scepticism, but now also need to be seen in the context of such analyses by Lee and Griffith.[35] Sheffield's revisionist history of the War has also referred to the 55th Division's tactical growth, learning the lessons of Guillemont in 1916 to be applied within a few short weeks at the end of September, and in the defensive training so vital to the stubborn British resistance to the German attack in April 1918.[36]

Embodied & Overseas

At the end of September, with around 400 local men in the Battalion, the Southport contingent marched or were driven to Headquarters at Bootle, and 100 of these went straight to Romsey to join up with the main element of the Battalion who were already there. Critchley recalled that he was digging ditches on Lord Derby's Knowsley estate, before heading for Romsey.[37] The *Southport Guardian* commented that the men had been promised they would stay together and would be allowed some choice in which Section they joined, along the idea of the Pals Battalions.[38] A later press report showed that the papers had been a little over-enthusiastic about numbers in the Battalion. When numbers in the 7th Battalion reached 1,000 men and thirty-five Officers, it was reported that this included 300 Southport men 'who had taken the place of the original ones who were unfit or unable to do foreign service.'[39] It seems that this 300 was the number of recruits in September, but it did not include the Southport men who were already in the Territorial Battalion before War broke out.

Giving impetus to the sense of regional identity, this first wave of volunteers were soon billetted on the south coast where 700 Kingsmen joined soldiers from all around Lancashire. Private Phillips wrote that the weather was hot, the people kind and that they were staying in large houses along the seafront.[40] The *Bootle Times*' sports pages reported from Southampton, where D Company was at the Dock Station in October 1914. A football encounter with St. Dennis Argyle had left Argyle 'routed with the terrible loss of 12 goals to 1'. The trench humour – and sporting entertainments – which they would have to rely on in France was much in evidence in Corporal Stanley's review of the game. The enemy's citadel was bombarded, there was quick firing, the 7th would not be driven out of enemy territory, there were fierce attacks on

34 As a Lancastrian, it was probably red rose-coloured.
35 Coop, *The Story of the 55th Division*; Tilsley, *Other Ranks.*
36 Sheffield, *Forgotten Victory*, pp. 181, 228–29.
37 Critchley.
38 *Southport Guardian*, 30 September 1914, p. 4.
39 *Southport Guardian*, 14 October 1914, p. 4.
40 *Southport Guardian*, 3 October 1914, p. 3.

their front line, backed by their rearguard, and when the order came to cease firing, D Company had won their first action 12:1![41]

Messages home from 2390 Private Jack Fearnhead, A Company, in Romsey showed that the Battalion was due to move to Sevenoaks on 18 October. After ten days there, they were sent on to Canterbury, where they were in their first beds for three months.[42]

Recruiting work by local organisations, by the newspapers and by rallies and meetings, continued throughout the Autumn. Working on garments and comforts was to encourage local involvement in recruiting as much as to ease the life of the soldiers who received them. Crosby Urban District Council even persuaded its Councillors to send cigarettes to G Company, out of their own pockets.[43] While the Mayor of Bootle and newspaper advertisements called for recruits for a third, reserve, for the 7th Battalion, local Bootle MP and Leader of the Conservative Party, Andrew Bonar Law, addressed a huge recruiting meeting with Lord Derby at the Metropole in Liverpool, which the *Bootle Times* reported verbatim.[44]

As the Battalion was on call for the defence of London over Christmas leave was cancelled, unlike Kitchener's and Home Service men.[45] Nonetheless, letters published in the local newspapers were designed to keep spirits up. They had a 'splendid Christmas' at Canterbury. After a route march on Christmas Eve, Christmas Day was given off and Christmas dinner was eaten on Boxing Day with each Company dining as a Unit (the author's Company ate along with G Company – one of the Southport Companies) on turkey, pork, sausages, potatoes, ham, minerals for the teetotallers, beer, plum pudding, mince pies and crackers.[46] Another letter from Bootle's Terriers in D Company, confirmed that it had been a good Christmas in Kent.[47]

However much the good people of Kent enjoyed their Christmas, apparently they were not so enthusiastic about New Year, so the men of the King's showed them how it was done in Liverpool. Partying through the town in fancy dress, playing the drums and singing 'Tipperary' and 'La Marseillaise', they aroused the interest of the local police who persuaded them that they had partied enough and should head back to their billets. On the way to their billet they paused to wake the Officers, who were staying in a big hotel, with more singing and drumming, wished a happy New Year to the residents of the town so privileged to billet the 7th King's, crossed hands and sang 'Auld Lang Syne', 'Rule Britannia' and 'God save the King', and went to bed. 'The

41 *Bootle Times*, 9 October 1914 p. 6.
42 Private collection PH: Jack Fearnhead correspondence, 17 October 1914, 6 November 1914 and 22 November 1914.
43 *Bootle Times*, 18 September 1914, p. 5.
44 *Bootle Times*, 4 December, p. 6; 18 December, p. 5; 24 December 1914, p. 4.
45 Jack Fearnhead correspondence, 18 December 1914.
46 *Bootle Times*, 1 January 1915, p. 4.
47 *Bootle Times*, 8 January 1915, p. 4.

A few soldiers of the 7th Battalion men billeted in Eastbourne. (Courtesy: Peter Threlfall)

people here afterwards said they had never seen anything like it – and they seemed to mean it.'[48]

It was important for the men to retain the link with home and the editors used these 'public interest' stories to keep up the recruitment campaign. Jack Fearnhead was less enthused with the positive and rather light-hearted activities, complaining that many of the presents and post for 7th Battalion had gone to the MOBs at Blackpool – 'Mother's Own Boys', that is, Home Service men. When enquiries were made it caused some disturbance, even though the Quartermaster hushed it up.[49] Nor was the *Bootle Times* shy of reporting some of the bad news too. With no leave over Christmas, New Year leave was then refused to any men who would not agree to be innoculated and there was uproar amongst men and their families. Vaccination had always been a contentious issue for the working classes. Letters complained about the issue and when it seemed that some men may be due home the following weekend, the Editor showed that the interests of the local lads were better served by having leave than by succumbing to the red tape of the Military Authorities.[50] A letter of thanks from a

48 *Bootle Times*, 8 January 1915, p. 4.
49 Jack Fearnhead correspondence, 29 December 1914.
50 *Bootle Times*, 22 January 1915, p. 4.

Formby company, 1/7th Battalion, King's Liverpool Regiment in France.
(*Formby Times*, 17 April 1915)

man in 7th Battalion later appeared as leave for most was granted, though it was still refused to those who would not be innoculated.[51]

This leave was the last time many of the men saw their families. Men continued to join the first group who had arrived in Romsey on Friday 4 September 1914, expecting to be sent to Egypt or India to replace Regular First Line troops who were coming back to fight in France.[52] The people of Romsey had soon made them feel at home, according to a letter from Colour Sergeant Ludlam of G Company, who along with the rest of the Battalion was soon guarding railway stock, sidings, stations and bridges.[53] As well as route marches, once stationed at Canterbury different Companies were trained through guarding strategic installations such as harbours and railway stations nearby, at Whitstable, Eastbourne and Ramsgate.[54] Divisional commanders in France were later to question the usefulness of this 'training'.[55]

For all the talk of Ireland, India or Egypt in the early days, their training and expectations turned to France. At the start of March they moved from Canterbury, to be replaced there by the advance parties of the 2/7th Battalion.[56] The newspapers at home barely reported the fact that the Battalion had arrived safely in France on

51 *Bootle Times*, 12 February 1915, p. 4.
52 *Southport Visiter*, 8 September, p. 5 and 10 September 1914, p. 6,
53 *Southport Visiter*, 12 September 1914, p. 7.
54 Jack Farrington correspondence, 27 January 1915.
55 TNA WO95/590 I Corps War Diary, Major-General Horne report.
56 *Southport Guardian*, 3 March 1915, p. 5.

Sunday 7 March 1915.[57] Private James Cook, No. 2388, 8 Platoon, B Company, just had time to record on a postcard for his family: 'Are in tents & it is very rough snow and rain falling… Very rough on this side of the Channel.'[58]

1/7th Kings in France, March – May 1915

After their training on the south coast of England, the 1/7th Battalion Kings Liverpool Regiment arrived in France on 8 March 1915 and spent some short time being assimilated into the 2nd Division. A period of minor action and trench duty was ended by the first major action for the Battalion as a Unit at the Battle of Festubert in May 1915.

The first ten weeks of the Battalion's time at the Front was a story of gradually building towards Festubert. The men were increasingly keen to become involved, although sanguine about their inexperience and the need to be properly respected as a fighting unit by the Regulars in the Brigade. The commanders allowed for bursts of involvement in the trenches, were grateful for carrying parties and were eventually ready to commit a full scale attack to their care. After a long lull in local press attention, when the Battalion was training in the south of England from September 1914, there was a sudden reawakening of interest once they were actually doing something newsworthy.

Seventh Battalion landed in two parties – officers and most of the men on the ship the 'Golden Eagle' and the rest on the 'Manchester Importer' – on 8 March 1915. Nothing but a small item in the local press heralded their arrival.[59] The first letter to appear in the *Southport Guardian*, from Private Carl Purser, C Company, the son of a local Councillor, writing on 14th, described his crossing in the cattle boat, 200 men and 300 horses, followed by marching in snow and bitter cold, a train journey in cattle trucks, packed like herrings and not being settled in one place until the end of the following week.[60]

Back home, the local population remained linked to the War effort. Local councils were engaged in the recruiting campaign for Territorial volunteers, responding to Lord Derby's request for open air meeting facilities and speakers from the Council[61] and in the establishment of a munitions factory in the Cunard properties in Bootle.[62]

57 *Southport Guardian*, 10 March 1915, p. 2.
58 Private Collection: James Cook correspondence, 8 March 1915.
59 *Southport Visiter*, 9 March 1915, p. 6.
60 *Southport Guardian*, 20 March 1915, p. 7. Purser's commentaries developed into him being an unofficial 'war correspondent' for the newspaper.
61 CL: Bootle County Borough Minutes Volume XXXII, 5 May 1915; LUD7 Litherland Urban District Council Minutes, 3 May 1915.
62 LUA: B4/44 Cunard Executive Board Minutes April-July 1915; *History of the Ministry of Munitions* Vol. VIII, Part II, p. 108.

Paddle Steamer *Golden Eagle*. (IWM ref. SP3037)

The Battle of Neuve Chapelle, on 10 to 12 March 1915, was soon in the headlines, although the heavy casualties sustained by 1st King's were not made public until over a week later.[63] By early April, some of the newly established nursing facilities on Merseyside were taking in the wounded from Neuve Chapelle.[64]

The 1/7th Battalion's War Diary noted their progress in the first few days from Le Havre to Vendin lez Béthune.[65] The Battalion spent the next few weeks assimilating, gaining experience and training, usually operating as companies, attached to different Regular units.[66] A sign of the lack of commitment of resources came in Marriott's letter of 12 March 1915 to his father, noting that the Battalion would not be used as a whole until they had all been issued with the short service rifle.[67] Rifle exercises, trench digging, inspections, drill and filling sandbags were the routines for the first ten days.

However, some of the Battalion did see action almost immediately. On the night of 17 March, while attached to the Guards, B Company were digging a communication trench and C Company filling sandbags in no man's land, when they were shelled

63 *Southport Guardian*, 20 March 1915, p. 7.
64 LCRO: 356WES 16/1(48) WLTAF Nursing Services Committee, 24 March 1915.
65 TNA: WO95/1360 1/7th Battalion Kings Liverpool Regiment War Diary, 8–12 March 1915.
66 TNA: WO95/1360 1/7th Battalion King's Liverpool Regiment War Diary, 12–30 March 1915; WO95/1352 6th Brigade War Diary, 14–31 March 1915; Southport Visiter, 15 May 1915, p. 2; *Southport Visiter*, 18 May 1915, p. 4.
67 Marriott correspondence, 12 March 1915.

by German artillery. One man was killed, and another died of wounds.[68] Private Griffiths mentioned it in a letter home, published ten days later.[69] Marriott, whose Company was involved, told his father they had been building a sandbag fort at the brick stacks, Cuinchy, when a flare went up and noted that Private Webb was the first man in the Battalion to be killed.[70] By the time the incident had reached the *Southport Guardian* however, it was a St. Patrick's Day baptism of fire![71] Rumours of it being a serious confrontation were quelled in subsequent reports.

Digging trenches at night still had its dangers and throughout the War men died in small but significant numbers. Nevertheless, each incident was examined, and the following day the Company Commanders of B and C Companies were interviewed by Generals Munro, Horne and Fanshawe.[72] A few days later, on 23 March, in a similar incident, Sergeant Schofield was killed and an unnamed man and Lieutenant Smythe injured.[73] According to Purser, it was simply misfortune that as the enemy were trying to find the British guns, a stray shell landed where they were digging out of the trenches.[74] Griffiths, who was part of the Company and close by, said they were digging in the communication trench to make it deeper.[75] Private Brenchley reported that Schofield 'was unrecognisable. His face was blown clean off'.[76]

The nature of that revelation was inevitably in great contrast to the letter which Company Commander, Captain Marriott sent to the family of Private Beveridge: 'He was detailed with a party under my command to work outside the advanced trenches and was killed instantly, much to the regret of the whole company, as he was not only a good soldier, but a very straight man, and one in whom I placed great reliance.'[77] Webb's date of death would seem to be slightly inaccurate as he seems to have died later of wounds while Beveridge was clearly killed by a shell and has no grave, and it is perhaps Beveridge who should be given the dubious honour of being the first man in the Battalion to die for his country. Notwithstanding this, Marriott's real views on the causes of most deaths during March – though presumably not these two – were clearer

68 TNA: WO95/1360 1/7th Battalion King's Liverpool Regiment War Diary, 17 March 1915.
69 *Southport Guardian*, 3 April 1915, p. 9.
70 Marriott correspondence 18 March 1915; Private R Webb, 2084, killed 17 March 1915, is buried in Béthune Town Cemetery. However, Private William Beveridge, 2087, was also recorded as killed on 17 March. His name appears on the Le Touret Memorial – *Indices of the Commonwealth War Graves Commission.*
71 *Southport Guardian*, 24 March 1915, p. 5.
72 TNA: WO95/1360 1/7th Battalion King's Liverpool Regiment War Diary, 18 March 1915; Marriott correspondence, 18 March 1915: Major-General Horne was Divisional Commander and Brigadier-General Fanshawe commanded 6th Brigade.
73 TNA: WO95/1360 1/7th Battalion King's Liverpool Regiment War Diary, 23 March 1915.
74 *Southport Guardian*, 3 April 1915, p. 9.
75 *Southport Guardian*, 3 April 1915, p. 9.
76 *Southport Guardian*, 3 April 1915, p. 9. Note that Schofield's date of death was inaccurately recorded in *Soldiers Died* as being 22 February, when in fact it was March 1915, p. 56.
77 *Southport Guardian*, 27 March 1915, p. 9

The 1/7th King's allegedly in the front line. (Front page of the *Daily Sketch*, 1 June 1915 and later reproduced in *The Year Illustrated 1915* (London: Headley Brothers, p. 90))

from his letter home on 28 March describing the occasional casualties as 'generally the man's own fault'.[78] Marriott pointed to new men who wanted to take a look over the parapet. This demonstrated the fascination and excitement which the War, sometimes tragically, engendered in the volunteers.

Although the next month's War Diary is missing, it is clear from letters and newspaper reports that the rest of April 1915 was spent in a similar routine. Private Rymer wrote to his sister on 10 April about a mine blowing up one of the British trenches nearby – also reported by Private James Cook – though they were now getting used to the shells; Fred Aldred described the many dead Germans lying on the battlefield, 'some of them are in a fearful state – faces quite black'; Corporal Caswell of the Machine-Gun Section was badly injured by a shrapnel shell, while Sergeant Cotton described refugees being hit by shells in a village.[79]

When Private Cook came out of the trenches after the latest four-day spell on 29 April, he called it 'the hardest yet.'[80] Other letters talk of billets, food, ruined villages and the awful weather, requiring the issue of goat and sheepskin coats – later withdrawn as being too cumbersome.[81] At the end of April what can be regarded as a starting figure for the Battalion's fighting strength was thirty Officers and 940 men.[82]

One of the reasons for all this training and these details was the need to bring the Battalion up to scratch for action on its own. The War Diary reported that the Battalion was allowed a portion of the Front Line on its own on 31 March, although Marriott did not expect more until early April.[83] The tardiness in entrusting Line and action solely to the Territorials appears to have been due to some disappointment amongst BEF commanders in France with the relevance and standard of training given to the men while they were in England.

The Regular divisions in France had been well prepared for the arrival of large numbers of the Territorial Force and seemed to greet it with some trepidation. In early February 1915, Lieutenant-General Robertson, Chief of the Imperial General Staff circulated a document highlighting the sorts of issues which divisional commanders needed to be aware of in advance of the Territorial Forces coming to France.[84] While based on the few Units who had arrived in France by that date, Robertson believed the advice was applicable to all newly-arriving Units.[85] Special attention had to be paid to rifle and machine gun training, march discipline, entrenching, communications and

78 Marriott correspondence, 28 March 1915.
79 *Southport Guardian*, 21 April 1915, p. 9; James Cook correspondence, 12 April 1915.
80 James Cook correspondence, 1 May 1915.
81 *Southport Visiter*, 15 May 1915, pp. 2, 4, 6.
82 TNA: WO95/1285 2nd Division War Diary Report of Fighting Strength, 24 April 1915.
83 TNA: WO95/1360 1/7th Battalion King's Liverpool Regiment War Diary, 31 March 1915; Marriott correspondence, 31 March 1915.
84 TNA: WO95/590 I Corps War Diary Letter from Lieutenant-General Robertson Chief of the Imperial General Staff to First Army Divisions, 4 February 1915.
85 TNA: WO162/7 Embarkation records.

platoon leading. Robertson identified a lack of proper sense of discipline, not maintaining the proper chains of command, boots being ill-fitting, a lack of understanding of the supply and ordering system, and poor instruction in billeting requirements.[86] General Horne, commanding 2nd Division, and a recipient of this circular, later made it clear to GHQ that the standards of training in England needed to be taken up with the appropriate authorities.[87]

The Army tried to match up the Territorial Battalions with related Regular counterparts as far as possible, presumably to secure an understanding and support mechanism for them. Certainly, the relationship between the Territorials and the Regulars in the King's Regiment was highlighted by the mutually supportive references in letters home in relation to the Battle of Festubert itself.[88] The Terriers of the West Lancashire Division were assigned to Regular Divisions with direct links to the local Regiments. The 5th and 7th King's were in 2nd (Regular) Division, with 1st King's. The 8th Battalion joined 4th and 5th King's Own, and 5th Loyal North Lancashires in 51st Division. The 9th King's were in the 1st Division, with the 1st Loyals. The 10th (Scottish) had been out since the previous Autumn, fully integrated in 3rd Division, and were joined by 4th South Lancashires and 2nd Loyals, while in the 4th Division the 1st King's Own and 2nd Lancashire Fusiliers were joined by 5th South Lancashires. Although the Territorial Division was not reconstituted until 1916, the individual units were still in close touch with their neighbours from home, as part of the deliberate policy of support and training for these fresh units.[89]

The immediate impression of the Battalion had been given in the Brigade War Diary, 13 March 1915 – 'They look a very useful lot.'[90] After only a few days, however, the appraisal was less glowing and, despite the fact that the CO reported that on 17 March they 'had all done very well under trying circumstances',[91] Division was less impressed. Brigadier-General Fanshawe, at Brigade level, a lot closer to the troops than his superiors, felt that both 5th and 7th King's were 'satisfactory' but that the

86 TNA: WO95/590 I Corps War Diary letter from Lieutenant-General Robertson Chief of the Imperial General Staff to First Army Divisions, 4 February 1915.

87 TNA: WO95/590 I Corps War Diary letter from Major-General Horne, 2nd Division, to GOC I Corps, 23 March 1915.

88 Additionally, the 24 April 1915 *Southport Guardian*, p. 6 included an anonymous letter: 'Our first line battalion are with us… Brave is not the word for it. They are a lot of dare-devils… The Germans know them as the 'cast iron' regiment. In fact … brigade known as the cast iron brigade'. This is particularly interesting in the light of Tilsley's use of the epithet to describe 55th Division, which did not include 1st King's, but did include 5th and 7th King's – Tilsley, *Other Ranks*, p. 4.

89 TNA: WO162/7 Embarkation records; Becke, A.F. Major *Order of Battle of Divisions Part I Regular Divisions* HMSO (1936) (repr. London: Ray Westlake, 1989) pp. 36–63; Morris 'The Leeds Rifles', p. 494.

90 TNA: WO95/1352 6th Brigade War Diary, 13 March 1915.

91 Marriott correspondence, 19 March 1915.

junior commanders needed greater confidence in themselves, and for them to improve discipline and training as a result. He also commented that the higher commanders were slow. Nevertheless, he did feel able to declare them fit for the Front Line.[92]

However, this view was overruled by Major-General Horne's interpretation of the report for First Army Corps, which said that neither Battalion was immediately fit for the Front, though they were being introduced gradually. His response was based largely on their smartness and ability in drill, rather than their prospective abilities in combat.[93] Typically for the Regular Command, the lower standard of drill and the more casual approach to smartness from the Territorials, were significant factors. Nevertheless, Horne did find the Battalion CO, Lieutenant-Colonel Stott, young and active with a good command of his officers and men. His most severe criticism was for the training methods in England, which are worth quoting at length as they demonstrate the inconsistency of approach within the Army Command to preparation for the Front:

> [B]earing in mind that these two battalions have been embodied for seven months, the standard of training is very disappointing… the battalion has been employed for some months guarding railways, etc. duties entailing many detachments and leaving little room for drills and exercises… drill and manoeuvre leave much to be desired. Little attention appears to be devoted in England to cultivate a smart and soldierlike bearing and to enforce strict discipline and cleanliness. This is noticeable, not only in these territorial battalions, but in the case of drafts sent to regular battalions.[94]

Horne was obviously less interested in musketry ability than having smart soldiers in his Division. The difference between Regular and Territorial style and ethos stood out very plainly, and the comments later in this chapter and elsewhere, which appear to show an inferiority complex amongst some of the Territorials in relation to the Regulars, were clearly the result of this kind of damning criticism. One can only imagine the regime which meant that 'these two battalions have improved out of recognition during the short time they have been with the division'.[95]

Private Purser gave his own appraisal of the Battalion in a letter at the end of April 1915:

92 TNA: WO95/590 I Corps War Diary Report of Brigadier-General Fanshawe 6th Brigade for GOC I Corps, 22 March 1915.
93 TNA: WO95/590 I Corps War Diary Report from Major-General Horne 2nd Division for GOC I Corps, 23 March 1915.
94 TNA: WO95/590 I Corps War Diary Report from Major-General Horne 2nd Division for GOC I Corps, 23 March 1915.
95 TNA: WO95/590 I Corps War Diary Report from Major-General Horne 2nd Division for GOC I Corps, 23 March 1915.

> So far I think the 7th Kings have come off very lucky, because they have been hard at it all the time. They have already gained a good name as 'real workers'. There isn't much of the 'swank' element in our battalion and we all try and act together, which accounts for the work getting done properly. Of course, I think there are many things which may be improved upon, but 'red tape' always has and always will exist, and it's no use saying more on the subject.[96]

Other Territorial Battalions fared much the same. By 6 April 1915, the Post Office Rifles had 'a great deal to learn' and were 'not trained in working at night'; 6th Battalion, City of London Rifles needed Regulars to left and right, but could hold the line with such assistance and supervision; while 7th Battalion London Regiment were however, quite competent to go into the line.[97] A consistent complaint was made about officers – in 15th (Civil Service) Battalion, and the 17th, 18th, and 20th Battalions, London Division, they were inclined to 'sit around and wait for a job to be done, lacked command, and required further work with the Regulars'.[98] In this context, 7th King's were on a reasonable par with members of one of the crack Territorial divisions.[99] The general appraisal of needs of the Brigade kept this and other Battalions hard at it through April – as Cook testified – until adjudged able to provide support at Aubers Ridge on 9 May.

The Brigade War Diary made reference to the various aspects of training and movements of the Battalions in the early days of May 1915 including forming part of the Corps Reserve for the attack by 1st Division on 9 May.[100] One correspondent reported that 1/7th Battalion had 'been acting as a "Flying Unit", moving from place to place at a moment's notice … attacking all along the line'.[101] The Diary reported the failure at Aubers Ridge of the first attack at 7:00 a.m. and also the second around 6:30 p.m., by which time the Brigade had moved up to support 1st Division at Richebourg St. Vaast. The Brigade was ordered into attack, but this was delayed by the blocking of trenches and approaches by wounded and returning troops from the 1st Division. 'This delay was just as well as the attack was cancelled. The orders to this effect barely reached the Brigade in time.'[102] The Diary gave a very clear indication of the confusion and error which could so easily have led to many more casualties, a situation replicated at many stages over the subsequent three and a half years. Orders were issued to attack on the 10th at 3:00 p.m., but this was cancelled at 10:30 a.m. and the troops returned to billets.[103]

96 *Southport Guardian*, 28th April 1915, p. 9.
97 TNA: WO95/1285 2nd Division War Diary Report, 6 April 1915.
98 TNA: WO95/1285 2nd Division War Diary Report, 16 April 1915.
99 The London Division. See Griffith, *Battle Tactics on the Western Front* p. 80 and Morris 'The Leeds Rifles', p. 494.
100 TNA: WO95/1352 6th Brigade War Diary, 30 April–9 May 1915.
101 *Southport Guardian*, 22 May 1915, p. 7.
102 TNA: WO95/1285 2nd Division War Diary, 9 May 1915.
103 TNA: WO95/1352 6th Brigade War Diary, 10 May 1915.

This incident also shows the different levels of information available to Brigade and Battalion commanders. While Brigade knew the details of the attack and the cause of its cancellation, as far as the Battalion was concerned they simply 'Stood by all day' on 10 May and on 11th 'Moved off to fresh billets'.[104]

For the men, there was a mixture of relief and disappointment not to be called on. Cook allayed his mother's anxiety, though, when he wrote the Battalion had not participated 'yet'.[105] Corporal Wainwright wrote at length of the day spent marching to reserve positions, eating dinner and tea, marching back and forth, leaving packs and donning capes, only to be returned to billets with unfulfilled excitement.[106] In a few short days and as many miles away, the Battalion would be back in the front line, leading an attack for the first time, at Festubert.

104 TNA: WO95/1360 1/7th Battalion King's Liverpool Regiment War Diary, 11 May 1915.
105 James Cook correspondence, 10 May 1915.
106 *Southport Visiter*, 15 May 1915, p. 4.

3

Avenge the *Lusitania*!

Two key events in May 1915 proved significant in contributing towards a community identity in Bootle and Southport which was to last through and beyond the conflict – the sinking of the *Lusitania* and the Battle of Festubert. While there is some evidence of the *Lusitania* disaster having an impact on the Battalion's attitude in action at Festubert, it is the impact on the local community which proved to be a defining factor. The rioting which followed in its wake was the most significant of all the anti-German feeling seen at Home.[1] In particular, this was an important element in the establishment of women's identity in Bootle. While the passengers on Cunard's *Lusitania* came from a variety of places, many being American, the majority of her crew and stewards were Liverpool people. The justification for the attack on the *Lusitania* as a legitimate target of War is another debate.[2]

The Sinking of the *Lusitania*

The *Lusitania* was not the first ship to be sunk by a German submarine in fact twenty-five merchant ships and the liner, *Falaba*, had gone down between February and the end of March of that year.[3] The *Lusitania* embarked from Liverpool on 17 April, arriving in New York on the 24th, on her regular monthly round trip, returning from New York on 1 May.[4] On the afternoon of Friday, 7 May she was holed by torpedoes and sank off the coast of Ireland with the loss of 1,201 lives.[5] The news spread quickly and the first outbreak of what was to prove a wave of unrest and violence occurred in

1 Panayi, 'The Lancashire anti-German riots of May 1915', *Manchester Region History* (1988), p. 3–11.
2 Preston, D., *Wilful Murder: The Sinking of the Lusitania* (London: Corgi, 2003).
3 C Simpson *Lusitania* (Wirral: Avid Publications, 1996), p. 83; *Southport Guardian*, 31 March 1915, p. 5; *Liverpool Echo*, 28 May 1915.
4 Simpson, *Lusitania*, pp. 90, 110.
5 Simpson, *Lusitania*, p. 9.

Liverpool the next day. It was reported that riots started in Walton Lane and then spread, although on the Saturday, they were mainly confined to the North End. They continued through the night and occurred again on Sunday, and on Monday 10th they spread, to Bootle, Birkenhead and Seacombe. The first riots in Manchester also occurred on the Monday.[6]

Three theories about why the riots occurred were put forward at the time: that they were hunger riots, that they were simply a reaction to the sinking itself and that they were inspired and fuelled by the press reaction. Panayi has concluded that there was more to it than a simple response to the event, that there is no real evidence that they were hunger riots, and that the press reaction merely reported what was going on rather than inspired it.[7] For Panayi's conclusion to be challenged evidence is needed that the rioters read the papers which were most vociferous in their anti-German columns and that their reports for instance of so-called 'atrocities' inspired locals to vent their anger. An appraisal of local papers shows that this was not the case.

Primarily the argument for blaming an inflamatory press can be refuted on the basis of the timings of the publication of local papers. The *Bootle Times* came out on a Friday, so it was a full week before they could report anything about the sinking or the aftermath. Even then its reports were limited to anything which occurred up to Tuesday night, implying that it was written on Wednesday, printed on Thursday and sold on Friday.[8] Similarly, the *Formby Times* and the *Crosby Herald* were published on a Saturday. The *Southport Guardian* came out twice a week, on Wednesdays and Saturdays, but the sinking happened too late to reach the editions of Saturday 8th May. The *Southport Visiter* was the first local paper able to print details of the disaster, and of the riots, as it came out on a Tuesday, Thursday and Saturday.

If the riots were inspired by the press it must have been the national papers, and it would need to be those on Saturday 8 May or Monday 10th, to have had any effect in Merseyside. The *Lusitania* was torpedoed on Friday 7 May at 2:10 p.m. In eighteen minutes she had sunk.[9] The first announcement reached the newspaper offices in London around 4:00 p.m. and the news was in late editions of the London papers.[10] Riots on the Saturday, Sunday and Monday, can only either have been spontaneous or dominated by local people who took the national papers. Evidence of circulation of such papers in Bootle at this time is non-existent. Riots broke out elsewhere too, even in Whitstable where Jack Fearnhead was guarding the harbour.[11]

The role of rumour cannot be discounted altogether. Undoubtedly, the travelling soldiers, administrators and civilians would have been part of the dissemination of

6 Panayi, *The Enemy in Our Midst: Germans in Britain during the First World War* (Oxford: Berg Publishers, 1991), pp. 237–238.
7 Panayi, *The Enemy in Our Midst*, pp. 229, 234–235.
8 *Bootle Times*, 14 May 1915.
9 Simpson, *Lusitania*, pp. 148, 150.
10 Simpson, *Lusitania*, p. 170.
11 Jack Fearnhead correspondence, 12 May 1915.

news of the tragedy. In the absence of any evidence it is not possible to establish the significance of this factor in reporting the news.

The riots may have been perpetuated by the national reporting fervour, but clearly the sparks of violence over that first weekend were the result of a pent-up reaction to Germany. In fact, the local editorials were censorious of the acts of rampage. On Friday 14 May, in his first opportunity to comment, the editor of the *Bootle Times* referred to the verdict of Monday's inquest into the disaster, held at Kinsale, which had found it 'Wilful murder', but he also wrote that the riots 'retard rather than advance our cause'. Emphasising where the energy should go, the editorial continued: 'the country wants soldiers not shopbreakers – keep the King's up to strength.'[12] The Tuesday edition of the *Southport Visiter* was indignant at this 'dastardly murder' and while reporting riots in London and Manchester in Thursday's paper, also reported Lord Derby's remarks that it was a 'senseless form of revenge', not to mention an 'extremely expensive one'. Derby stressed that the right form of retribution was to enlist in the Army.[13] One correspondent with Bootle MP, Andrew Bonar Law, expressed the fears of families with men held by the Germans as Prisoners of War, that their lives may be in jeopardy as a result of this 'foolish' and 'illegal' action. Bonar Law agreed with the need to stop the riots but also expressed the hope that one result would be that 'America may join us in the War.'[14]

The *Bootle Times* reported the riots in detail. Between 150 and 200 shops were attacked on both sides of the Mersey and damage was calculated at up to £50,000. Saturday night violence was confined to Fischer's butchers in Walton Lane and Dimler's in County Road. Both shops were again attacked on Sunday, ransacking the upstairs living quarters. The paper called them 'patriotic pillagers'. George Vogel, who had four sons serving in the British Army, also had his shop wrecked. A fire was started at Franz and Co. sweet factory in Everton. On Monday the crowd moved on to Bootle, headed by 'shawled women'. The report continued: 'a confectioner's shop bearing a Teutonic name Smash! Crash! and the window was in smithereens. The crowd gave a cheer and cursed the Kaiser'.[15]

The reports were ambivalent in their approach to the mob – creating a story of excitement from which can be drawn parallels with later reports of the action in France. There are references to the 'curious crowd', to the actions of a woman with an axe, and later, 'a new leader was discovered at the head of affairs in the form of a well-dressed young lady.' The item referred to the 'savage spirit' of the crowd. There was looting of butchers, confectioners, jewellers, and general destruction of furniture

12 *Bootle Times*, 14 May 1915, p. 4.
13 *Southport Visiter*, 11 May 1915, p. 7 and 13 May 1915, p. 7; *Southport Guardian*, 12 May 1915.
14 House of Lords Record Office Bonar Law MSS Vol 2 37/2/17 and 37/5/24, correspondence between James Graham Watson, Midlothian (12 May 1915) and Andrew Bonar Law MP (14 May 1915).
15 *Bootle Times*, 14 May 1915, p. 6.

and fittings – a piano was brought out of one house in Hapsford Road 'and one of the crowd obliged with a few patriotic selections before the instrument was utterly destroyed.' There were some suggestions that on Monday there had been a 'plan of campaign', with different groups taking Stanley Road, Hawthorne Road and Derby Road but no other evidence of this has been found.[16]

There were several references to women in the mob. One report claimed the trouble was started by women who had lost relatives in the disaster. Apparently, one of the women stood on a chair in Stanley Road and preached an eye for an eye. The newspaper thought it 'deplorable' that there were so many young girls in the crowd.[17] The involvement of women is borne out by an analysis of the court cases over the following few days. The Bootle magistrates dealt largely with theft and receiving, sitting on Saturday 15th and then a further three days the following week. Five women were convicted on Saturday, twenty-four women out of a total of thirty-two defendants on Monday, eighteen on Tuesday and another twelve on Wednesday – a total of 59 women from Bootle alone. Several of the defendants were only fifteen or sixteen years old. Of forty cases at Liverpool magistrates on Tuesday 18 May, the 'majority were women and a few young girls.' Fines ranged from five to forty shillings and there were a number of imprisonments, ranging from five to fourteen days, the women receiving the lighter punishments of five or seven days in prison, if they could not pay the fine.[18]

This predominance of women could support Sylvia Pankhurst's argument that these were riots in protest at the shortage of food. However, the nature of the charges reported in the local press shows that they were not targeting food shops. German butchers were attacked as being German, not for their food – although clearly any looter would not have turned down the opportunity. The majority of charges related to stealing other things – chairs, cushions, skirts, dolly tubs, prams, chests of drawers, mirrors, trays, pans, mattresses, tables, a sofa, clocks, jewellery, plates and saucers. And a piano lid.[19] All this points to widespread but opportunistic and untargetted looting and certainly nothing to do with being a hunger riot. Nor were there any pronouncements by local suffragists on the matter.

As far as the Battalion was concerned, they went into battle at Festubert with the name *Lusitania* on their lips. There is no logical direct connection between the riots and the men attacking 'in the name of the Lusi' and their war cry may have been no less spontaneous than that of the rioters. An assertion in the *Bootle Times* of 21 May that the Battalion was also hit by the loss clearly referred to the news of the sinking rather than proving a causal link between the riots and the Battalion attack.[20]

16 *Bootle Times*, 14 May 1915, p. 6.
17 *Bootle Times*, 14 May 1915, p. 6.
18 *Bootle Times*, 21 May 1915, p. 6; 28 May 1915, p. 2.
19 *Bootle Times*, 21 May 1915, p. 6; 28 May 1915, p. 2.
20 *Bootle Times*, 21 May 1915, p. 4, – Pte. J.Hughes letter, 1/7th Battalion King's Liverpool Regiment.

The institutional response to the sinking was perforce more restrained, dealing more in what could come out of the tragedy, but this too concentrated on the immediacy of the event and there is evidence that for many authorities the importance of the loss was shortlived. Litherland Council, meeting on Monday 10 May expressed sympathy for the relatives of those lost, but no mention was made of the disturbances.[21] Formby recorded its abhorrence at this 'wanton and murderous deed.'[22] The Liverpool Chamber of Commerce, under the chairmanship of Lord Derby, passed a resolution expressing sympathy and condolence.[23] A Memorial Service was held at St. Peter's Church, Liverpool on Thursday 13th, attended by representatives from the local authorities, Cunard, the Mersey Docks and Harbour Board, and a number of survivors and grieving relatives.[24] Towards the end of May, Bootle organised a Benefit Concert and a Mayor's Fund was set up to raise money for the relatives.[25] Most subsequent references in the press or in local council minutes concerned the riots and their costs.[26]

Cunard eventually set up a Fund for a Motor Ambulance called the *Lusitania* and also a Number 2 Fund, as a memorial. After the first six months grant expired – £400 – it was reported to the Board that there were still two ambulances operating at the Front in the name of the *Lusitania* so the grant was extended.[27] Cunard also erected a war memorial outside its headquarters on the Pier Head, Liverpool, in 1921, dedicated to the men and women employed by the company who had been lost during the War, but made no other permanent contribution to the victims of the *Lusitania* in particular. They did pay a modest sum toward the upkeep of graves in Kinsale until 1926 and subsequently, as they fell into disrepair, desired to remove the Cunard name from the plot. It was left to an American committee to pay for and erect a memorial to those lost in the disaster. Due to complications it was not unveiled until 1953, but with no involvement from Cunard.[28]

The evidence from reports in the press and from Council meetings confirmed that the riots were a spontaneous outburst of anti-German feeling. Panayi's conclusion, that the riots were racist and anti-German, albeit within the context of spy hysteria and intolerance of aliens during a War situation, appears to be the most reliable one.[29] This may also have been locked into a build-up of antipathy, fuelled partly by publicity

21 CL: LUD 7 Litherland Urban District Council Minutes, 10 May 1915.
22 Lancashire Record Office (LRO): UDFo 2/4/3 Formby Urban District Council Minutes, 12 May 1915.
23 *Southport Guardian*, 12 May 1915.
24 *Bootle Times*, 28 May 1915, p. 5.
25 *Bootle Times*, 28 May 1915, p. 5.
26 *Bootle Times*, 21 May 1915, p. 5.
27 LUA: B4/46 Cunard Board Executive Committee Minutes, 21 October 1915, Vol. 46.
28 Wilton, D., '"Their name liveth"; analysing the approaches to First World War Remembrance using records in Liverpool and Worcester', Unpublished MARM thesis, Liverpool University, 1998, pp. 8, 28, 29,32.
29 Panayi, 'The Lancashire anti-German riots of May 1915', pp. 3–11.

about German methods of warfare, particularly the gas attack at Ypres, and partly by stories of atrocities in Belgium. At the same time as the reports of the sinking of the *Lusitania* were appearing in the papers, the *Southport Visiter* for one was carrying stories of these reported atrocities such as 'a sergeant of the Cheshires crucified to a tree with bayonets and a farm with one hundred wounded in it being blown down'[30] and of questions in the Commons when the War Office denied any knowledge of three Canadians who had been similarly crucified with bayonets by the Germans.[31]

It may have been further fuelled by the tone and descriptions employed by the press, even in their condemnation of the rioting, as shown in the reports described above. As much as two weeks later the *Bootle Times* still referred to the cases before the courts as 'pilfering patriots'.[32] Mostly, however, it was an opportunity for the local civilian population to feel part of the War, to show that they were physically involved as well as the Battalion. It provoked a rush to recruit in the local area which is not reported elsewhere in the country,[33] further suggesting that this at least began as a very local, Merseyside reaction to a local tragedy. Derby and others did not lose the opportunity to promote a recruiting drive, as they did with subseqent attacks on the Western Front. Recruiting posters appeared with the phrase 'Avenge the Lusitania' well into 1916.[34] There was even a brief suggestion that the surge in recruits in West Lancashire should be used to form a 'Lusitania Battalion'.[35]

The Battle of Festubert 1915: '7 days in hell'[36]

Festubert needs to be seen in its context as the third in a series of attempts in the La Bassée sector to break through the enemy lines in the Spring of 1915, in support of the attacks being made by the French Tenth Army to the south.[37] Griffith noted that the battles in the La Bassée area in early 1915 were part of a gradual adaptation and understanding of the tactics needed to secure a breakthrough.[38] These included the artillery's creeping barrage, Lewis guns, trench mortars, smoke, gas, signals and aircraft, although this understanding was patchy, and not until Loos did it begin to

30 *Southport Visiter*, 11 May 1915, p. 8 letter from Private C.C. Jopling 6th Northumberland Fusiliers, convalescing at the Grange, Southport.
31 *Southport Visiter*, 13 May 1915, p. 6.
32 *Bootle Times*, 28 May 1915, p. 2.
33 *Bootle Times*, 14 May 1915, p. 8, reported that recruiting in the previous week had surpassed previous figures and 'over 60 have joined in the last week'.
34 *Southport Guardian*, 12 May 1915, p. 8; Simpson, *Lusitania*, p. 18.
35 *Southport Guardian*, 12 May 1915, p. 8.
36 James Cook correspondence, 21 May 1915.
37 Only one contemporary account from an eyewitness drew attention to the combined campaign: 'the best of all was that we cleared the way for further French advances on our right.' – Threlfall, *The Story of the King's*, p. 169.
38 Griffith, *Battle Tactics of the Western Front*, p. 53.

come to fruition. The barrage at Festubert was extensive, based on the supposition that Neuve Chapelle and Aubers Ridge might just have been more successful if the enemy had been obliterated, before the infantry attacked.[39]

Militarily, three key aspects stand out in this action: firstly, it was reported as the first night attack of the War; secondly, it did not start out as a planned battle in its own right, but became that by default; and thirdly, the generals' decision to use relatively new troops in the assault was a calculated and somewhat cynical decision. Despite being seen as the first night attack of the War,[40] little critical attention seems to have been given to this fact.[41] Haig's strategic conference demonstrated that, originally, the renewed attack at Aubers Ridge on 10 May 1915 was planned to be either at night with bayonet and no artillery, or during the day with fresh troops.[42] In the event, there was no renewed attack at Aubers on 10th May. The dilemma for High Command was always that a huge barrage forfeited the element of surprise – a night attack would at least provide some protection to the infantry. Unfortunately, at Festubert, the dark hindered the attackers and led to confusion. Additionally, the barrage did not damage the defences or machine gun emplacements to the level expected.

References to the battle have drawn attention to its failure to advance very far and the high casualty list. Taylor stated that it further demonstrated the futility of this kind of attack on such a narrow front against a heavily fortified line.[43] Griffith has pointed out that there were moments when they were close to success, implying that massed columns of men could breach the enemy defences.[44] Nonetheless, the culmination of the expenditure on shells, coupled with the failure to break through at Aubers Ridge or Festubert, was highlighted by Sir John French's contact with his friend, Lord Northcliffe, in *The Times*, when he began the campaign against Asquith on the basis of the 'Shell Scandal'.[45]

The failure of the assault on 9 May was blamed on inadequate preparation and so when the bombardment, which began on 13 May, did not, apparently, prepare the way for the infantry, it was continued and the attack postponed from the night of 14th to the night of 15 May.[46] Reports referred firstly to the unpreparedness of the Indian

39 Holmes, *Fatal Avenue*, pp. 112–3; Clark, *The Donkeys*, p. 126.
40 Messenger, *Terriers in the Trenches*, p. 18.
41 *The Official History* did not draw any particular attention to the fact, although Festubert was only the third major attack by the BEF after the trench lines had been established at the end of 1914: Official History – 1915, Aubers, Festubert and Loos, pp. 40–77.
42 TNA: WO95/155 First Army War Diary Conference notes, 9 May 1915.
43 Taylor, *The First World War*, p. 83; others have referred to the high casualty rate and lack of ground gained or breakthrough made: Brown, M., *The Imperial War Museum Book of the Western Front* (London: Sidgwick and Jackson, 1993), p. 71; Holmes, *The Western Front*, pp. 65–66.
44 Griffith, *Battle Tactics of the Western Front*, p. 53.
45 Gilbert, *First World War*, p. 162.
46 TNA: WO95/155 First Army War Diary, 14 May 1915.

Corps[47] and secondly to the failure of a number of shells to explode when hitting the German parapet.[48] However, it is clear from First Army War Diary that the attack at Festubert should really be seen as a continuation of the Aubers Ridge battle, after a series of delays from 11 May.[49]

Haig later noted that Horne's plan of attack was straightforward. The assault would be by night across ground 'now so well known, in order to gain a footing in the first two lines of the German trenches before dawn.' After the first success, however, he proposed to await daylight as … obstacles … [would] dislocate further advance in the dark.'[50] The three brigades of the 2nd Division would attack employing 10,000 men, including 6th Brigade and 1/7th Battalion King's Liverpool Regiment in the first assault. This attack would be over 1,000 yards of waterlogged fields, muddy trenches and barbed wire to the first objective of La Quinque Rue.[51]

Originally, 6th Brigade were notified that the new attack would be at night on 14 May, and orders given, but then withdrawn, as stated, due to the wet and muddy ground over which the 7th Division would later have to advance in daylight.[52] The daylight attack subsequently proved to be less successful on that Front. The reinforcing attack by the 7th Division had to be by day as they were new to the area, but the success of the assault required both 2nd and 7th Divisions to carry out a more deliberate attack, rather than the failed 'rapid assault' at Aubers.[53] The Battalion Commander had a 'Conference with GOC Brigade' on 14 May, but the troops were resting and there is no indication at Battalion level of the postponement from 14 to 15 May, unlike the entry in the Brigade Diary.[54] Kearsey placed the bombardment over the 60 hours of 13 to 15 May although this 'Official' implication that the event was originally planned to be a night assault on 15th following a prolonged bombardment is not supported by the evidence in the War Diary which clearly shows that the initial plan was for an attack twenty-four hours prior to that.[55]

The third element in considering the preparations for the battle was the blooding of new troops. In the 2nd Division the explicit method of attack was to use the raw troops as live bait to draw the enemy, who could then be punished by rested, seasoned troops waiting in reserve. Fanshawe's policy was to employ the 'expendable' element of his Division to allow his more experienced men to launch a renewed attack on a tired

47 TNA: WO95/591 I Corps War Diary, 14 May 1915.
48 TNA: WO95/591 I Corps War Diary, 15 May 1915.
49 TNA: WO95/155 First Army War Diary, 9–14 May 1915.
50 TNA: CAB44/20 Draft chapter on Festubert for the *Official History*.
51 Kearsey, Lt. Col. A., *1915 Campaign in France: The Battles of Aubers Ridge, Festubert and Loos considered in relation to the Field Service Regulations* (London: Naval and Military Press, reprint 1929), pp. 10–11; TNA: WO95/1285 2nd Division War Diary Battle Instructions, 13 May 1915.
52 TNA: WO95/1352 6th Brigade War Diary, 14 May 1915.
53 TNA: WO95/591 I Corps War Diary, 10 May 1915.
54 TNA: WO95/1352 6th Brigade War Diary, 15 May 1915.
55 TNA: WO95/591 I Corps War Diary, 10–15 May 1915.

enemy, or to resist a counter-attack. In a memo from General Whigham referring to new troops it was stated that: 'to encourage the enemy to attack it will be better for us to employ them and keep our seasoned troops in reserve.'[56] This and other clear evidence related earlier, showed the view taken by Regular Generals of their new Territorial charges. It is doubtful that this deliberate policy was common knowledge within the lower levels of the brigade's command structure. It should, however be contrasted firstly with the reports after the Battle concerning the response by those same Generals, and secondly with the enthusiasm with which the men in 7th King's took to their job.

The long bombardment was clearly vital to Haig, as he made several notes to this effect on Edmonds' draft chapter,[57] but it transpires that it had only continued for so long because the initial date was put back twenty-four hours due to the failure to hit the target effectively and problems in preparation amongst the attack troops. Neither the *Official History* nor Haig's notes link the battles at Aubers and Festubert as closely as now appears to have been the case from evidence in the First Army War Diary.[58]

Private Carl Purser showed that the significance of the barrage laid down by the British, and the German retaliation, was not lost on the troops, either in relation to the physical and mental effect on the soldiers, or to the need for more resources.

> Artillery may win the war; infantry will certainly be sufferers throughout, [he wrote] if they can afford to bombard as they have done this last few days it does not show much shortage, and for us to keep up with them, or rather, to get the better of them, we shall have to buck up and have less talk about shells and actually get on to the making.[59]

The *Southport Guardian* demonstrated part of the growing anxiety at the shortage of shells and guns, indicating an editorial line subtly against the Government.

Most other correspondents seemed simply anxious to let their families know what it was like and their accounts are graphic, hardly sparing those at home from the worry over the danger their menfolk were in. Finn's study referred to a call in the *Formby Times* seeking letters from the Front and the results were stark enough to demonstrate that, contrary to much historiography, people at Home can hardly have failed to see the reality of battle.[60] The accounts of the artillery barrage before the attack, for instance, demonstrated the sheer powerlessness of the infantry. Private Erlam Greaves' comments about the Germans would equally apply to the British, although he was not going to admit it: 'our guns commenced their task of destroying the barbed

56 TNA: WO95/590 I Corps War Diary Orders from Brig.Gen Whigham, 8 April 1915.
57 TNA: CAB44/20 Festubert draft chapter for the *Official History*.
58 TNA: WO95/155 First Army War Diary.
59 *Southport Guardian*, 29 May 1915, p. 9.
60 Finn, 'The Realities of War'.

wire entanglements in front of the German lines and the cannonade continued all through the day. The noise was simply awful and I do not know how the Germans stood it'.[61] The immediate success of the attack seemed to show that at least the battery was able to clear a path for the infantry, though there was no specific mention of it in the reports. What is also clear from the letters is that men of different units talked to each other about the War. Private Dobson wrote about the bombardment that 'the Regulars who were alongside us say they've never been under such hot fire',[62] while Arthur Butterworth noted that 'The men in the artillery say that Neuve Chapelle was dangerous, but that beat it'.[63] Arthur's brother, Harold, wrote to tell his parents that 'it was murder in the fire zone'.[64]

The nature of the attack carried out by A and B Companies can be detected from a variety of sources. The official reports focused on tactics and events, justifying the actions and encouraging recruitment. The accounts from individual soldiers concentrated on the emotions of the events, whether it was the bravery of their comrades or the pitiful appearance of their enemy. The Battalion War Diary stated simply that 'A & B Coys in attack, moved over parapet about 10:45 p.m. & waited. Attack successful. German line carried'.[65] Kearsey confirmed that the principles of Field Service Regulations in relation to night attacks were carried out, thus ensuring the initial success of the operation.[66] The *Official History* said that 6th Brigade advanced 'at a silent walk with bayonets'.[67] Orders from Division were to render a surprise by advancing at a walk in total silence until the last minute. Lieutenant-Colonel Louis Vaughan made particular reference to synchronising watches, as one of the problems at Aubers had been mistrust of officers' watches.[68] Conan Doyle later described the attack when 'in three minutes they had swarmed across the open and poured into the trenches.'[69] In reaching the German support trenches, the objectives were apparently met before dawn. Two styles of soldiers' accounts are apparent from the newspapers – the description from afar by observers of this attack, and the accounts given by men from A and B Companies who took part. The observers' stories depict heroism and sacrifice: the attackers' tales belie their shock and fear and do not attempt to hide the realities of war. Despite, or perhaps because of, the more unsuccessful follow-up by C and D Companies in the morning, the emphasis of the reporting was on the great

61 *Formby Times*, 5 June 1915, p. 5; *Southport Guardian*, 5 June 1915, p. 7.
62 *Southport Guardian*, 29 May 1915, p. 9; *Southport Visiter*, 27 May 1915, p. 6; *Waterloo and Crosby Herald and Formby, Bootle and Seaforth Gazette*, 29 May 1915, p. 5 (hereafter *Crosby Herald*).
63 *Southport Guardian*, 5 June 1915, p. 7.
64 *Southport Visiter*, 27 May 1915, p. 6; *Crosby Herald*, 29 May 1915, p. 5.
65 TNA: WO95/1360 1/7th Battalion King's Liverpool Regiment War Diary, 15 May 1915.
66 Kearsey, *1915 Campaign in France*, pp. 32–34.
67 *Official History 1915*, Vol. 2, p. 58.
68 TNA: WO95/1285 2nd Division War Diary, 13 May 1915.
69 Conan Doyle, A., *The British Campaign in France and Flanders 1915* (London: Hodder and Stoughton, 1917), p. 128.

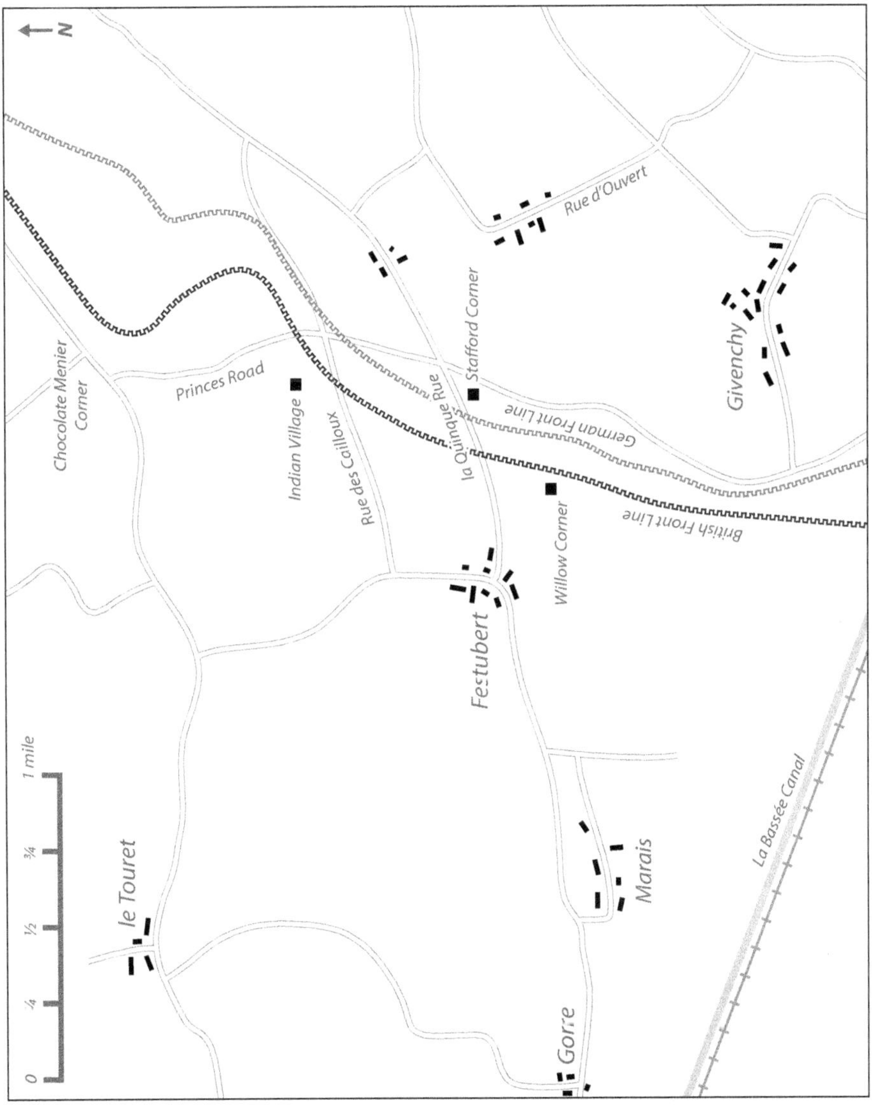

Map 1 Festubert, May 1915.

bayonet charge rather than what had been referred to in the *Official History* as a silent walk.[70]

The difference between a walk and a charge is partly explained by the natural enthusiasm for exaggeration and partly by the restrained and sober reflection typical of the *Official History*. When this volume was written in 1927, Festubert did not hold much significance in the context of the entire War, whereas the immediacy of the battle for these young men, writing only one or two days afterwards, was completely different. The different reports suggest that there was a silent walk until they were seen and then they charged on to the trenches.[71] Nonetheless, the experience was a defining one, as Private Farrington reported: 'Our company was the first over the parapet and led the way onto the battlefield. To be more correct, I should say "slaughter house".[72]

Private Greaves, A Company, observed:

> no sooner had we got over the parapet than the Germans commenced rapid fire on us … I can tell you it was not very palatable waiting there with thousands of little pills whizzing over your head…we were encouraged by one of our sergeants who kept shouting, "Come on the King's, avenge the Lusitania" … The Germans do not like the bayonet … they came running out of their trench crying "Mercy, mercy, Comrade boon" … It was a horrible sight the next morning, looking across to our lines, the ground strewed with dead and wounded. It is a sight I do not want to see again. If I have to witness such a spectacle I pray to God He will bring me safely through.[73]

James Cook, a Private who later received a commission described it as 'a dream … there must have been divine help on our side'.[74]

Private George Kerr wrote from his hospital bed:

> We had at least 500 yards to go before we reached their trench. Well we started advancing on our stomachs for about half-way when the Germans spotted us

70 *Official History*.
71 Also in the attack was Private J.H. Ross: 'The platoon I am in was the very first… over the parapet. We had 300 to 400 yards to go and at first we walked; soon, too soon, they saw us, star shells went up all round, rifles cracked, and machine guns went zip, zip, zip. …All this time we had been advancing, and men had been falling; it was like going through a hailstorm, but the hailstones were hard bullets…' *Southport Guardian*, 5 June 1915, p. 7; Richard Tyrer, an A Company private, wrote 'We made a bayonet charge … and captured two lines of trenches by 1 a.m. It was an awful thing charging amid bullets from left and right, so many of our brave lads fell, and I am exceedingly sorry to tell you young Bobby Mercer was accidentally shot. Arthur Band is very badly wounded. Dean's boys, Erlam Greaves and Sandy Bourhill are all safe and well.': *Southport Visiter*, 29 May 1915, p. 5.
72 *Southport Visiter*, 27 May 1915, p. 6; *Crosby Herald*, 29 May 1915, p. 5.
73 *Formby Times*, 5 June 1915, p. 5; *Southport Guardian*, 5 June 1915, p. 7.
74 James Cook correspondence, 21 May 1915.

with their star-lights. Well, that did it. They set their Maxim guns on us; also rifle fire, shells and bombs. My word, I thought we would never get through it... We dashed into the trench with a loud cheer. There was moaning and groaning, and clatter of bayonets. It was awful, the blood was flying all over; the Germans were crying for mercy. Of course there was heavy loss on our side as well.[75]

2898 Private Bobby Mercer of Formby, killed 17 May 1915, commemorated on the Le Touret Memorial, Panels 6–8. (*Formby Times*, 5 June 1915)

In contrast, Private Thomas Murray, Lieutenant Adams' servant and well out of the fighting, was typical of the other strand of writing when he wrote to his mother:

The night was pitch dark except from the fire from bursting shells...Over our trench crept No.4 platoon, under Lieut. Adams, with the platoons of the other regiments (from KRR, 1st King's, Staffords, Berks, 5th King's)... Our men had crept within 100 yards of the Germans, who were 600 yards from our trenches...Alas! they were spotted. Out from dozens of Maxims came the terrible bullets, and shell began bursting round them. It was hell on earth but on they went through the murderous fire. Our men were cut down like grass... It was here poor Bob Balshaw was killed. He died fighting like a lion. Poor Lieut. Adams was shot on the trench, urging his platoon on, who mostly follow him... "Don't forget the Lusitania"...Our men drove the Germans out. The 1st King's got at them. They would not have the bayonet, and started coming into us in hundreds under the white flag.[76]

2175 Private Robert Balshaw of Formby, died of wounds 20 May 1915, buried at Boulogne Eastern Cemetery Grave VIII.D.31. (*Formby Times*, 5 June 1915)

75 *Southport Guardian*, 5 June 1915, p. 7.
76 *Southport Guardian*, 29 May 1915, pp. 5 and 9; *Formby Times*, 29 May 1915, p. 5.

Murray's story was similar to the others, but lacked the passion of the combatant, substituting it for something more Kiplingesque.

The letters contained tactical information which these days may not have been made so public. Private Norman Heaps, 13 Platoon, D Company, watched A and B Companies prepare to attack: 'each man being as lightly equipped as possible and with white cloths attached to their hats in order to distinguish each other in the darkness', although the *Official History* referred to patches on the front and back of tunics, not hats.[77] Heaps' matter-of-fact description of preparations immediately prior to an attack seemed tinged with regret at not being involved and respect for those who were.

The *Crosby Herald* relied almost entirely on letters for its reporting of the action, under a headline of '7th King's in Action'.[78] However, it did carry the 'Eyewitness' account, from the British Headquarters three miles to the rear and this makes for interesting comparisons with the foregoing letters:

> May 16th ... The landscape stretching before me was typical of this part of France. Through innumerable thickets and plantations of trees peeped out red roofs of houses and cottages, while further away on the skyline the chimneys of coal mines in the Lille district reared their heads up against the blue sky... over Festubert hung a dark pall of smoke that seemed to grow in intensity. As I watched the shells were bursting the whole time – a dazzling flash, a cloud of smoke, and then a dull boom. Green fumes of lyddite mingled with a black cloud produced by 'Jack Johnsons' and over all screamed shrapnel, leaving a little speck of white as it burst. It seemed impossible that anything could live in such a storm.

On the contrary, it sounded positively idyllic! The communique also observed:

> Along the roads leading up to the trenches, lorries of all descriptions carrying stores, and above all ammunition, could be seen, while the severe nature of the fighting was testified by the Red Cross wagons that occasionally passed along to the casualty stations in the rear of the firing line...Back in the town, only a few miles from the firing line, everything was going on as usual, only the passing of a few Red Cross cars laden with wounded showed that an engagement was proceeding so near. [The reporter described the convoy of prisoners from the 57th Westphalian Regiment]: Their uniforms, it is true, were new and good, but the men themselves were almost without exception of the poorest physique, and marched along with downcast heads...Besides the keen, well-cut faces of their bronzed guard they showed up in very poor contrast.[79]

77 *Crosby Herald*, 29 May 1915, p. 5
78 *Crosby Herald*, 29 May 1915, p. 5.
79 *Crosby Herald*, 22 May 1915, p. 2.

This last description of British and German appearances is interesting, given the wintry weather which had been experienced up until this point.

Problems grew as light came on 16 May, when 7th Battalion Diary reported reinforcements 'were wiped out by machine gun fire'.[80] After describing the charge by A and B Companies, while he was in Reserve, Purser (C Company) wrote that D Company had to reinforce the attack at 5:00 a.m. and half the company had to cross about 360 yards in broad daylight and under a hail of machine gun fire as trenches to the right flank had not been taken. As the dead and wounded piled up in the communication sap, the Major stopped any further attempts. A new move was made at 11:00 a.m. by C Company, again a platoon at a time in broad daylight. 'It was a brave attempt, and every man who went over knew it was almost a certainty of death or being wounded.' After four platoons – 180 men – had tried, Purser's platoon was next, but again the machine guns cut terrible losses into C and D Companies.[81]

Purser's account was complemented by Marriott, writing to his father:

> C and D were ordered to charge in broad daylight – it was a mad idea and I knew the result before we started... The first platoon went over under McClelland... They were mown down. Then the 2nd platoon was mown down. I was just going with the 3rd when the order came to stop us.[82]

Marriott's independent and unpublished account corresponds with Purser and lends weight to the accuracy of the rest of his account. It is interesting to note that the Lieutenant called the idea mad, while the Private thought it brave. Clearly Purser knew his letters were being published while Marriott wrote purely to his family. This disparity may also reflect the differences between the informed and experienced view of an Officer who, while not dispassionate, was perhaps more objective and that of the enthusiastic volunteer seeing his first taste of real action.[83] As a cub journalist, Purser's account is strong on the bravery and tenacity in the face of the enemy, tinged with humour when reporting his involvement in carrying ammunition and rations up to

80 TNA: WO95/1360 1/7th Battalion King's Liverpool Regiment War Diary, 16 May 1915.

81 *Southport Guardian* 29 May 1915 p. 9.

82 Marriott correspondence 21 May 1915.

83 Another account came from Private Heap, D Company: 'We were moved along the line relieved of our packs, the heaviest and unessential part of our equipment and each two men took hold of a box of ammunition, with a third man behind them. We then moved out through an opening in the barricade. We then quickly learnt what the third men had been sent with us for, as a Maxim gun was trained on us and a number of men were hit ... Just before daybreak word was passed along to 'dig yourselves in' as the trench had been practically demolished by our artillery during the day. We had with us our entrenching tools, the blades of which are only about four inches square – not very promising implements with which to make a hole big enough to conceal yourself. However, we set to, and I assure you I never worked harder in my life than I did in that half-hour. At any rate, by daybreak, I was well below the level of the ground': *Southport Visiter*, 5 June 1915, p. 12.

the front, across shell holes, mud and dead bodies – 'I was covered from head to foot with mud, and had a huge biscuit tin to carry. Swear! I am afraid I cursed frightfully'.[84]

Early on 17 May a number of Germans attempted to surrender, but were shelled by artillery. Several letters refer to these events, noted in the *Official History*: [At 7:00 a.m. on the 17th] Germans retired with white flags and ran unarmed towards the trench of 1/7th King's Liverpool, east of Chocolat Meunier Corner'.[85] The *Official History* notes that Germans fired shells on them, probably thinking they were British as they thought their own trenches had by now been evacuated. The British artillery also shelled them, and none made it to the trench. Shortly afterwards, another 450 tried to surrender, and despite further fire were more successful.

The correspondents had mixed feelings about these men, ranging from Arthur Butterworth, C Company, who wrote to his father of 'The cowards, after turning machine guns on our wounded, hoisted the white flag. Germans came running towards our trench…and one of our shells burst right in the midst of them and that was the last of them';[86] to the rather more sympathetic line of Richard Tyrer:

> We got about 500 prisoners. It was a great sight to see them waving white flags and running to our trenches…Some of them were wounded and we helped them to the dressing station. They would not do that for us, but that is where the Britisher shows humanity, a thing in which the Germans lack.[87]

For others, the event seemed to catch the imagination with increasing excitement and exaggeration.[88] Perhaps Private Sharrocks summed up the views of the men, keen to get at the enemy, but overruled not just by an Officer but by an apparent morality of the sort which ordinary men on either side of no-man's-land seemed to feel for their opposite numbers caught in the war machine: 'hundreds of Germans came rushing towards us with their hands up…We felt inclined to shoot them, but our officers would not let us…They looked a dejected lot. Some of our chaps were carrying wounded Germans …'[89]

84 *Southport Guardian*, 29 May 1915, p. 9.
85 *Official History 1915*, Vol. 2, p. 66.
86 *Southport Guardian*, 5 June 1915, p. 7.
87 *Southport Guardian*, 29 May 1915, p. 11; *Southport Visiter*, 29 May 1915, p. 5; *Crosby Herald*, 29 May 1915, p. 5; *Formby Times*, 29 May 1915, p. 5.
88 Private W.H. Wright was in the captured trench 'while Monday night… but a whole group of them [Germans] surrendered… They came running across the field like rabbits, with their hands up and waving white flags.' See *Southport Guardian*, 29 May 1915, p. 11. An officer whose letter was printed in the Bootle paper wrote: 'we suddenly saw a forest of white flags go up over their trenches to our right, and they came streaming in hundreds over the parapet and made a bolt for our original front line opposite them. Our guns dropped any number of them before their fire could be stopped.' See *Bootle Times*, 28 May 1915, p. 5.
89 *Southport Guardian*, 29 May 1915, p. 11.

An 'eyewitness' quoted by Threlfall appeared to get the account of the capture of prisoners confused with the success of the attack:

> The Germans made a desperate attempt to hold their ground… but it was all useless. Once that tide of angry Liverpool men had got going there was nothing made in Germany strong enough to stop it… They seemed to lose all heart. Some threw away their rifles. Others tried to run, only to be shot or bayoneted. None of them seemed to have the gumption to surrender, until one of their officers stepped forward and held up his hands. At that signal hands went up all round and then the place that had been the scene of so much of the noise and roar and madness of battle only a few minutes before was quiet as a Quakers' meeting.[90]

As far as the newspapers were concerned, the capture of the enemy was a coup for the Battalion, and an important little victory over the enemy. For the professional soldier, it was an event of little significance. Marriott only gave it a passing mention in his letter. After the first group had run out and a shell landed in the middle, Marriott told his father another '500–600 came out with their hands up. They were full of watches, money, cigars which they gave to our men as they came in'.[91] The 7th King's Diary referred to fatigue parties found to supply rations to 1st King's, burial parties, and the continuous shelling from German lines. The Battalion was relieved during the night of 19th/20th under heavy shelling.[92]

The Orme brothers, from D Company, demonstrated the dangers of reporting events second-hand. They related tales – not actually witnessed – about German atrocities. No evidence was produced but the stories were well received at home, coming hard on the heels of the Lusitania riots and the publication of Lord Bryce's report into alleged German atrocities.[93] Though subsequently seen to be a flawed report, writers such as Sanders and Taylor have pointed to its significance for the Home population's morale at the time.[94] The 'atrocities' in Belgium referred to in the report and the sinking of the *Lusitania*, had been emphasised before a concert at the Christ Church Soldiers Institute in Southport on 13 May, justifying the actions of rioters and looters in the North West, referred to above.[95] Drummer Alfred Orme observed:

> When they took a few of the Black Watch prisoners the other week we found out that they stripped them of their clothes and sent them in front of their trench and riddled the Scotsmen with a Maxim. A fine lot of rascals to be fighting, but

90 Threlfall, *The Story of the King's*, pp. 167–169.
91 Marriott correspondence, 21 May 1915.
92 TNA: WO95/1360 1/7th Battalion King's Liverpool Regiment War Diary, 20 May 1915
93 *Report of the Committee on Alleged German Outrages* (London 1915).
94 Sanders and Taylor, *British Propaganda during the First World War*, p. 144.
95 *Southport Visiter*, 15 May 1915, p. 2.

> we have had a bit of our own back, and if I have the luck to get home I'll be able to tell you something.[96]

Orme seems to have suggested that the British were not above underhand tactics, which was probably true. It was unusual to see as much admitted in the press, however. His brother, Lawrence gave a similar story:

> With regard to the atrocities you will have read about them. It is all true. In the trenches recently taken I am told a Guardsman had been crucified against a dug-out door, his body having been shockingly mutilated. There were also some Highlanders who had been stripped of their kilts, sent back to our trenches and then shot down in cold blood when half way across.[97]

While there is no direct evidence available of these events, the stories were clearly rife in D Company for, as well as the Orme brothers, Corporal Critchley's account made reference to it too in an oral interview: 'At the beginning of May the Jocks did a bayonet charge but were cut up and prisoners taken. The Germans took their kilts and turned them loose and opened up machine guns on them.'[98] Although interviewed in 1981 Critchley also remembered 'we were like wild animals, we took no prisoners'.[99]

Stories of atrocities were routinely used throughout the War to castigate the terrible Hun and later commentators have shown that officials working on such propaganda did not deny their involvement in such falsehoods.[100] The fact that the tales from D Company all corroborate each other should not be taken to mean they were an accurate reflection of events. No direct evidence has come to light to support this story, although March's 6th Brigade Diary report may indicate where its foundation lay. The entry for 16 March 1915 included reference to the return of some wounded men:

> Four wounded have recently crawled back, or been recovered from close to the enemy lines after enduring great hardships – it is apparent from their statements that our wounded can expect little mercy from the Germans. If not actually shot, they are stripped of equipment and even of clothing…In some instances, the shooting of our wounded as they lay out close to the enemy trenches seems well substantiated. The brigade has an account to settle – we hope at no distant date.[101]

96 *Crosby Herald*, 29 May 1915, p. 5; *Southport Visiter*, 5 June 1915, p. 7.
97 *Crosby Herald*, 29 May 1915, p. 5; *Southport Visiter*, 5 June 1915, p. 7; *The Times* had run the now infamous story of a crucified Canadian soldier on the Ypres Front on May 15, a story quickly repeated and expanded in the trenches – Gilbert, *First World War*, p. 162.
98 Critchley.
99 Critchley.
100 Sanders & Taylor, *British Propaganda during the First World War*, p. 264.
101 TNA: WO95/1352 6th Brigade War Diary, 16 March 1915.

The threat in the final line of the report in the official War Diary appeared to sanction similar action in retribution, enforcing the strength of feeling at the highest level. Notwithstanding that, the incident was back in March, and was clearly unrelated to the Scots' charge at Aubers the previous week. The similarities were such, however, that this type of act may have had some of its roots in fact, although any promulgation of it was designed to stiffen resolve. As well as the *Times*, the soldiers' access to other national or local newspapers was likely to have fuelled their imagination. Such reports and the stance taken by senior officers marked a significant difference to the attitude of the men and company officers when faced with hundreds of German prisoners being shelled by both sides.

According to the subsequent Report in 6th Brigade Diary, 1/7th King's (referred to in the report as 7/8th using the old nomenclature for the Regiment – 8th Foot) swung a little to the left of their objective and did not actually take it, although this was not known at the time.[102] In fact, Private Cook claimed that in taking three lines of trenches, they accomplished what had been 'deemed improbable' – perhaps feedback of information to the troops was not very good.[103] The Report went on to note that machine gun fire and shelling were heavy and attempts to move other units up to the captured trenches were fruitless, though by daylight on 16th men in ones and twos were able to get to the German line. With these trenches thick with troops, it was fortunate that German shelling was more on British trenches, though these were also congested.[104] The 7th Battalion were amongst those withdrawn to British trench breastworks on the night of 16th/17th, while 1st King's took the objective originally thought to have been secured by 7th Battalion.

Reliefs from the Guards and Sirhind Brigades took over the attack on 18th, leaving the line to be held by 1st and 7th King's only, and they were withdrawn on 19th. According to the report, nearly 1,000 yards of enemy trenches were won and 200 prisoners taken. The artillery cooperation was described as 'very satisfactory', but casualties were around 2,500 for all ranks. Brigade Diary reported that the forming up of the men for the attack in successive lines outside the parapet, and pushing men out gradually as flares subsided, had been successfully carried out. The Brigade report clearly felt the operation had been reasonably successful.[105]

A number of writers including Private Dobbs, claimed that a passing general praised the Battalion.[106]

102 TNA: WO95/1352 6th Brigade War Diary extracts from Narrative of Operations from night 15/16 to 19 May 1915.
103 James Cook correspondence, 21 May 1915.
104 TNA: WO95/1352 6th Brigade War Diary extracts from Narrative of Operations from night 15/16 to 19 May 1915.
105 TNA: WO95/1352 6th Brigade War Diary extracts from Narrative of Operations for night of 15/16 to 19 May 1915.
106 Private Sherwood also felt it worth mentioning when he wrote home: 'We were praised by the General. No doubt you will see something of it in the papers by now', *Southport Guardian*,

> We came through with the highest honours…we fought a great battle and came out with flying colours…Of course there were more regiments in it besides ours…They all spoke well of us. The general gave us a good name, and he waved his hand to us as we were leaving the village.[107]

Marriott's letters home confirmed what had appeared to be a rather anecdotal claim.[108] Subsequent gallantry awards also appeared to confirm that view of the hierarchy with the award of a Military Cross, a DCM and several Officers and NCOs 'Mentioned in Dispatches'.[109]

The *Official History* summed up the battle as 'tantalizing'.[110] Objectives had been reached by some units and if the British had had as much artillery as well as equipment for close-quarter fighting as the Germans clearly had, then success could have been complete. This was the story of so many of the battles of the War, a British attack held up apparently for want of men and equipment. The difference in emphasis with 6th Brigade's view is explained by the fact that other elements of the attack were less successful. The *Official History* put it down to 'British unpreparedness for war' – a verdict warmly welcomed by Haig in 1927: 'I am glad you put this in' and 'I hope that the British people will realise what 'unpreparedness for war' cost the Empire in flesh and blood'.[111] At the time of planning the Festubert battle, however, Haig did nothing to address these shortages or unpreparedness and, had it not been for other factors, would have carried on the assault at Aubers Ridge regardless. Kearsey pointed out, however, that to await better preparation would have saved casualties but would not have fitted into the general plan of combining with the French.[112] The failure to knock out German machine-gun positions did contribute to the heavy casualties on the second and third days and the delay in being able to pursue the attack caused congested trenches which were prone to enemy shelling. More effective planning might have dissipated these shortfalls.

After the battle, as if to reinforce the feeling of being on a long and exciting excursion, some soldiers were keen to collect souvenirs and send them home as proof that

29 May 1915, p. 9. The *Southport Guardian,* 5 June 1915, p. 7 printed an extract from a letter from an officer which read that: The Brigadier is very pleased with us, and said to a sergeant of ours, 'Well, your regiment has made a name for itself anyway.' Corporal Wainwright, who also wrote to the Mayor, was wounded in the charge. In his letter to his parents he concluded 'my section were advancing like heroes, through a downpour of shells and bullets, and the Liverpool Terriers, if never before, made a name for themselves. To be in the first line of charge was a thing never expected by our boys. The way the good old regulars charged an encouraged our chaps I shall never forget.' *Southport Guardian,* 22 May 1915, p. 7.

107 *Southport Visiter,* 27 May 1915, p. 6.

108 Marriott correspondence, 21 May 1915.

109 Threlfall, *The Story of the King's,* pp. 192–7.

110 *Official History,* 1915, Vol. II, pp. 76 and 77.

111 TNA: CAB44/20 Festubert chapter draft for the *Official History.*

112 Kearsey, *1915 Campaign in France,* pp. 11–12.

they had been there when the 7th King's made their charge. As noted above, surrendering Germans handed over some of their possessions. Private Sharrocks 'got a German helmet, a belt, a knife, a cigarette case, a water bottle etc. One chap got a cat-o-nine-tails'.[113] James Cook had a water bottle and belt, but found the helmets too bulky to carry.[114] Private Farrington sent his sister a rather gruesome souvenir:

> One of the Germans came running in my direction. I let him have a couple in memory of 'Lusi' and other things besides. I have got his helmet. I am going to send it to you along with some more souvenirs. If you get it all right you can put it in your shop window.[115]

At least Arthur Butterworth recognised what was going on when he wrote 'I think the horrors of war make one unusually callous. During the scramble it was most amusing to see the men looking for souvenirs. Helmets were the order of the day, though bayonets, buttons, watches, and even clocks came into our hands'. Private Greaves was not one of them – 'I was only too glad it was all over'.[116]

One of the immediate after-effects of the action was illness. On 24 May Private Cook reported that he had had diarrohea for the last three days and put this down to the change in and rationing of food while they were in the attack, together with the rain, lack of sleep and having no change of clothing. He wrote: 'Xcuse writing (sic) but I have to keep still & lie on my back. There are lots of others with the same complaint'. He had earlier referred to resting shattered nerves, hardly surprising having had a bullet through his hat too.[117] Again, the home community should not have been in any doubt as to the conditions under which their sons were fighting. For instance, Drummer Orme reported:

> I can tell you it's been awful. You could have got plenty of souvenirs, but the sight of men blown to pieces, fed me up, and I do not wish for any souvenirs of that massacre. A better name would be scientific murder. You were walking over dead men all the time, and the smell was suffocating.[118]

Private Pirrie of the Machine Gun Company provided another account:

> After the charge the battlefield was a terrible sight. There were thousands of dead. When going into the German trenches we could not help walking over them. Last week the Scotch Guards and a few other regiments made a charge

113 *Southport Guardian*, 29 May 1915 p. 11.
114 James Cook correspondence, 24 May 1915.
115 *Southport Visiter*, 27 May 1915, p. 6; *Crosby Herald*, 29 May 1915, p. 5.
116 *Southport Guardian*, 5 June 1915, p. 7; *Formby Times*, 5 June 1915, p. 5.
117 James Cook correspondence, 21 May and 24 May 1915.
118 *Crosby Herald*, 29 May 1915, p. 5; *Southport Visiter*, 5 June 1915, p. 7.

> in the same place, but did not come off successful, and believe me we fetched in some of the wounded who had been lying out all week.[119]

In the early years of the War, officers were targeted and certainly suffered disproportionately in casualties, although this was also partly due to their practice of leading from the front; the 7th King's were no exception. Marriott wrote that he was 'the only double company commander to [come back untouched].'[120] Nonetheless, his Company suffered the second highest casualties behind A Company. He buried his friend (and brother-in-law) Kingston Adams, and was promoted to second in command. According to Tyrer, 'Lieut. Adams was simply worshipped by the men, of whom he was very proud',[121] a view Pirrie confirmed. '"Come on the 7th" shouted... Lt. Adams...nothing could have inspired us more than seeing him fall, for we all loved him, and we went into them with cold steel'.[122] Other officers also came in for similar praise, and their position in leading the men on was clearly significant. Their loss was keenly felt, noted by Sergeant James Taylor – 'Amongst the officers killed were Captain Harvey, Lieut. McClelland, both my old officers. Our officers died like what they were in life – gentlemen.'[123]

All accounts tell of the large number of casualties. Divisional casualties for the 16 – 25 May 1915 were other ranks: 536 – killed, 3,725 – wounded, and 1,006 – missing; officers: 46 – killed, 120 – wounded, and 12 – missing.[124] These figures came from the *Official History*, written in 1927, by which time figures should have been reasonably accurate. These were not the first casualties for 7th King's and they had certainly seen death by May, but it was the first time that they had been involved in action which saw casualties on a large scale. This was also the case for the communities at home, although other Liverpool Regiments had seen action and it was partly through this realisation that a sense of community evolved. When links were forged after the War, the emphasis was on those places where the dead had fallen.

For the men the casualties were obvious very quickly. Ross recounted the feeling after the relief, 'A good meal – the first we had had for a week...Then we looked around. Oh! the faces that were missing. My three intimate friends were all missing.'[125] Stephens was another to show quite graphically the impact on the ranks: '...out of our platoon, which numbered 49, we have only eight left, having 20 killed and 21 wounded...Over a dozen Maxim guns played on us, and our poor fellows kept

119 *Southport Visiter*, 27 May 1915, p. 8; Crosby Herald, 29 May 1915, p. 5.
120 Marriott correspondence, 23 May 1915.
121 *Southport Guardian*, 29 May 1915, p. 12; *Southport Visiter*, 29 May 1915, p. 8; *Crosby Herald*, 29 May 1915, p. 5; *Formby Times*, 29 May 1915, p. 5.
122 *Southport Visiter*, 27 May 1915, p. 8; *Crosby Herald*, 29 May 1915, p. 5.
123 *Southport Visiter*, 27 May 1915, p. 8.
124 *Official History*, 1915, Vol. II, p. 74.
125 *Southport Guardian*, 5 June 1915, p. 7.

dropping like rats'.[126] William Campbell's unnamed brother-in-law also referred to the high casualty figures with some degree of passion. When it came to his brother-in-law however, his tone immediately changed. The first part of his letter contrasted with the more idyllic, sacrificial death described in the second:

> Men were dropping but still we kept on, and captured the first trench and the second, but at great cost. When daylight broke on Monday, May 17th, we had a roll call, and the cost was appalling. I soon found Will was missing, and asked permission to search for him. I went on my own, and discovered he had been shot through the brain. He looked very peaceful. He was hit while leading his men on.[127]

This was not untypical. Particular deaths were heroic; the general were appalling.[128]

It is difficult to arrive at an accurate figure for the Battalion casualty list. The Battalion War Diary noted nine Officers killed or missing, and four wounded, on 16 May; along with 220 Other Ranks (OR) killed, wounded or missing.[129] Marriott noted in a letter to his father that nine Officers had been killed and three wounded, while of the other ranks there were c.300–400 casualties. His own Company had been reduced from 252 to c.100 and one Officer.[130] The Brigade Diary recorded casualty figures but unfortunately the report of operations and the table were lost, and when a typed form of the precis was done in 1924 and added to the Diary, the table was not reproduced. Thus, all we have is a note that there were c.2,500 casualties in all, nearly half the fighting strength of 6th Brigade. The Diary does note that the Battalion strength afterwards was fifteen Officers and 639 OR. This compared with twenty-eight Officers in 1st South Staffordshire Regiment, and 601 OR in 1st King's, 801 OR in 1st Royal Berkshire Regiment.[131]

126 *Southport Visiter*, 3 June 1915, p. 8; Stephens' figures were confirmed by another Private from 12 Platoon, *Southport Visiter*, 27 May 1915, p. 6; *Crosby Herald*, 29 May 1915, p. 5.
127 *Bootle Times*, 28 May 1915, p. 7.
128 Private Harold Butterworth described the death of Harry Cave in similar vein – 'Harry, acting as one of the bomb throwers along with our Major, went in advance of the men, and both acted with great courage and bravery before they fell mortally wounded. It was a glorious death looked at in a military light, for it was their courageous conduct that enabled our men to capture the trenches without many casualties.... Southport has been hit heavily in this engagement, and the town should know how gallantly her sons have fought under murderous conditions and, what is more, came through victoriously. Before the Germans are pushed back thousands of lives must inevitably be sacrificed, but then, if we are successful the price will ungrudgingly be paid.' *Southport Guardian*, 5 June 1915, p. 7.
129 TNA: WO95/1360 1/7th Battalion King's Liverpool Regiment War Diary, 16 May 1915.
130 Marriott correspondence, 21 May 1915.
131 TNA: WO95/1352 6th Brigade War Diary, 25 May 1915.

Most of the men are now buried in one of the many small cemeteries in the area, such as the Guards Cemetery at Windy Corner, Post Office Rifles Cemetery, Brown's Road in Festubert, which now includes those originally buried at Cheyne Walk, Givenchy and Le Plantin (South) or Le Plantin (Welsh), and Cuinchy Communal Cemetery, which includes those from the now defunct cemeteries of the Royal Berkshires and the King's Claire, both originally in Cuinchy too.[132] In Marriott's letters he wrote of burying Arthur Hughes where he had fallen, but of taking back Kingston Adams to the British lines and burying him after the rest of the Battalion had been relieved. Later in his correspondence he reported on his return to the area in 1918 and locating graves of Kingston Adams, Hughes, McClelland, Hannon and Captains Tweedale and Chisholm amongst the battle debris.[133]

Wyrall, who tabulated casualties by year, listed 109 deaths in the Battalion.[134] Written in 1935, this was not too far away from the 'official' figure of 115 found in *Soldiers Died*, although his total number of deaths for the War was 100 less than that in *Soldiers Died*. Simply from this research, it is known that there are also a few omissions in *Soldiers Died*. 115 represented nearly 12 percent of the total deaths for the Battalion 1914–19 of 960. Of those 115, 98 had enlisted at Bootle, Seaforth, Southport, Crosby or Birkdale. That figure of 98 does not include those who were born or lived in the catchment area, but enlisted elsewhere, including Liverpool itself.[135] By any calculation, therefore, this was a severe blow to the area. It must also be remembered that 6th Brigade contained the 1st and 5th King's Liverpool Battalions, and their casualties also impacted on the area and on the Regiment as a whole. The impact of officer casualties was severe: all of the nine had pre-War Territorial commissions and the officer contingent was practically halved. The effects of this would have repercussions for the following years. Analysis of a similar nature for Givenchy 1918 shows a further 79 men killed and this explains the importance of the area to Liverpool and Southport in the years after the War.[136]

Reports of the Battle stressed the honour of the Regiment, and this would have been helpful in securing more recruits for the Front. While Purser had much praise for other units, including the 5th King's, the Irish and the stretcher bearers, as well as the officers and men who risked a lot to save their friends, his point was to refer to the local appeal. 'No wonder the Liverpool regiments have a good name out here. They deserve it and the General sent good praise for our battalion.'[137]

Relations between the ranks was a key issue. The attitude toward officers who had been killed (see examples relating to Harvey and McClelland above) tends to confirm Sheffield's and Morris' findings, that the amount of deference and respect accorded

132 *Indices of the Commonwealth War Graves Commission.*
133 Marriott correspondence, 10–11 December 1918.
134 Wyrall, *The History of the King's Regiment*, pp. 230–231.
135 *Soldiers Died,* pp. 48–58.
136 *Soldiers Died,* pp. 48–58.
137 *Southport Guardian*, 29 May 1915, p. 9.

the officer was related to their battlefield performance.[138] It was also undoubtedly to do with the role played by company officers, in particular in routine matters. This factor was recognised in orders in November 1915 of 22nd Brigade, 7th Division:

> It is most noticeable that both the spirit of the men and the amount of work done is far better in those battalions where the Officers are constantly amongst their men, inspiring them to work and even taking a hand themselves. Everyone can learn from the experiences and difficulties of others.[139]

Another element of the success in the field was to enhance the reputation of the Battalion and the Regiment. There was a real regimental pride in being part of the Liverpool Regiment, as well as the more localised identification with the Southport Terriers. This will be seen throughout this study, somewhat contrary to the findings of other writers. For instance, Fuller has argued that rapid dilution in 'local' battalions took away any sense of local identity and that the local identity which did exist was very specific and did not extend to a sense of regimental identity.[140] Any dilution which did occur is explored in subsequent chapters, but it had not begun in 7th King's until after this first action thinned the ranks.

It was also important for the men to know that others had respect for them. Private Percy Oliver said: 'The 7th King's can always say they have fought and beat some of the cream of the Kaiser's Prussian Guards. We have won a grand name from our Brigade staff'.[141] Ormerod wrote: 'We have covered ourselves with glory, and have gained great respect from the Regulars. The Irish Guards, I am told, say we take 'The cake and biscuit too'.[142]

The Territorials had had a poor reputation, and their levels of discipline in particular had been a key feature of Kitchener's decision not to send them out in autumn 1914. Nonetheless, a number of units had already left for the Front by Christmas and, as Simkins has pointed out, there were mixed views about their deployment.[143] Despite the high number of volunteers for overseas service and the fact that Home Defence was now in the hands of Third Lines and troops in training, Beckett noted that Kitchener did not alter his opinion of the Force.[144] This was a line well known by the Terriers themselves, and this was one reason why it was so important to prove their ability and enhance their own reputation, as well as that of Territorials in other Divisions. This sense of inferiority caused some officers to lead their men shouting,

138 Sheffield *Leadership in the trenches*, pp. 146–148; Morris 'The Leeds Rifles', p. 919.
139 TNA: WO95/1660 22nd Brigade War Diary, 4 December 1915.
140 Fuller, *Popular Culture and Troop Morale*, p. 57; Beckett has also referred to the high extent of dilution in these units: Beckett, 'The Territorial Force', p. 147.
141 *Bootle Times*, 28 May 1915, p. 7.
142 *Crosby Herald*, 29 May 1915, p. 5; *Southport Visiter*, 5 June 1915, p. 12.
143 Simkins, *Kitchener's Army*, p. 44.
144 Beckett, 'The Territorial Force', p. 131.

as reported by Private Pirrie, 'We are only Territorials but we'll show them what we are made of'.[145] Presumably the intention was to encourage the men to show that the Territorials were more than able to hold their end up.

Some signs of the strains between Home and War Fronts began to surface in some of the correspondence, although it was in the minority. An unnamed writer, printed in the *Bootle Times* complained that: 'When one is hard at it out here doing one's level best and then picks up a paper and reads of some of the blighters striking for more pay it makes one disgusted'.[146] However, the concerns were generally more directed at persuading people to enlist, such as Private Webster's entreaty from his hospital bed:

> I have not yet realised being in England, it seems too good to be true, and yet there is so much to be done and so many brave lives to be sacrificed before the Hun murderers are crushed once and forever. I wonder how long will it take for those who know that they are needed to add their names to Southports's Roll of Honour. They have been set a fine example by our late young Captain, who will be sadly missed by the men of 14 Platoon. He was an officer and a gentleman.[147]

Despite this prevailing view regarding their success and the need for recruits to get the job done, the experience had demonstrated to the men that, given a choice, they would rather be at home. This attitude could perhaps be summed up by James Cook's report of a review by Lord Derby on 7 June, who told the men that in a few hours he would be in Liverpool: 'we were all saying "lucky chap" under our breath and derived no pleasure from his speech'.[148] Cook's subsequent career shows that he was no recalcitrant soldier but simply had a very understandable perspective towards the Earl's rather insensitive words.

The general reaction at home, gauged largely through the press, was one of pride and excitement. Reports show a number of memorial services and the casualty lists kept coming into late June, but more was made of the notion of sacrifice than the fact of loss. Recruitment was an important aspect of the home reaction too, and as later evidence will show, Festubert proved an important element in Southport's reconstruction after the War.

The first report of the battle appeared in the *Southport Visiter* on 18 May 1915, though there were few details.[149] The first in-depth reports did not feature until 22nd (*Southport Guardian*, *Crosby Herald*, *Southport Visiter*), while the first mention in the *Bootle Times* was 28 May, and in the *Formby Times* the 29th. This is largely explained by the different publishing dates. The attack started on Sunday 16 May, the troops

145 *Southport Visiter*, 27 May 1915, p. 8; *Crosby Herald*, 29 May 1915, p. 5.
146 *Bootle Times*, 28 May 1915, p. 7.
147 *Southport Guardian*, 22 May 1915, p. 7.
148 James Cook correspondence, 8 June 1915; TNA: WO95/1360 1/7th Battalion King's Liverpool Regiment War Diary, 7 June 1915.
149 *Southport Visiter*, 18 May 1915, p. 6.

were relieved from the trenches on Thursday night (20 May), and the first detailed reports appeared in time for the papers on 22nd, but just too late for the *Bootle Times* which had to wait a further week.

Some historians have said that the public knew little of casualties, of the attrition, of the real nature of the War, until much later, and certainly not in 1915–16.[150] However, the evidence of the Southport papers suggests that the information was abroad. As Finn has commented, little attention has been paid to looking at the impact of letters and reports in local papers.[151] The local press had a different perspective on the War to the national press. Certainly, the papers would be unlikely to be as easily available to the enemy, although the sending back of local papers to the lads at the Front was a common occurrence. There was clearly no censorship imposed by the local papers of the horrors of War. Nor was there any attempt to hide the fate of individuals, or spare their families grief. However, this attitude could be seen as reflecting the community spirit, asking the whole town to share in the success and the loss together. In an attempt to make the losses bearable, this notion of shared community experience was vital in keeping morale at home at a high level and was assisted by having a particular local battalion with which to identify. Through such accounts in newspapers, the level of understanding and sense of belonging between the War and Home Fronts was built up at an early stage.

The sparsity of official news of local soldiers was therefore of some concern to the press and anything which broke through that 'fog' of GHQ war information was a bonus. The Press had a dilemma however. They were keen to present a story, but obviously were also aware of the need to maintain interest and increase recruitment levels. Unpalatable descriptions may have hindered that balance but equally honesty may have increased respect. Knightley has suggested that when, in the later 1920s, the truth about the War became known, this was a turning point for the press as a whole in this country and confidence in the newspaper to tell the truth to the public was lost.[152] However, the local publication of harsh accounts by local men demonstrates that, at least in 1915, the home public heard much of the reality of war.

The *Bootle Times* based its report of the action on a few letters, but the *Formby Times*, the *Southport Visiter* and the *Southport Guardian*, produced extensive reports and details under bold titles such as 'Praise for Local Lads', 'Seventh's Glorious Charge', and 'Southport's Heroic Soldier Sons'.[153] These titles and interpretation of events sounded like propaganda, in contrast to the content of actual accounts and letters. There was no attempt to detract from the casualty list as alongside these reports were lists of men killed, and personal details of many of the men who had been lost.

150 Knightley, *The First Casualty*, p. 108; Farrar, *News from the Front*, p. ix.
151 Finn, M., 'The Realities of War', pp. 26–31.
152 Knightley, *The First Casualty*, p. 81.
153 *Formby Times*, 29 May 1915, p. 5; *Southport Visiter*, 29 May 1915, p. 7; *Southport Guardian*, 29 May 1915, pp. 9 and 11.

In fact, the *Southport Visiter*, which was able to steal a march on the others as a result of its publishing dates, led with: 'Southport's Battalion's Heavy Losses'.[154]

The editorial of the *Bootle Times* was quite clear in emphasizing the local identification with the battle: 'The famous charges will long form the subject of admiring talk in this neighbourhood, which is so closely associated with this regiment and goes to prove that the young manhood of Bootle is doing its share towards crushing that monster of organised brutality which is named militarism'.[155]

The local orientation of reports backfired a little when the papers reached the Front. The emphasis on the Southport men in the 7th King's caused a few ripples of discontent when copies of the *Southport Visiter* reached the troops, prompting a 'Sandgrounder' to write: 'there are one or two Liverpool or district boys in this battalion…and I think they would have appreciated a word or two on their behalf…now just give a word of praise to the Liverpool boys'. The Editor inserted a by-line reading, 'Of course the whole of the 7th King's Liverpool Battalion has done splendidly, and the designation "Southport Battalion" includes the Formby, Bootle and other men from this district'.[156] This reinforces the assumptions of the thesis that the spatial identity of the Battalion extended beyond the immediacy of Bootle and Southport.

It is interesting to note, however, that the praise heaped on the Territorials was not restricted to the very local press. The *Liverpool Echo* also carried the story. Of course, a number of Battalions of the Regiment were in the fight and so there is a slightly wider Regimental outlook, but even so the headlines tell the story: 'King's in thick of the Fight. Fine work in the battle of Festubert a tribute to gallant local officers. Splendid record of bravery. How our Territorials and Regulars stood the great test of courage.'[157] In fact the emphasis on the brave work of Territorials and Regulars together was a clear message of the solidarity and uniformity in the Regiment as a whole.[158]

The *Southport Guardian* reported on the increase in recruiting on 29 May:

> Obviously the young men of Southport who up to the present had not decided to join the colours, have by this now famous charge at last been moved…the last seven days have constituted a record recruiting week for this popular regiment.

154 *Southport Visiter*, 27 May 1915, p. 6
155 *Bootle Times*, 28 May 1915, p. 7
156 A 'Sandgrounder' was one born in Southport; *Southport Visiter*, 8 June 1915, p. 6
157 *Liverpool Echo*, 29 May 1915, p. 3
158 'No words can fittingly describe the pluck and gallantry shown by our troops, Regulars and Territorials alike, during the recent fighting in the Festubert district' – *Liverpool Echo*, 29 May 1915, p. 3; a report on 'The Fighting Fifth – Liverpool Terriers in the thick of it' was followed by another on 'Seventh Liverpool's Fine Work – Storming German trenches' – *Liverpool Echo*, 26 May 1915, p. 3: Another report included some letters, such as that from Private James Blackwood, B Company, which had not appeared in the Southport or Bootle papers – *Liverpool Echo*, 28 May 1915, p. 5

> Over 150 men have been passed by the doctor. The record exceeds anything that has been done by any other Territorial Battalion in the West Lancashire Division, over 1,800 recruits having been obtained for the 7th King's and quite half of these have come from the Southport and Birkdale district. The Second Battalion is considerably over strength, the Third Battalion is nearly complete, and there are rumours of a Fourth Battalion to be formed.[159]

The paper was quoting the recruiting officer, Captain Campbell, and although there is no other corroboration available for the figures, a Third Battalion was fully formed and was engaged on Home Defence for the duration, suggesting that the action was instrumental in providing a boost to recruiting in the area. It did, however, coincide with Derby's call as Chairman of the West Lancashire Territorial Force Association, for local Councils to increase the recruiting campaign in early May.[160]

Some letters from the Front were making the point about the need for recruits, including Corporal Wainwright in his letter to the Mayor: 'I cannot say what our casualties are not having seen the list, but I am afraid it will go hard against the town, but trust others will soon come forward to take our places'.[161] The 1 June 1915 edition of the *Southport Visiter* printed a list of recent recruits alongside more letters from the Front, and the report of a memorial service to Private W.A. Scott, who had been killed in the action, thus stressing the importance of continuity and encouraging recruitment with tales from the Front while recognising the sacrifices that had to be made.[162]

The local Councils had important roles to play on the Home Front in leading, organising and facilitating the many aspects required to deal with the situation. Two of these roles were also to lead the comment and the mourning. In both aspects, they were strangely muted. While they had responded positively to the recruitment campaign, as noted above, there was no particular civic response to the many casualties. This was perhaps because of the recruitment campaign. People could read about the casualties in the local papers but the Councils were determined to put a positive spin on the battle, emphasizing the call to arms. Nonetheless, it had become the habit for Councils to express sympathy to Councillors who had lost members of their family, and Litherland UDC passed a vote of sympathy to those who had lost relatives on the Lusitania,[163] and later in the North Sea battle in May 1916.[164] The absence of this public statement on the casualties may have been due to the close allegiance of a coastal area to maritime events – but it is more likely to have been a conscious decision to not discourage volunteers.

159 *Southport Guardian,* 29 May 1915, p. 7.
160 CL: Bootle County Borough Minutes Volume XXXII, 5 May 1915; LUD7 Litherland Urban District Council Minutes, 3 May 1915.
161 *Southport Guardian*, 29 May 1915, p. 9; *Southport Visiter*, 29 May 1915, p. 4.,
162 *Southport Visiter*, 1 June 1915 p. 3.
163 CL: LUD 7 Litherland Urban District Council Minutes, 10 May 1915.
164 CL: LUD 7 Litherland Urban District Council Minutes, 5 June 1916.

Significance of Festubert

Although the battle of Festubert was carried out in conjunction with the operations being pursued by the French, a realistic study of it must place it in the context of the earlier battles in the La Basée area, at Neuve Chapelle and Aubers Ridge, part of the first attempts to launch breakthrough attacks on the German line. As such, it was tactically important as the first planned night attack of the War and was also significant for its involvement of Territorial battalions in the first wave of the assault (although this was not the first occasion on which this had happened). The immediate success was tempered by the failure to follow through with the attack sufficiently to make the break count. Casualties were high and these affected the 1/7th King's particularly severely. This impact had the result of helping to evolve the sense of community identity within the Battalion, within the Home communities, and between the Home community and the Front Line. It also contributed toward a reasonable reputation for combat effectiveness in the Unit.

Festubert was also significant because it marked the end of the wide ranging freedoms in press reporting and the introduction of the official War Office briefings. Reports of the battle of Loos, September 1915, in local newspapers were noticeably less reliant on soldiers' letters home, as editors became more reliant on the War Office and less inclined or less able to print the less palatable soldiers' truths. The press reports around Festubert were significant, however, in galvanising support for a flagging recruitment campaign, albeit temporarily. Despite these key elements attached to it, Festubert has not had the same level of historical attention as either Neuve Chapelle or Aubers Ridge. The historiography has demonstrated this distinction, perhaps because it was less important in terms of the bigger picture of 1915. Nonetheless, the particular elements of the battle, such as the success of the night attack and the immediate relevance of the loss of the *Lusitania,* have deserved more critical attention than they have received. Despite this, Festubert itself has retained a key place in the Battalion's history and the history of the communities from which it was drawn.

4

The Cast Iron Division: Local identity and morale[1]

Local identity was a central tenet of the Battalion at the outset of the war and continuing references to 'Festubert men' indicate that, even as that local identity came under threat from casualties and drafts, it remained a potent tradition. Whilst during 1915 it had been the physical weight of numbers from the local area which was the principal driver for this sense of local community increasingly it became their combat history.

It was the established view that combat effectiveness was based on good morale. Not only in their general deployment and length of time spent in the trenches but also in assault, the 7th King's were as more or less effective as any other in the Division. There is also evidence to show that after the disastrous failures to take Guillemont in August 1916, the 55th Division's ability to learn and assimilate their new general's tactics and training meant that the assault at Gueudecourt, a few weeks later, was more successful.

Not that this success was achieved cheaply, as the casualty list demonstrates. The mounting deaths and injuries severely affected the numbers of men from the local area who could maintain that local focus. Nevertheless, by the end of 1916, the Division and its constituent parts appeared to have already progressed in terms of tactical awareness and to have a high level of morale rooted in their sense of belonging to the Lancashire Division.

With the introduction of the Military Service Acts, voluntary service all but ceased in 1916 and the direct connection between community and Battalion began to come under pressure. The danger of this was that the localness which was so important for a concept of community identity within the Battalion began to be undermined. Conversely the Battalion was rejoined with other Territorial battalions in the re-formed West Lancashire Territorial Division – the 55th – under Major-General Jeudwine

1 This reference to 55th Division (Tilsley) as 'Cast Iron' can be compared to a similar epithet for the whole King's as the 'Cast Iron Regiment' recalled by Critchley. See Tilsley *Other Ranks*, p. 48. Its use implies that the senior partners in the Division were the Liverpool battalions.

and this saw a comprehensive process of 'Lancastrianisation' in an attempt to reinforce the local community identity of the Division as a key element of maintaining troop morale.

For Jeudwine, morale and discipline were key elements to building a cohesive and effective combat force and he understood that the Territorials' morale, much like that of the more often studied 'Pals' units, was built around a sense of belonging to a home community and that this was reflected in their battlefield performance. Ultimately, this sense of community and belonging was about reliance, support and cohesiveness and these are also the key requirements for an effective combat unit. In one of his first instructions on training to the new division in January 1916 he wrote: 'Every endeavour should be made to inculcate mutual confidence, cohesion, and the spirit of combination'.[2]

Major-General Sir Hugh Sandham Jeudwine by Walter Stoneman, bromide print, 1917. (© National Portrait Gallery, London)

There was more than one sense of identity holding the Battalion together. There was a plurality of identities that contributed to an overall sense of belonging to the geographical base of the Battalion. As the actual numbers of 'sandgrounders' declined, the battle honours and combat record of the unit grew, creating an emerging Battalion mythology around the Festubert veterans. The fresh drafts from the county and the concept of a 'Lancashire Division' resulted in a growing sub-regional identity which built upon, yet also compensated for, a relative decline in direct local community identity.

In the 7th King's the connection between Home and War Front was maintained throughout the War, and indeed after it. This was founded on a sense of identity and belonging which was felt within the Battalion towards the home community, and by the community in Southport and Bootle towards the 7th King's Battalion. This sense of identity was at the heart of the Battalion's level of morale and combat effectiveness.

The nature of this sense of identity in the Battalion needs to be viewed in the context of the long and established history of the Volunteer and Territorial tradition in West Lancashire. The Battalion was an active part of the pre-War Liverpool Brigade and West Lancashire Division,[3] and evidence from the original regimental numbers

2 TNA: WO95/2899 55th Division General Staff War Diary, 7 January 1916

3 Mileham, P., *'Difficulties be damned': The King's Regiment 8th, 63rd, 96th: A History of the City Regiment of Manchester and Liverpool* (Knutsford: Fleur de Lys Publishing, 2000), p. 231.

indicates that a large body of pre-War Territorials enlisted for foreign service and certainly the majority of officers and NCOs were serving before 1914.[4]

Territorial battalions have been considered to place less emphasis on discipline than the Regular troops, but Morris identified their *esprit de corps* as the crucial element in their levels of morale. She interpreted this as having a feeling of 'belonging to a community'.[5] In his study on morale, Baynes's five key factors – regimental loyalty; officer-men relations; strong discipline; a sense of duty and sound administration – were supplemented by other elements including *esprit de corps*, battle success, punishment and social factors.[6] Sheffield, Beckett and Morris have added to these basic factors and it is therefore possible to create a more complete list of the key constituents of morale from the historiography:

- *Esprit de corps* including Battalion, Regimental and Divisional loyalty, community identity, battle effectiveness, attitude to the enemy
- Officer/men relations including leadership by NCOs, junior officers, unit commanders, GHQ, 'Staff', relations with other units
- Discipline including training and punishment
- Living and working conditions including contact with home, resources and equipment, battle conditions, recreational activities, health and welfare
- Social factors including class, religion, politics, age, occupation, marital status, sexuality, nationality
- Aims and objectives including ownership, influence and motivation in the War.[7]

Ferguson would agree with this list, but he would place it in a different order, with the soldier's comfort being of prime importance.[8] In delivering the 55th Division's training, Major-General Jeudwine considered that discipline should be delivered ahead of tactical and other training, specifically conduct, smartness, appearance; morale and *esprit de corps*; leadership; discipline; and physical fitness.[9] However, Bourne, writing in general about soldiers rather than just about Regulars or Territorials, saw the loyalty to community and comrades as the 'chief strategy for survival'.[10] It is this commitment

4 TNA: WO329/809 – 838, 2637 – 2643 and 2947 War Medal Rolls Liverpool Regiment; *Soldiers Died*, Newspaper reports also named individuals – for instance at the Annual Camp *Southport Visiter*, 4 August 1914, p. 6; Major Burnie, later temporary Lieutenant-Colonel, was to be referred to as an 'old Volunteer and territorial': *Bootle Times*, 10 November 1922, p. 2.

5 Morris, 'The Leeds Rifles', pp. 950–951.

6 Baynes, *Morale,* pp. 253–254.

7 Sheffield, *Leadership in the Trenches.* pp. 180–181; Beckett, I.F.W., *The Great War 1914–1918* (London: Pearson Education Limited, 2001), pp. 220–221; Morris, 'The Leeds Rifles'.

8 Ferguson, *The Pity of War,* pp. 446–7.

9 LCRO: 356 FIF/13 55th Divisional School of Instruction Syllabus, 27 February 1917, Jeudwine MSS.

10 Bourne, J., 'The British Working Man in Arms' in *Facing Armageddon*, p. 349.

to the local community which can be evidenced through studying 1/7th King's and, as the spatial identity shifted slightly over the course of the War, the 55th Division.

However, the analysis cannot focus solely on the notion of a single identity. Even on the basis of a geographical identity it is clear that there were significant differences between men who had enlisted from Bootle and those who had enlisted from Southport. As the Battalion moved further away – in time and distance – from those home towns, their allegiance became wider, more Merseyside or Lancastrian when operating in a larger unit, such as is seen after Givenchy in 1918. Nevertheless, the very local identities were also maintained.

In addition to the differing spatial identities, a variety of individual and group identities functioned together to create a sense of community and belonging. Many different identities blurred and overlapped. Joyce, in particular, has demonstrated the importance of understanding that a plurality of identities exists within any unit of society and that these identities are in conflict with each other, to a greater or lesser extent.[11] In their introduction to *Authority, Identity and the Social history of the Great War*, the Coetzees stressed the relevance of the number of different levels of identification which may be felt at different times.[12] Thus, different elements of identification, depending on the needs or circumstances of the time, could co-exist and sustain the individual.

A soldier could identify himself in a variety of ways; as a man, as a conscript, as a Regular, as a Territorial, as a volunteer, as a Derby man, by sexuality, by ethnicity, as coloured or, more likely, Scottish, Irish, Welsh, a cockney, tyke or scouser, as a Catholic or a Jew, an NCO, a sergeant, a corporal, or a private, married, a father, a son, a miner, a railwayman, from the corporation trams, as a footballer, a cricketer or a rugby player; as a stretcher bearer, a bomber, a Lewis gunner, a rifleman, a musician, from Bootle or Southport, Crossens or Banks, Freshfield or Formby, from the docks, an insurance company, a small law firm, from Lancashire, in the Liverpools, the Loyals or the King's Own, of the West Lancashire Division, or as a Festubert veteran. Equally importantly, he was seen differently by others; by a Regular, by an NCO, by the General, by the Liverpool Scottish, by his firm, by his family, by his Mayor and Council. In the press, he was a Southport man, a Lancashire man, a 'Kingsman', a father, a hero, a son, or, sometimes, a sacrifice.

The anecdotal differences between the volunteers, and even 'Derby' men, and the conscripts of the Military Service Tribunal system, for example, has only recently started to receive critical attention.[13] Tilsley wrote that although one veteran 'was heard to sneer something about tribunals and starred trades', surprisingly 'the newcomers looked a more intelligent crowd than the war-beaten men they joined'.[14]

11 Joyce, P., 'The end of social history?', *Social History*, Vol. 20, No. 1, p. 82.

12 Coetzee, F., and Shevin-Coetzee, M., (eds), *Authority, Identity and the Social History of the Great War* (Oxford: Bergahn Books Providence, 1995), pp. vii-xix.

13 Bet-El, I.R., *Conscripts: Lost legions of the Great War* (Stroud: Sutton Publishing, 1999).

14 Tilsley, *Other Ranks*, p. 150.

The importance and significance of these overlapping identities should be borne in mind through any study of morale, discipline and combat. However, there remains room for consideration of those major categories of identity which dominated individuals' perceptions. For Waites,[15] the major generic remained class but for the purposes of this study, it is the sense of belonging, related to the geographic area of, and within, Lancashire. Despite the plurality and diversity of complex identities within any given sociological unit, such as a battalion, Joyce was clear that major categories, such as class, region or community, remain an evident and acceptable categories for consideration.[16] For the purposes of this study, community identity is to the fore against a background of others.

The 55th (West Lancashire) Division

From 1916 the West Lancashire Division was a significant formation encapsulating strong morale, good discipline and growing combat effectiveness. A crucial aspect for the 55th Division's level of morale was its sense of community identity. Lee emphasised the importance of the sense of belonging to a division, referring to the 55th specifically as a good example.[17] Griffith had some reservations about the significance of 'divisions' in terms of loyalty, but he did define an elite group of divisions which he considered had developed a corporate identity that involved various factors, including a good or bad reputation for aggression, cohesion and discipline.[18] The Commanding Officer was important, but the traditions of the unit more so. Units such as 7th King's, which stayed together longest, were able to develop this cohesion better than others. Griffith linked this 'inner essence' with a group of Divisions who formed what he called an elite within the BEF.

Notwithstanding his classification of Divisions in terms of tactics, for morale Griffith focused on the enduring structures such as Battalion and Regiment as being most important.[19] Bourne has pointed out that the Battalion was the most important thing to a soldier, although he was also keen to stress that the most loyalty or identity was felt with the unit closest to the men with whom he ate, slept, fought and often died.[20] At the Front, there was a widening series of groups to whom a man owed loyalty – from simply his mates, to his section, platoon, company, battalion,

15 Waites, B., *A Class Society at War: England 1914–18* (Leamington Spa: Berg Publishers, 1987).
16 Joyce, P., *Visions of the People* (Cambridge: Cambridge University Press, 1991), p. 12.
17 Lee, J., 'The British Divisions at Third Ypres' in *Passchendaele in Perspective*, p. 225.
18 Griffith, *Battle Tactics of the Western Front,* pp. 79–83.
19 Griffith, P., 'Tactical Reform in the British Army' in Griffith, *British Fighting Methods*, p. 6.
20 Bourne, *Britain and the Great War,* pp. 215 and 220.

brigade and division. Bourne went on to include the particular 'trade' of a man – Lewis gunner, sapper or infantryman.[21]

Certainly battalion identity was maintained – in *Other Ranks* Tilsley often referred to 'Festubert men'. So too was regimental loyalty – the 'Liverpool Brigade' was reunited in the new Division, but the reuniting of the whole Lancashire Division was recalled by Critchley as being most important. He said '[the Division] were all Lancashire lads … we were fighting as a Division for the first time and we soon made our name. Our motto was 'We win or Die'.[22]

The evidence demonstrates that, as well as retaining a significant local presence in terms of the men's origins, the notion of community identity and Battalion loyalty was actively fostered at all levels, but especially by Major-General Jeudwine. The Divisional General displayed a consistent determination to emphasise the importance of the Lancashire connection within the Division. This was shown in his correspondence and actions when, in January 1916, days after the formation of the Division, Jeudwine wrote to XIV Corps requesting that 1/1st West Lancashire Field Company be transferred from 4th to the 55th Division.[23] Corresponding with Lord Derby in March, he noted that this had happened.[24] Jeudwine was keen on retaining that local identity because he felt it was a vital aspect of his unit's combat effectiveness. His determination was an example he expected to be followed, and it was a determination shared by Lord Derby.

Derby's links with Jeudwine as Chairman of the West Lancashire Territorial Association led him to visit France and inspect the troops, visiting the trenches of 1/7th King's on 7th June 1915. This kind of contact and ceremonial inspection was designed to enthuse the troops as well as make these important personages feel they were making some contribution. The following month, a party of 1/7th King's formed a Guard of Honour for Kitchener at Vendin, and Derby made another visit, this time to his 55th Division, in early February 1916.[25]

Jeudwine was keen on parades, inspections and the distribution of gallantry awards, the publication of which was designed to inspire future action as well as to recognise and praise past deeds. At the first such Divisional occasion, at the end of July 1916, a number of men from 1/7th Battalion were recognised for their action in the field: 1973 Corporal McQuilton, 2577 Corporal Bowles and 4937 Private Currie received Military Medals for their part in the raids on 26 and 28 June 1916, while Captain

21 Bourne, 'The British Working Man in Arms' in *Facing Armageddon*, p. 349.
22 Critchley.
23 TNA: WO95/2899 55th Division War Diary Letter from Jeudwine to XIV Corps HQ, 24 January 1916.
24 LCRO: 356 FIF/42 Letter from Jeudwine to Derby, 2 March 1916, Jeudwine MSS.
25 TNA: WO95/1360 1/7th Battalion King's Liverpool Regiment War Diary, 7 June, 8 July 1915 and 2 February 1916. The link was maintained beyond the War: at the twentieth anniversary dinner, Derby 'paid high tribute to the qualities and leadership of General Jeudwine' – *Southport Guardian*, 13 April 1938, p. 4.

Robinson, RAMC was awarded the Distinguished Service Order.[26] Awards were routinely recorded in the pages of the Battalion War Diary. In February 1918, on the second anniversary of the formation of the Division in the field, and later in the same year, Jeudwine had statistics compiled listing all gallantry awards by unit, again to recognise combat effectiveness, boost morale, and help create a sense of identity for the Division.[27]

Less formal social contact to boost morale was also promoted in life away from the action and the 1/7th Battalion were fully engaged in such activity. In considering the maintenance of troop morale, Fuller established that entertainments, and sport in particular, were crucial elements in maintaining morale, building on other aspects of social cohesion. These entertainments included music hall and, in terms of sport, particularly football. In other words, the pleasures of the rank and file, rather than those of the Officers, were what kept spirits up. This encouragement to replicate the culture of Home was significant.[28]

General entertainment and social interaction, sport and formal parades were all important aspects of the Division's morale building exercise. In the West Lancashire Division these activities were given an extra element which, in presenting the unit as a social whole, gave men a sense of belonging. Returning men to their own units after injury or reforging links between local battalions that had spent the first year of the War in different divisions, were the first steps in engendering the Lancastrian spirit in the Division. As a unit, the men's morale was therefore based upon a physical sense of identity and locality fostered by the Divisional leadership.

Almost before they made it to the trenches, the 7th Battalion was playing football. On Wednesday 18 March 1915, the Battalion team beat a combined team from 1st and 5th King's 6:2, the day after the first two men from the Battalion had been killed.[29] The Battalion fostered a good team and played a lot of football, culminating after hostilities ceased with a successful run in the Divisional competition. By Christmas they had beaten the West Lancashire Field Ambulance, 6th King's, 5th King's and 165th Brigade Headquarters. In the semi-final they beat 2/5th Lancashire Fusiliers 3:2 and in the final they won 4:2 against 166th Brigade Headquarters.[30] War Diaries also record cross-country runs, Battalion, Brigade and Divisional sports, gymkhanas

26 TNA: WO95/1360 1/7th Battalion King's Liverpool Regiment War Diary, 26 and 31 July 1916.

27 LCRO: 356 FIF/16 Honours and Awards List 55th Division, 16 February 1918; LCRO: 356 FIF/16 Annotated Nominal Roll of Recommendations for 'Immediate reward' 55th Division, July 1918, Jeudwine MSS.

28 Fuller, *Troop Morale and Popular Culture*, pp. 175–6.

29 TNA: WO95/1360 1/7th Battalion King's Liverpool Regiment War Diary, 18 March 1915.

30 TNA: WO95/2927 1/7th Battalion King's Liverpool Regiment War Diary, 19, 23, 26, 29 November 1918, 16 and 28 January 1918; WO95/2907 55th Division General Staff War Diary, 28 January 1919.

and boxing tournaments. All these activities contributed to maintaining the morale of the unit and brought it closer together, as well as maintaining fitness and providing welcome relief from the trenches. Critchley recorded that after the campaign on the Somme, they regrouped, playing 'football, a cross country run and all kinds of sport.'[31] Competitions were also held in more practical fields such as in a shooting competition in February 1916 and in January 1918 1/7th King's won the Divisional wiring competition, beating the Liverpool Scottish and 5th North Lancashires.[32]

Entertainment to bolster morale came in other ways. There was a Battalion concert in Béthune on 19 March 1915 and a regimental concert room with 'cinematograph and band' which opened in November that year.[33] Lord Derby put some of his fundraising efforts into helping establish a 55th Division band. Jeudwine wrote to thank him: 'We can soon get a band together when they arrive – we can then retaliate on the Germans who have lately been giving way to music across the fence.'[34] When the Battalion dined together to celebrate a belated Christmas on 1 January 1917 in the church at Ypres, they were treated to a concert of songs, recitals and monologues.[35] The Divisional theatre party – called the 'Roses' – was so popular that they had a three day residency at GHQ in January 1918, raising money for St Dunstan's. The 'Roses' also gave two local performances in the Divisional canteen.[36]

In the trenches too, identification with home was important and could be maintained quite simply by, for example, the use of familiar roads and streets given to trench networks and camps. Critchley noted that trench names around Givenchy included Scotland Road, Old Haynes Road, Southport Road, Crosby Road – all familiar from the Liverpool area.[37] In June 1917 1/7th Battalion was based first at Mersey Camp and then at Derby Camp, on the outskirts of Poperinghe.[38]

A further element introduced to engender cohesion within the Division was the trench magazine, *Sub Rosa*. Fuller believed trench magazines were an important element of unit cohesion and some were produced on a monthly basis, although the 55th Division only had two editions – June 1917 and June 1918.[39] This may have been because that need did not exist to the same extent as some other units, perhaps due to the success of other factors contributing to unit cohesion explored in the previous

31 Critchley.
32 TNA: WO95/1360 1/7th Battalion King's Liverpool Regiment War, Diary 4 February 1916; WO95/2910 55th Division A&Q Branch War Diary, 29 January 1918
33 TNA: WO95/1360 1/7th Battalion King's Liverpool Regiment War Diary, 19 March 1915; WO95/1636 7th Division A&QMG War Diary, 10 November 1915
34 LCRO: 356 FIF/42 Letter from Jeudwine to Lord Derby, 2 March 1916, Jeudwine MSS
35 TNA: WO95/1360 1/7th Battalion King's Liverpool Regiment War Diary, 1 January 1917; 7th Battalion signed Menu Card, King's Regimental Museum, Liverpool.
36 TNA: WO95/2910 55th Divison A&Q Branch War Diary, 23 January 1918.
37 Critchley.
38 TNA: WO95/2927 1/7th Battalion King's Liverpool Regiment War, Diary June 1917.
39 Fuller, *Troop Morale and Popular Culture*, p. 4; IWM MS/E/S 851 *Sub Rosa,* June 1917 and June 1918.

chapter. The evidence of the 'Lancashire' togetherness demonstrates that the reason cannot have been that there was no divisional loyalty to work with in the first place. It is possible that magazines at Battalion level were more relevant to the troops and that these two issues were simply secondary efforts to maintain morale designed to bolster the more widespread aspects such as football, entertainment and red rose badges. However, the existence of such magazines in other Units of the Division is unknown. Although there was an editorial note in the inaugural edition to the effect that all ranks were represented in contributions, and there were caricature cartoons of the General Staff, the inclusion of lists of gallantry awards, the number of contributions apparently from officers, and the use of the official rose motif, demonstrate that the magazine had unofficial sanction at the highest level. The Latin title – *Sub Rosa* – certainly implied that it was initiated from amongst the officer class.

Cartoon of Major-General Jeudwine, 55th Division trench magazine *Sub Rosa*, June 1917.

The timing of these publications may give the clue to their main purpose of lifting morale at particularly difficult moments. The first edition, in June 1917, had a number of cynical articles, including a mock intelligence report compiled by A. Nobon, Captain, and General Strafe, and a sardonic report of an MP's visit to the Line. A Platoon Commander's instructions included points to check when doing the rounds which used accent and dialect to draw particular attention to the class distinction between officer and man: 'Are all my rifles charged with "Five i' th' tin box and wun i' th' funnel"?' and 'Where are my listening pests?' The friendly disregard of Officers, War policy and politicians demonstrated that the magazine had a relatively relaxed attitude towards the usual sensibilities.

The 1918 version had less of the cynical contributions, and the clause stating that it was the 'work entirely of serving soldiers' went on to say that not all contributions had been printed, some being 'deemed unsuitable.' A facetious collection of patrol reports was submitted by such typical patrolmen as Horatio Bottomley, G.K.Chesterton, George Robey and G.B. Shaw, the latter who was purported to have reported: 'It was a bloody battle (but not my blood).'

Amongst the poetic contributions in 1918 were two from Major Blumberg, 1/7th King's, including 'Wipers', reproduced at the end of the next Chapter. While he was a senior officer from Southport, Blumberg's poem used the language and dialect of the men in the ranks.[40] It may not be a piece for literary acclaim but it may have been more appealing than perhaps some others written by officers about the War. It also demonstrates that the magazine itself was aimed at the readership amongst the Other Ranks.

The most heartfelt comment lay in the witty (and, as it turned out, accurate) report in the 1917 edition: 'the war will certainly end before 1930. This is official'.

Fuller found that many trench magazines only ran to five or less editions, so it may be that there is nothing untoward in only having two. However, both were published in June. In June 1917 it had been several months since the Division had been in a direct attack. Not only had there been time to work on a publication but also the assault at Ypres on 31 July, was looming. Perhaps this was an opportunity to give another boost to the morale and unity of the Division before that attack. The content was distinctly Lancastrian. The edition in June 1918 came after a difficult winter, followed by the German Spring Offensive. The magazine in June was an opportunity to boost morale again after the very successful, but costly, stand at Givenchy in April. It came out too far in advance of the Division's Advance a few months hence, but the halting of the German Offensive and crucial battles on other areas of the Front, were signs of a turning tide. Again, Divisional command needed to put out another subtle message of loyalty and commitment, emphasising its Lancashire focus.

The red rose of Lancashire, which appeared on the front of *Sub Rosa*, was an emblem noted by the Major-General as 'an object of deepest reverence ... there was no more dreadful punishment ... than to order the individual to remove the Rose from his shoulders or the unit erase it from their transport'.[41] When the booklet produced to celebrate the stand at Givenchy in April 1918 had an early version of the logo, Jeudwine was incensed, noting on his copy 'This is not the correct badge'.[42] In theory, every officer and man had the badge on both shoulders and it was painted on every item of transport and artillery. The rose had been adopted as the motif during 1916, however the motto, 'We win or die', was adopted in 1917, coming from a poem by Lieutenant L.G. Wall, A Battery 275, 1st West Lancashire Brigade, who was killed on 9 June 1917:

40 Compare with Private Peet's note after Festubert and the relevance of dialect to social identity – Joyce, *Visions of the People*, p. 279.

41 LCRO: 356 FIF/57 'A History of the Rose', Jeudwine MSS.

42 IWM Ref. 72/82/1 Jeudwine MSS Imperial War Museum.

When Princes fought for England's Crown
The house that won the most renown
And trod the sullen Yorkist down
Was Lancaster

Her blood red emblem, stricken sore
Yet steeped her pallid foe in gore,
Still stands for England ever more
And Lancaster

Now England's blood like water flows,
Full many a lusty German knows
We win or die who wear the Rose
Of Lancaster[43]

The badge and motto of 55th (West Lancashire) Division. (Author's private collection)

Dilution in the ranks – True or false?

From 1917 onwards the morale of the unit was under attack from various quarters. The effects of the Military Service Acts had meant that new drafts to the colours were conscripts with little or no direct link with the unit to which they were assigned, unlike the volunteers to the Pals and county territorial regiments in 1914 and 1915. Thus, local identity within the army unit was liable to deteriorate and if identity was the key to good morale, this too would be affected. At the same time, the longevity of the War was questioned from within and without the War Front as disillusionment threatened the War effort. Bourne pointed to the early months of 1917 on the Home Front and the winter of 1917–18 on the battle front, as being periods when morale was particularly low.[44]

The efforts made by Division command to maintain the local or regional identity of the unit were not aided by the conscription legislation, one effect of which was to send the men to any unit regardless of abode. However, there is some evidence that this local link remained important, at least to the Military Service Tribunal itself. On one occasion in Southport the Military Representative, Colonel Eaton, promised to write for a schoolteacher who had not been exempted by the Tribunal, to secure him a place in the 7th King's, the same Battalion as his brother.[45]

43 LCRO: 356 FIF/57 'A history of the Rose' Jeudwine MSS; IWM Ref.72/82/1 Jeudwine MSS Imperial War Museum.
44 Bourne, *Britain and the Great War*, pp. 209, 223.
45 *Bootle Times*, 17 March 1916, p. 6.

Jeudwine was keen to baulk the system which had removed this continuity within a soldier's unit. In correspondence with Lord Derby in late August 1918 he was still emphasising the importance of the 'localness' of the Division when urging the return of wounded men to their own units. After Critchley had been wounded at Festubert, he had been able to return to the same Battalion eight months later, by then in the new Division.[46] In his letter to Derby, Jeudwine reiterated that 'our Boys are very proud of their Division ... and they ask nothing better than that they may continue to fight side by side with their comrades ... if possible to add further lustre on the emblem they have so proudly worn'.[47] The Major-General noted one particular instance in his personal notebook: 'Burrows No.14 Platoon 7 Kings – application to return referred to B. Moss'.[48]

Even with the new drafts of men in 1917 (reinforcements under the conscription legislation) Battalion strengths were never as high as they had been in the summer of 1916 and this added further pressure on tired and exhausted men whose units were to be rearranged in early 1918. However, the successful defence of Givenchy in the spring of 1918 and the subsequent march from France into Belgium and Germany in the autumn were driven by the effectiveness of the combat units. Jeudwine continued to develop and maintain the local identity and significance of his West Lancashire Division, despite dilution and reorganisation. His success in this was best seen after the stand at Givenchy in spring 1918 and the impact of Givenchy on the sense of community identity in the Battalion and at Home mirrored the earlier engagement at Festubert.

There remained throughout the war a very significant number of local men amongst the ranks of the 1/7th Battalion King's Liverpool Regiment. Even with official attempts to encourage and maintain a sense of local identity within the Division and within Battalions, these would have had little effect had it not been for this matter of numbers. Unusually, especially for a Territorial Battalion, 1/7th King's remained predominantly a unit founded in Bootle, Southport and the surrounding area. Even those who transferred into the Battalion were predominantly from Lancashire, so limiting the extent of dilution in regional identity for the unit.

The evidence of recruiting reports in the local press indicated that when the 1/7th Battalion left for France in March 1915 it was mainly made up of local men. Before Festubert there had been few casualties and numbers were at the optimum. After the battle, the fighting strength was reduced to 639.[49] There were more casualties in the summer and, as highlighted in the previous chapter, in early August 1915 the Battalion was detached for training as a Pioneer Battalion. However, ranks were filled by a draft

46 Critchley.
47 LCRO: 356 FIF/45 Letter from Jeudwine to Derby, 28 August 1918, Jeudwine MSS.
48 LCRO: 356 FIF/40 Jeudwine Notebooks, [June 1918?], Jeudwine MSS.
49 TNA: WO95/1352 6th Brigade War Diary, 23 May 1915.

of 164 men arriving on 9 August 1915, with a further 76 coming on 7 September.[50] In early January 1917, 550 reinforcements who had been training at Musketry School, swelled the ranks of all three Brigades.[51] The only other significant draft of men to the Battalion came in early 1918 when 202 joined from sister Battalions as a result of the reorganisation of the Army.[52]

The full extent of the dilution of the Battalion can be established by examining the details presented in *Soldiers Died*.[53] The analysis below is based on the 960 Other Ranks listed in *Soldiers Died*. Over the course of the War, 70 percent of the men killed were from the Merseyside area, including 55 percent coming from the specific recruiting bases of Bootle, Southport, Crosby, and so on. A further 16 percent had enlisted in Lancashire. Table Eight and Chart One show the numbers of local men killed over the course of the War. The first figure relates to men whose residence or place of enlistment was Southport, Bootle, Crosby, Formby, Waterloo or Birkdale. The second figure includes men who enlisted in Liverpool. Thus, in 1915, the Battalion's fatalities were all from the Liverpool area with nearly 90 percent of these men coming from the specific recruiting area of the Battalion, though this had dropped to just over a quarter in 1918. In 1918, only 26 percent were specifically local, but considerable numbers remained, with 45 percent in total from Merseyside and 45 percent from the rest of Lancashire. As deaths increased in 1917 and 1918, the ratio of deaths from the local area fell. Less local numbers being killed despite the overall increase in deaths indicating that there were less men from the area left in the Battalion to be killed. However, the figure shows that there was a still a significant percentage of men from the region. These figures compare favourably with those provided by McCartney for 6th and 10th Liverpool Battalions.[54]

50 TNA: WO95/1360 1/7th Battalion King's Liverpool Regiment War Diary, 9 August and 7 September 1915.
51 TNA: WO95/2909 55th Division War Diary, AQMG Branch, January 1917.
52 TNA: WO95/2910 55th Division War Diary, A&Q Branch, January 1918.
53 *Soldiers Died*, pp. 48–58; Beckett utilised the source for similar purposes in 'The Territorial Force', p. 147 There are other caveats which must be placed on these statistics, including the fact that the list in *Soldiers Died* covered all three Line Battalions indiscriminately. While the numbers who died in 3/7th were very small as the Battalion did not leave England as a fighting unit, 2/7th was a fully-fledged Battalion within the 2nd Line West Lancashire Territorial Division – 57th. They entered the War in June 1917 and should be recognised in relation to deaths during the last eighteen months of the War.
54 McCartney, *Citizen Soldiers*, p. 61.

Table 8 Proportions of local men in the 1/7th King's Battalion[55]

Year	Local–Specific %	Local and Merseyside %	Lancashire%
1915	88	100	–
1916	85	87	13
1917	50	68	19
1918	26	45	45

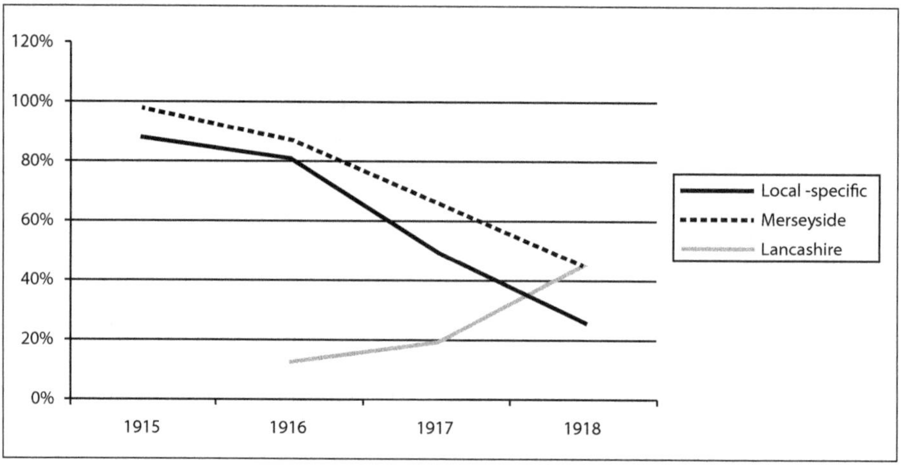

Chart 1 Proportions of local men in the 1/7th King's Battalion.

The notion of a Battalion which had a solid identification with its local community has been said to be a fallacy. Fuller felt that such identification, or 'demarcation' was thin from the start.[56] However, it was possible that, even with a decreasing number of 'local' men, a Battalion could still retain this allegiance on the basis of tradition and the 'cultural seniority' of original members. The Irish or Scottish Battalions from Liverpool, Tyneside and London were the most obvious examples, retaining a strong regional or ethnic identity despite the influx of men from many other parts of the country. A similar situation, creating a Lancashire identity, was created in 7th Battalion, something also found in other Liverpool Battalions.[57]

It is possible to establish the source of regimental drafts. For instance, the transfers arising from the reorganisation of 1918 saw some of those from the first line Liverpool Battalions being amalgamated with their second lines and others drafted

55 *Soldiers Died*, op cit., pp. 48–58.
56 Fuller, *Troop Morale and Popular Culture*, p. 58.
57 McCartney, *Citizen Soldiers*, p. 58.

to 1/5th, 1/6th and 1/7th Battalions. The Battalion War Diary noted specifically 137 Other Ranks and five Officers transferred from the Liverpool Irish (8th Battalion).[58] Another large group came from the Manchester Regiment. This is clear from the numbers recorded in *Soldiers Died* and the dates when they started being killed. There were not high numbers of men joining the 7th Battalion from alien units except for this large draft from Manchester, mainly Tameside, whose timing matches the dates for new drafts in August and September 1915, recorded in the 1/7th Battalion War Diary.[59]

The numbers of local men in the 1/7th Battalion clearly did decline during the War but this 'local' link was never broken. It is very clear that the Battalion remained predominantly a Lancastrian one, even if the Merseyside element fell below 50 percent. As with the study of the Leeds Territorials, where Morris found that despite losing high numbers of local men, the 'local spirit' of the Battalions remained, the maintenance of this social cohesion and *esprit de corps* was also prevalent in 1/7th King's.[60] A great deal of this was due to the activities of the Division, bolstered by the publication of the trench magazine. While evidence of the local connection is more limited in 1917, the reaction to the defence of Givenchy in 1918, examined later, does demonstrate the importance of the local identity of the unit for its morale.

Disciplinary Matters

A unit's disciplinary record was an indicator of morale and thus also related to its combat effectiveness. The record of 1/7th King's appears to have been a good one with relatively few cases overall, although there is a recognisable difference between their time in the Regular Divisions in 1915 and the impact of Jeudwine a man known for his emphasis on training and discipline when there is evidence of increased attention to disciplinary matters.[61] However, it also seems apparent that the efforts of the Battalion and its Colonel, Marriott, within the Division, had first to overcome the memory of a rout at Loos in September 1915. Difficulties with discipline have been highlighted in 1917. Beckett summarised that 'military crime invariably rose after heavy casualties', noting particular problems following Passchendaele. He also noted that despite the notoriously difficult winter of 1917–18, an analysis of Fifth Army records showed 'little sign of any serious morale problems' and an examination, below, of discipline in the 7th King's Battalion's time in Fifth Army confirms this.[62]

58 Wyrall, *The History of the King's Regiment (Liverpool)* p. 608; TNA: WO95/2927 1/7th Battalion King's Liverpool Regiment War Diary, 31 January 1918.
59 TNA: WO95/1360 1/7th Battalion King's Liverpool Regiment War Diary, 9 August and 7 September 1915.
60 Morris, 'The Leeds Rifles', p. 993.
61 Griffith, *Battle Tactics of the Western Front,* pp. 81–83.
62 Beckett, *The Great War 1914–1918,* pp. 221– 222.

During the whole war Courts Martial heard 141 cases from 7th King's, constituting 124 individuals (a number of men were tried on more than one occasion). This was 0.1 percent of all cases recorded in the Field General Courts Martial records, shown in Tables Nine and Ten. The only consistent comparison of discipline that can be carried out is in terms of death sentences. An analysis of all units by Oram indicated that the King's Liverpool Regiment as a whole had 62 death sentences passed; twenty-two in the first four Regular Battalions, twenty-six in the Territorials (5th–10th Battalions) and fourteen in the New Army and Service Battalions.[63] This indicates that discipline amongst Territorials was not noticeably worse than amongst Regulars and would imply a cohesive unit committed to comrades and the cause.

Table 9 Nature of alleged disciplinary offences in 7th King's Battalions 1915–1919[64]

Offence	Number
Drunkenness	28
Misc. s.11	12
Misc. s.40	38
Disobedience	16
Breaking out of camp	15
Insubordination	5
Sleeping/Quitting post	8
Striking an officer	5
Theft	1
Cowardice	2
Desertion	20
Indecency	1
Offence against inhabitant	1
s.20	2
s.29 (false evidence)	1
s.18 (self-inflicted wound)	1

63 Oram, G., *Death Sentences Passed by Military Courts of the British Army 1914*–1924 (London: Francis Boutle, 1998).
64 Collated from TNA: WO213/3–26 Field General Courts Martial Registers 1915–1919.

Table 10 1/7th Battalion King's Liverpool Regiment – Monthly disciplinary cases[65]

	1915	1916	1917	1918	1919	Total
January		2	4	3	1	10
February		14	4	1		19
March		3	4	3		10
April			4	2		6
May	3	1	6	3		13
June	1	14	4	3		22
July	2	2	5	2		11
August			2	4		6
September		1	1	5		7
October	3	1	2			6
November	1	1				2
December	1		2			3
						115

Note: The figures in the table have only counted the trials of: Private A.J. Hilton (8th and 10th July 1915), Private J. Hale (2nd and 7th June 1917) and Private J. Duffy (15th and 28th June 1918) once, although in each case two hearings were necessary

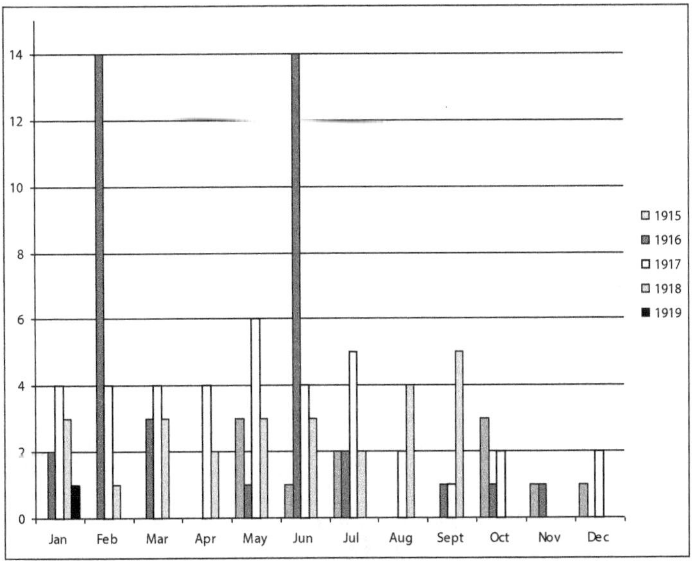

Chart 2 Number of disciplinary cases brought each month.

65 TNA: WO213/3–26 Field General Courts Martial Registers 1915–1919.

Of the death sentences, six were for men in the 7th Battalions, representing 23 percent of all the Liverpool Territorials sentenced – the same as 9th Battalion, but less than 8th (eleven). The 10th (Scottish) were the only one of the six Territorial Battalions to have no-one sentenced to death.[66] Only six of the Liverpool Regiment's sentences were carried out with two Regulars, two Territorials (from the Liverpool Irish) and two New Army men being shot.[67] Six executions out of the Regiment's total 62 sentences correspond with the overall ratio of executions during the War being 10 percent of the 3,080 sentences.[68] Another two men from 7th King's are not amongst the official court records but were reported as absentees being sought by the Military Police.[69] Their fate is unknown.[70]

The large majority of other disciplinary cases in the Battalion involved Privates. There is no reliable indication of the soldiers' social backgrounds but there is some limited evidence of the ethnicity of the men involved. In their studies on executions Putkowski and Sykes have shown that northern English units suffered disproportionately.[71] Oram has drawn out the latent trends and fears showing that there were racial and other considerations involved. An indication of this may be seen in the fact

66 TNA: WO213/4–27 Field General Courts Martial Registers 1915–1919.

67 Putkowski, J. and Sykes, J., *Shot at Dawn: Executions in World War One by Authority of the British Army Act* (Barnsley: Wharncliffe Publishing, 1989), pp. 286–291. These men were executed on 16 July and 2 November 1916. Two other men from 55th Division were executed, one also on 16 July, the other on 25 October 1916.

68 Putkowski & Sykes, *Shot at Dawn,* p. 11.

69 TNA: WO154/8 List of Absentees up to 8 December 1916 reported to the Provost Marshal GHQ in the War Diary of Assistant Provost Marshal IX Corps; List of Absentees up to 30 June 1917.

70 The six were Privates Bolton (2/7th King's, November 1918), Braithwaite (July 1915), Halsall (July 1916), Hilton (July 1915), Robson (April 1917) and Tolley (September 1918), although Oram stated that, with the exception of Bolton, they were in the Isle of Man Battalion in Salonika. Robson was clearly not in Salonika, in any Battalion, as he appeared on the List of Absentees in the Western Front section, not in the sections on other theatres. Nor is there any mention in the Courts Martial records of the trial being in Salonika. Oram himself refers to the trials of Braithwaite, Hilton and Tolley being in France and Flanders. Halsall is recorded as being tried at Bretencourt. The source of Oram's misunderstanding appears to be that the Isle of Man Battalion in the Liverpool Regiment, which derived from the Volunteer battalions of the pre-1908 reforms, was styled as 7th (Isle of Man) Volunteer Battalion. According to James it formed a service company which was attached to16th King's in March 1915 and then transferred to 3rd Cheshire Regiment in October of that year as 1st Manx (Service) Company. The Company became 'A' Company of 2nd Cheshire's and joined them in Salonika on 12 January 1916. Sources: Oram, *Death Sentences Passed by Military Courts*, p. 107 inter alia; Frederick, J.B.M., (ed.) *Lineage book of British land forces 1660–1978* (Wakefield: Microform Academic Publishers, 1984); Brown, 'The King's Regiment (Liverpool) – Liverpool's Volunteers and Territorials and their Shako, Helmet and Cap Badges', pp. 23–7; James, Brig. E.A. (compiler), *Historical records of British Infantry Regiments in the Great War 1914–1918* (London: Samson Books, 1976).

71 Putkowski & Sykes, *Shot at Dawn,* p. 23.

that the Irish 8th Battalion had more men sentenced to death than any of the other Liverpool Battalions. Conversely, the Liverpool Scottish had none at all. Oram was clear that it was the Irish who were seen as the 'threat' to military order.[72] It is possible to make a crude assessment of the ethnic origin of those charged from their surnames. On this basis, maybe up to thirty-eight (30 percent) of the 124 cases recorded could be men of Scottish, Welsh or Irish descent. Compared with the earlier assessment of names listed in *Soldiers Died*, that 10 percent of the Battalion were Celtic, this much higher proportion of men with apparently immigrant roots who were charged would tend to support Oram's conclusions. However, there is no evidence that the transfer of men from the Liverpool Irish in January 1918 created a significant change in the disciplinary record of 1/7th King's.

There was an average of just over one case per month in 1915, whereas this more than doubled each year for the rest of the War.[73] Apart from two men sentenced to death for sleeping at their post and a Private tried for desertion in December, the cases were largely low level misdemeanours, usually drunkenness.[74] There does not appear to be any link between these serious 'crimes' and a particular event.[75]

If the individuals' behaviour indicated a Battalion of good discipline, one incident relating to the whole Battalion damaged that gloss to some extent. In November 1915 Major Paul Hemelryk, acting Colonel of the Battalion, was sent home in unusual circumstances, and this coincided with a long leave of absence for Colonel Potter, resulting in Captain Marriott being put in command of the Battalion. Writing in a letter to his father dated 25 October 1915 Marriott later observed:

> [T]he poor old battalion had a severe trial the other night which had a rather unfortunate sequel. It was a misty night, chaos in the front line when you could not state definitely if the trench was ours or the Bosch… sudden outburst of bombing near a large body of men. The men were already overstrung and half a dozen got out of hand. A report and request for names has been made but none are forthcoming and two days later on adverse reports were sent in. There was not much about the Battalion as a whole and the General said the Officer's conduct was splendid.[76]

72 Oram, G., *Worthless Men: Race eugenics and the Death Penalty in the British Army during the First World War* (London: Francis Boutle, 1998), pp. 60–73, 116.

73 Not all cases appear to have been recorded: Critchley claimed to have spent '10 days in jankers in the cookhouse' for keeping a Uhlan horse after shooting the enemy trooper when out on a patrol with some Regulars in the summer of 1915, but there is no record in the registers.

74 TNA: WO213/4 and WO213/6 Field General Courts Martial Registers 1915.

75 TNA: WO95/1360 1/7th Battalion King's Liverpool Regiment War Diary May, June, July, November, December 1915.

76 Marriott correspondence, 25 October 1915.

The letter referred to the 'last fighting' and in a letter at the end of September he had written: 'We have been forward again since my last and things have happened which unfortunately I am not allowed to speak about.'[77] Marriott later inserted these paragraphs into his text in the letter of 25 October. The chronology of correspondence clearly places the incident in question during the battle of Loos. There is a note made by the cataloguer of the collection in Liddell's Archive to the effect that the CO was sacked and sent home.[78]

This was a conclusion corroborated by a further reference in Marriott's correspondence where he referred to 'the unfortunate affair of the night attack on the Battalion leading to the CO's sacking.'[79] Certainly around this time, Potter appears to have disappeared but this seems linked either to an injury – Potter was in a list of casualties of 25 September which Marriott recounted later in his letters,[80] – or to personal problems: Marriott wrote: ' the CO is quite fit but his business and father are bad and I think he gets special leave tomorrow.'[81] On 1 November 1915, Marriott wrote: 'The CO has had his marching orders… await actual instructions when I shall take over,' and this appears to refer to Potter because a subsequent letter records that Hemelryk and Stott were candidates for the promotion awarded to Marriott.[82]

This was a confused and confusing episode. It is clear that Hemelryk departed in bad favour as he appeared in the Army List as CO of 3/7th Battalion at home.[83] Marriott referred to it on a number of occasions in later letters: '… the authorities have forgotten or forgiven the incident which led to Hemelryk's departure, but I have found it many times a millstone round the neck'; 'I know Division is pleased as they sent 2 bottles of whisky, 1 of Port and a tin of Egyptian cigars. This, compared with the reception after Loos under Hemelryk shows we are alright.'[84]

In the absence of service records for either Marriott or Hemelryk, little more is known of the affair. There were no references in War Diaries at Battalion, Brigade, Division, Corps or Army level.[85] It is only possible to assume the date of the incident based on Marriott's letters as there is no obvious reference in the Battalion War Diary.[86] Nor was there any noticeable disciplinary action taken against men of the

77 Marriott correspondence, 28 September 1915.
78 Marriott correspondence, 30 October 1915.
79 Marriott correspondence, undated [25–30 October 1915].
80 Marriott correspondence, 4 November 1915.
81 Marriott correspondence, 6 October 1915.
82 Marriott correspondence, 1 November 1915 and 5 December 1915.
83 *Army List*, January 1916.
84 Marriott correspondence, 19 June and 14 August 1916 (referring to 8 August action).
85 TNA: WO95/1360 1/7th Battalion King's Liverpool Regiment War Diary; WO95/1343 5th Brigade War Diary; WO95/1286 2nd Division War Diary; WO95/592 I Corps War Diary; WO95/158 and 159 1st Army War Diary.
86 '24 September – Battalion in trenches and several working parties detailed to various Battalions of the Brigade. 25 September – The Battalion took part in the operations of the 5th Brigade covering the left flank of the Brigade and finding several working parties…The

Battalion, at this juncture.[87] Marriott was gazetted in December 1915.[88] After he returned to England in late summer, 1916, it was Colonel Potter who returned to take over command, apparently signifying that there was no slur against him at least.[89]

While writers have observed that territorial discipline tightened up during the War, the new Divisional General, Jeudwine, was particularly keen.[90] Baynes has listed good discipline as an element of morale but Jeudwine said just the opposite, that morale was an element of good discipline.[91] The transformation in discipline brought by Jeudwine was felt by the Battalion Commanders. Marriott wrote home in March 1916 saying: 'The old Territorial ideas have gone by the board. We are Regulars pure and simple. Last time we were in rest I had 31 men tied to the wheel at the same time'.[92] By March 1916 only thirty-one cases had gone through the courts in the whole of the previous twelve months. It is possible that Marriott's exaggeration was based on fact, possibly the half dozen men sentenced under s.11 on 28 February.[93] However, not all cases were processed through the system by Battalion Officers, though a crime meriting Field Punishment No. 1 should have been significant enough to have done so.[94]

Battalion was withdrawn to Billets in ESSARS late at night. 26 September … spent "cleaning up" 27 September … relieved the Glasgow Highlanders in the trenches. 28 September – Battalion were relieved at 8.20 from trenches by 1/1st Ghurkas. Returned to ESSARS late at night.' – WO95/1360 1/7th Battalion King's Liverpool Regiment War Diary.

87 TNA: WO213/5 and 6 Field General Courts Martial Registers August – December 1915. The only other scrap of evidence about this incident could relate to Second Lieutenant Herbert Watson's relinquishing of his commission, the subject of his own court hearing back home in Southport. Watson's own evidence was reported as follows: 'Defendant gave evidence in support, and added that he was between nine and ten months in France and was at the battle of Loos. In consequence of some action when the men were being brought out of a farmyard he got a moment's (sic) order to go to England'. See *Southport Guardian,* 23 September 1916 p. 8. The report could be read as linking the two events, although this was probably unlikely as it took until May 1916 to issue the order, and Marriot was so fulsome in praising Watson despite the breach of discipline for which he was sent home.

88 *London Gazette,* 7 December 1915.

89 Potter rejoined sometime in late August/early September 1916, and was wounded again on 25 September at Gueudecourt. He was back in the Battalion on 6 November 1916 – TNA: WO95/2927 1/7th Battalion King's Liverpool Regiment War Diary.

90 Sheffield, *Leadership in the Trenches,* pp. 27–28.

91 Baynes *Morale* pp. 253–254; LCRO: 356 FIF/13 55th Divisional School of Instruction Syllabus 27 February 1917 Jeudwine MSS.

92 Marriott correspondence to his father 17 March 1916. According to the War Diary WO95/2927 the last time the Battalion was 'at rest' was in Beaumetz between 8–14 March. Prior to that they had been in the trenches and support areas since 15 February.

93 TNA: WO213/7 and 8 Field General Courts Martial Registers, January–March 1916.

94 Field Punishment No.1 consisted of putting the man in fetters or handcuffs, or both, and attaching him to a fixed object for a period of up to two hours every day. He could not spend more than three out of four consecutive days cuffed or tied to the object. He was also subjected to labour, the like of which could be similar to hard labour. Field

On another occasion ten men were charged with 'disobedience' and were also sentenced in June to 90 days Field Punishment No. 1.[95] This may have been a particularly significant and co-ordinated act of disobedience, or the punishment may have been just to set an example in advance of the raids and fighting described in the previous chapter. Tilsley noted that 'a man who is crucified to a wheel before all his comrades suffers a degrading, demoralising punishment. His battalion is often kept in the line longer than the recognised spell'.[96] His storyteller, Bradshaw, had been in doubt about the existence of Field Punishment No.1 until he had seen 'a Lancashire of the old Festubert days tied to a limber wheel near the cookhouse. Men passed by indifferent and spiritless; the Aussies would have cut him free very quickly'.[97]

There is no record in the War Diary of this event. June was spent in 'Usual trench routine', working parties, classes and instruction around Wailly. May 1916 had been much the same, including a visit by Jeudwine on Sunday 28th, who had congratulated the Battalion on its 'excellent turnout and appearance.'[98] Appearance was another of Jeudwine's concerns, emphasising the need for smartness and discipline in saluting.[99] There were several references to being congratulated on its appearance in the Battalion War Diary – 6 April 1916 by the Corps Commander and 28 May by Jeudwine for example – although Marriott wrote that 'the general is alternatively cursing or praising us. He likes our vigorous methods but says we are dirty when in billets. He is right to an extent as we recruit from the slums of Bootle.'[100]

A study of the cases around Third Ypres in 1917 proves interesting as it coincides with a period generally reckoned to have been of lower morale and tests the assertion that discipline was tightened in advance of a 'Big Push'.[101] The incidence of convictions in the Battalion increased during 1917 suggesting either an increase in poor discipline or a tightening up of discipline. Two cases of cowardice occurred in July, while the Battalion was supplying working parties on the outskirts of Ypres and there were three other cases, for being drunk and an offence against an inhabitant, for striking a

Punishment No.2 consisted of being handcuffed or fettered and labouring, but the soldier was spared the attachment to a fixed object: *Manual of Military Law* (London, 1914).

95 TNA: WO213/9 Field General Courts Martial Register, April–June 1916.

96 Tilsley, *Other Ranks,* p. 180.

97 Tilsley, *Other Ranks,* p. 124.

98 TNA: WO95/2927 1/7th Battalion King's Liverpool Regiment War Diary, June 1916.

99 TNA: WO95/2899 55th Division War Diary Training Notes circulated by Cochrane, 7 January 1916; LCRO: 356 FIF/13 55th Divisional School of Instruction Syllabus 27, February 1917 Jeudwine MSS Liverpool Record Office; various references in Jeudwine's notebooks to saluting (356 FIF/38) march discipline (356 FIF/40) and uniform (356 FIF/41).

100 TNA: WO95/2927 1/7th Battalion King's Liverpool Regiment War Diary, 6 April and 28 May 1916; Marriott correspondence, 20 April 1916.

101 Oram, *Death Sentences Passed by the Military Courts,* p. 14.

senior officer, and one under s.40 of the Army Act.[102] This considerably higher number in July could have been related to the imminent attack on 31st at Ypres.

These two cases of cowardice were the only ones recorded in 7th King's. Table Nine shows the nature of offences alleged against men during the hostilities. It is interesting to note that charges under s.11 were prevalent in 1916, but for the rest of the War the miscellaneous charge under s.40, for offences prejudicial to order and discipline, was more common.[103] Sleeping or quitting a post did not occur in the Battalion after 1916. However, desertion was much more prevalent in 1917 and 1918 indicating a growing disillusionment and demoralisation in the War. The extent of self-inflicted wounds is not clear, as a Fifth Army circular reminded officers that men to be tried for self-wounding should usually be charged under s.40 and not s.18(2).[104] In the Fifth Army as whole, the number of convictions for self-inflicted wounds under s.40 from June to September 1917 was 101 out of 1,771 individual classified charges – 5.7 percent.[105] As the cases of Barker and McFarlane in July were 'Cowardice s.40', it is possible that these were incidences of self-inflicted wounds.[106]

Comparative information for the period the 55th Division spent in Fifth Army between June and September 1917 exists in the detailed conviction statistics extant in the War Diary.[107] Evidence in the following chapter shows that much of this time was spent in the Front Line areas. During this period the Division's rate of convictions varied from 1 percent to 2 percent of that Army's convictions, and in July it was at its highest with fourteen convictions (2 percent). Five of these were from 1/7th King's

102 TNA: WO213/16 and 20 Field General Courts Martial Registers, July 1917–February 1918.

103 Section 11 of the Army Act stated that it was an offence to disobey garrison or general orders. Concealment of venereal disease could be dealt with under this order. Disobeying a specific order or command relating to a military duty came under Section 9, which, if associated with wilful defiance, could be punishable by death. Section 40 was a useful catch-all which declared it an offence to carry out 'any act, conduct, disorder, or neglect to the prejudice of good order and military discipline.' Neglect needed to be wilful and the court had to be satisfied that the act was prejudicial to both good order and military discipline. Sometimes Section 20 – permitting the escape of persons in custody – was used in association with this Section. Charges coming close to desertion or abandonment which were not sufficient to be catered for under Sections 4 and 5, would be covered by Section 40. The other commonly used Section was 19 – drunkenness: *Manual of Military Law* and amendments to *The Army Act, 44 & 45 VICT.* c.58.

104 TNA: WO95/525 Fifth Army War Diary Adjutant and Quarter Master General Circular 1902, 15 June 1917.

105 TNA: WO95/525 Fifth Army War Diary Adjutant and Quarter Master General. The percentages rose more or less month by month from June to July, August and September 1917. The figures were: 5.3 percent, 4.9 percent, 5.7 percent and 6.8 percent respectively.

106 Thomas Hope recounted the organisation of a mutiny in a Lancashire Battalion which received agreement from men in his own Battalion, against a likely execution in October 1917. A man was charged with sleeping at his post and then deserting but as the death sentence was commuted to ten years in prison the threat abated. See Hope, *The Winding Road Unfolds*, pp. 191–212.

107 TNA: WO95/525 Fifth Army War Diary Adjutant and Quarter Master General.

Liverpool. In October 57th (West Lancashire 2nd Line) Division joined Fifth Army more or less as the 1st Line Division left, and of six convictions in that Division, only one was from 2/7th King's Battalion. The statistics demonstrate that both Divisions had low levels of indiscipline compared to other units in Fifth Army at that time. As the winter passed into 1918 there were six cases of serious indiscipline between December and February, including desertion, breaking out and under s.40, and a series of isolated convictions for breaking out, desertion and disobedience went on into April, resulting in eight men being given Field Punishment No. 1.[108] Although still relatively few in number, this corroborates the period being one of low morale.

There were further charges in 1918, including two desertions in May, two in June, one in August and two more in September.[109] Critchley recalled an incident when he had struck an officer which seems to have occurred during the stand at Givenchy, or possibly soon afterwards. It does not appear in official records but he recorded it in his interview:

> I was on duty in an advance post and no-one came out in daytime … this officer had only just come out to France … and he broke our rule of not being disturbed [during the day]. When he came into our sap I let fly at him … I got 90 days field punishment number one … I was lucky because I could have been shot but at my trial I had my Adjutant to act for me in my defence. When the officer was asked could he identify me as the one who hit him, he shuffled and said I think so … but the Court knew I'd done it so I got field punishment no. 1 but spared my life. All pay was stopped and I lost two stripes – but when the punishment was over I got them back … All my lads had been asked and they all said they did not see me and they told the Court no-one was allowed in the sap in the daytime – my defence by the Adjutant was that I may have thought he was a German.[110]

The statistical evidence shows that Jeudwine's considered approach to discipline had an impact, as the number of cases rose dramatically within the Battalion once it had joined 55th Division. However, the incidence remained low. There is some evidence that charges increased in advance of an attack, for instance in July 1917. This reflects the officers' need to instil some resolve and demonstrate to the men the futility of indiscipline. The more consistent rumbling number of convictions for desertion and breaking out which continued from late 1917 through 1918, could be an indication of low morale amongst the men, rather than over enthusiastic officers making a point.

108 TNA: WO213/19–21 Field General Courts Martial Registers, November 1917–April 1918.

109 TNA: WO213/22–26 Field General Courts Martial Registers, April 1918–September 1918.

110 See Critchley. The precise date for this event is not available but it appears to have happened around the time of the German attack in April 1918 and before the British advance began in the late summer.

The notion and reality of community identity in 7th King's and in the 55th Division was an important one. It was encouraged and maintained by the Commanding Officer and was seen as a crucial aspect to maintaining morale, itself a key contributor to better performance in combat engagements.

5

The 'Learning Curve': From the Somme to Passchendaele

Before studying specific engagements of the Battalion during 1916 and 1917, it is worth considering the overall deployment of the 1/7th King's during the War. This evidence relates firstly to the number of days spent in action; secondly, the number of casualties suffered; and thirdly, the relative strength of the Battalion. A study of these elements provides a context for the study of particular actions, the level of discipline and the relevance of the dilution of local men in a Battalion which relied so heavily on a sense of community identity. The number of days spent in frontline action demonstrates the level of their deployment by GHQ; the casualty figures indicate the level of intensity of the actions in which they were engaged; and the relative strength of the Battalion shows their level of operational efficiency. It appears that fewer men were fighting harder for greater lengths of time as the War progressed but was this a sign of greater efficiency or a gradual wearing down of resources? Whatever the answer, it does not seem to have had a detrimental effect on the community identity of the Battalion.

The principal locus of attention for 1/7th King's, of Bootle and Southport, reinforced what was becoming the wider allegiance to Lancashire during the second part of the War. This 'Lancastrianisation' process had begun in January 1916 and was under way before the numbers of men from the local area started to show significant decline (seen earlier in Table Eight). As this regional identity fostered high morale in the Division, so GHQ grew more confident in the Division's abilities and this confidence was reflected in their deployment in a number of theatres on the Western Front.

General Deployment 1915–18

In terms of the general deployment of the new 55th Division the 1/7th King's Regiment saw action on fourteen occasions and as this was achieved excluding any action in 1914 or 1915, it compares favourably with others who had served the longer period of the War.[1] As a Unit, 1/7th King's were in 2nd and 7th Regular Divisions in 1915, adding three more engagements. Griffith found that the average frequency for a Territorial Division to spend in action was sixteen occasions, concluding that this demonstrated a 'low level of trust [by GHQ]'.[2] Despite this Griffith did recognise that an, albeit informal, hierarchy of Divisions had emerged by the end of 1916, including 55th Division amongst the more trustworthy units who were grouped as an elite for assault.[3] There had also emerged a group of senior commanders who were clearly more effective and who led the strategic thinking and training through the rest of the War. Griffith listed 19 names, including Jeudwine. It was these men who formed the 'assault spearhead of the BEF' in 1917.[4] Coop pointed out that having gained the confidence of Army Command by the end of July 1917, the Division was chosen to carry out the assault at Ypres on its own front – 'an honour which it both appreciated and entirely vindicated'.[5]

Table 11 Percentage numbers of days spent in the Front areas by 1/7th King's 1915–18[6]

Year and potential days in the field	Days in Action, Front Line and Support Trenches	Total days in 'forward area', including trenches
1915 – 305	73 – 24%	158 – 52%
1916 – 366	164 – 44%	234 – 63%
1917 – 365	121 – 33%	171 – 47%
1918 – 315	177 – 56%	182 – 57%
Total for entire war	38%	55%

1 Battle honours for the 55th Division ascribed in Becke, A.F., *History of the Great War: Order of Battle of Divisions* Parts 2A and 3A (London, 1936 and 1938), pp. 138–9.
2 Griffith, *Battle Tactics on the Western Front*, pp. 81–2. Note that the average number of months spent by a first line Territorial Division in a major theatre of War was thirty-eight. While 55th Division had thirty-five, from 1916, 1/7th Battalion was at the Front for forty-four months: Fuller, *Troop Morale and Popular Culture* p. 9.
3 Griffith, *Battle Tactics of the Western Front*, p. 82. Not all commentators shared his view. Simkins was more sanguine about the inclusion of 55th Division, providing a much wider list of claimants and thus diluting Griffith's elite spearhead: Simkins, P., 'Co-Stars or Supporting Cast? British Divisions in the "Hundred Days", 1918' in *British Fighting Methods in the Great War*, p. 64.
4 Griffith, *Battle Tactics of the Western Front*, pp. 79, 83.
5 Coop, *The Story of the 55th Division*, p. 46.
6 These Figures have been calculated from an analysis of the Battalion War Diaries. The yearly averages have been used in the cases of April 1915, May 1916, and July 1917, which are missing from the series of monthly War Diaries.

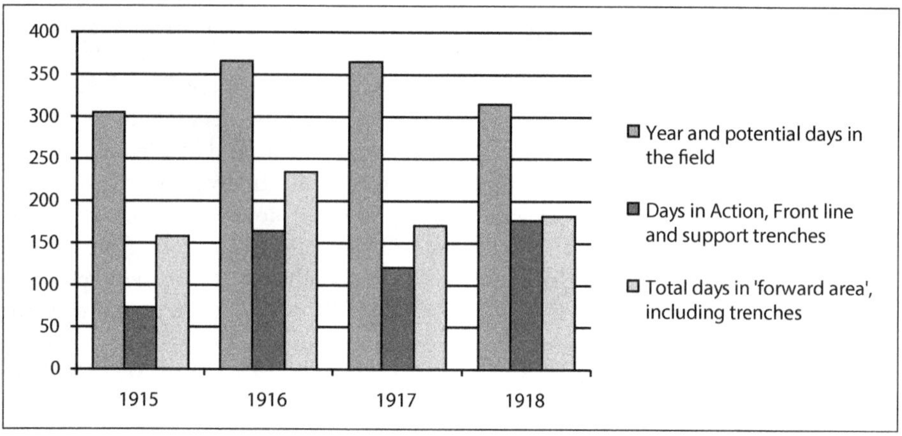

Chart 3 Percentage numbers of days spent in the forward area 1915–18.

The number of engagements can be more sharply defined in terms of the numbers of days spent in the forward lines, calculated from War Diaries. The evidence from this Battalion is that they spent only 45 percent of their time in the 'rear' and the remaining time at the Front. This high ratio of time deployed in the Line indicates that they were relied upon by Army Command in that role. Table Eleven and Chart Three show that 1/7th King's spent a total of 55 percent of their time in the trenches and the forward area, where they were sufficiently close to be running working and digging parties during the nights. Fuller assumed that 60 percent of any unit's time was spent in the reserve or rest,[7] although as Malcolm Brown pointed out, even when away from the Front Line and at 'rest', troops were making up working parties, carrying parties, burial parties, and digging trenches and mines.[8] When in the Regular Division 7th Battalion spent 52 percent of 1915 in the forward area. This was more than the time spent by the 55th Division in 1917 and close to the Divisional commitment in 1918 when GHQ apparently had a greater confidence in the unit's abilities.

This detailed study of the days at the Front in 1/7th King's also confirmed what Morris established had happened in the Leeds Rifles, with the planned routine of trench life being a rotation of six days in the Front Line, six in Reserve, six in Second Line and six at rest, breaking down very early on. Morris found that the Leeds men could be in the trenches for up to twenty-five days and have much shorter rest periods.[9] While the Kingsmen spent the whole of December 1915 and January 1916 away from the Front, this was a period of transition into the new 55th Division. In the

7 Fuller, *Troop Morale and Popular Culture*, p. 58.
8 Brown, M., *The Imperial War Museum Book of the Western Front* (London: Sidgwick & Jackson, 1993), pp. 64–68.
9 Morris, 'The Leeds Rifles', p. 573.

middle of 1916 they were in the trenches from 12 June until 19 July, with only three days designated for working parties; even those three included taking part in a night raid. In 1917, they spent the second half of June forming working parties for the Front, but were in the trenches for virtually the whole time between 17 September and 5 December. In 1918 they were away from the Front, taking part in training in Divisional Reserve on a routine, almost monthly, basis. Furthermore, in 1918, from September onwards, they were not simply in the trenches but formed the Line of Resistance, Support, Outpost Line or Advanced Guard, as the enemy was pursued back into Belgium. All this deployment demonstrated their perceived reliability and dependability across a range of sectors in the Front Line.

A further indication of the perceived effectiveness of the unit is given by the fact that on three separate occasions when an opportunity arose to disband the Battalion, it was not taken. Other units did suffer that fate. Firstly, in August 1915 there was a strong chance they would turn into a Pioneer Battalion, but instead were transferred from 2nd to 7th Division and subsequently to the reformed 55th.[10] Then in January 1918 there was widespread reorganisation of Brigades and three Battalions of 55th Division were dismantled and merged with their Second Lines in 57th Division – 8th and 9th King's, and 5th Loyal North Lancashires.[11] Much of 1/8th Battalion was actually merged with 1/5th, 1/6th and 1/7th Battalions.[12] Thirdly, shortly after the War, the Territorial Association instructed the West Lancashire County Association to make some reductions, but a consideration of the various Battalions in the Association resolved that 7th King's had built a reputation during the War which meant they were too good to be disbanded.[13]

Table 12 Average monthly deaths in 7th King's Battalions[14]

Year and Number of Months in Action	Average Number of Deaths per Month
1915 (10 months)	16.6
1916 (12 months)	16.5
1917 (12 months)	25.1
1918 (10 months)	29.1

10 TNA: WO95/1360 1/7th Battalion King's Liverpool Regiment War Diary; Marriott correspondence 26 August 1915. K.W. Mitchinson. *Pioneer Battalions in the Great War: Organized and Intelligent Labour* (London: Leo Cooper, 1997) p. 63–68 proposes that it was precisely this re-formation that prevented the change.

11 Becke, *Order of Battle* Part 2A, pp. 133–9.

12 Wyrall, *The History of the King's Regiment*, Vol. III, p. 607.

13 LCRO: 356WES 1/1 (1) WLTAF Minute Book – Special meeting, 7 June 1921 to decide the dismantling of one Territorial Battalion – agreed to merge 6th and 10th Liverpool's.

14 *Soldiers Died*, op cit., pp. 48–58.

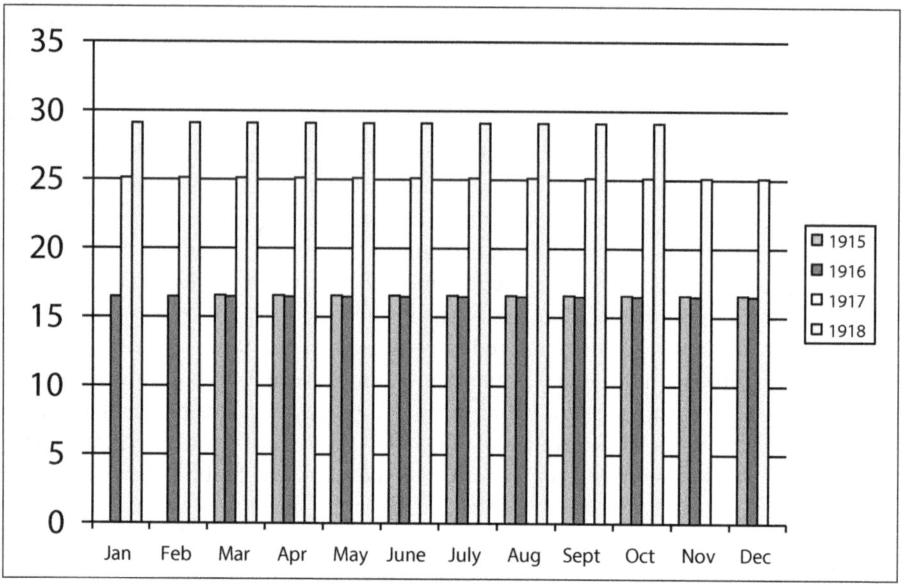

Chart 4 Average monthly deaths in 7th King's Battalion.

In addition to spending such a large proportion of their time at the Front, the increasing number of deaths in the Battalion demonstrates an increasing commitment to action where casualties could occur. Table Twelve and Chart Four show monthly averages for each year of the War for 1/7th King's. However, some caution should be exercised in relying on these figures too heavily as they are a record of both 1st and 2nd Line Battalions – 2/7th King's were in action on the Western Front in 57th Division from late 1917. Overall casualties were high in 1918 as a result of the Spring Offensive and the Final Advance, when, for example, 180,000 casualties were sustained by the BEF in the first 50 days.[15] Finally, the nature of fighting in the last two or three months of the War changed and casualties were generally reduced.

The casualty figures serve to indicate the increased use of Territorials from 1916 onwards. This can be further demonstrated by the fluctuating ranks of the Battalion as the War continued, shown in Chart Five. The chart pinpoints Battalion strength on a quarterly basis, on or around 25 of March, June, September and December. The Battalion's fighting strength on the eve of Festubert, on 15 May 1915, was 931, higher than the figures when they landed in France. However, in July 1915 it reached its lowest point of 567 and this explains why there was a discussion about transforming it into a Pioneer Battalion.[16] As it was decided not to do this, more drafts joined and the

15 Sheffield, *Forgotten Victory*, p. 244.
16 TNA: WO95/1285 2nd Division War Diary Strength of Units, 15 May and 17 July 1915.

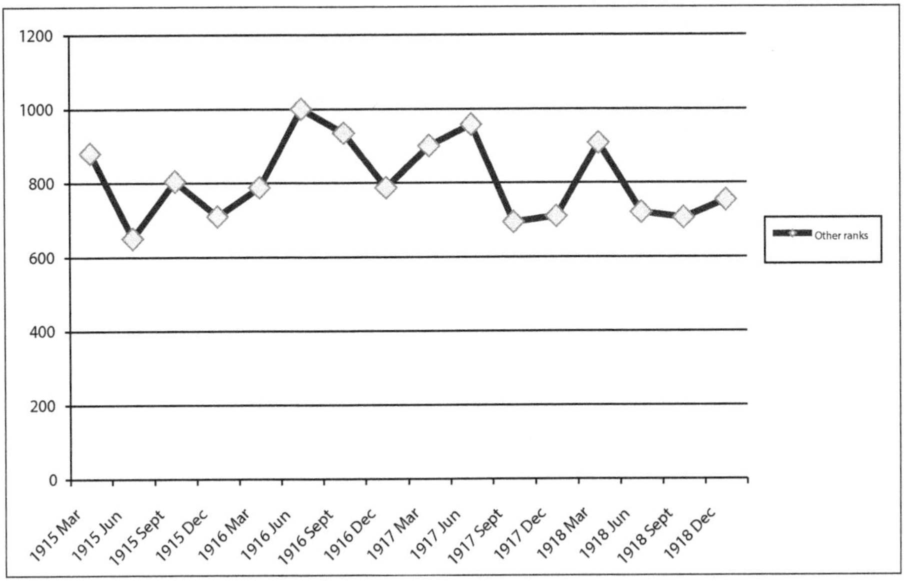

Chart 5 Other ranks: Quarterly figures.

numbers rose steadily until, on 2 September 1916, they reached their highest point at 1072.[17] The pattern is particularly instructive when related to the battles they fought. After starting at Festubert with 931 men, and suffering losses, they were back to 805 when they supported the attacks at Loos.[18] Almost ten months later, in the new Division, they fought on the Somme with over 1,000 men, and when they finished that summer campaign after taking considerable casualties they had fallen to a new low of 745. By November they had barely 700 men in the ranks.[19] After rebuilding through 1917 they went into Third Ypres with less than 900 men, comparable to Festubert in 1915.[20] Their losses brought them back to a figure similar to that of that first summer. The defence at Givenchy looks all the more impressive when it is considered that it was made by just 946 men.[21]

During the Final Advance numbers fluctuated between 795 and 694. These considerably smaller numbers were fighting more efficiently and effectively on an all-arms basis, as opposed to the need for ranks in depth on account of the nature of the attacks on the Somme and at Passchendaele. Overall, the figures seem to indicate that an optimum fighting strength of around 900 men was achieved in time for each major

17 TNA: WO95/2909 55th Division War Diary Strength of Units, 2 September 1916.
18 TNA: WO95/1287 2nd Division War Diary Strength of Units, 25 September 1915.
19 TNA: WO95/2901 55th Division War Diary Strength of Units, 7 October and 11 November 1916.
20 TNA: WO95/525 Fifth Army War Diary Strength of Units, 29 July 1917.
21 TNA: WO95/2950 55th Division War Diary Strength of Units, 6 April 1918.

engagement of the War, until the Hundred Days. This represented a major achievement of recruitment and organisation and the determination to maintain these figures implies a desire by GHQ to keep 1/7th King's as a viable fighting unit.

By reconstructing the triangle of evidence in Tables Eleven and Twelve and Charts Three, Four and Five it can be seen that in 1915 the Battalion spent 52 percent of their time in the forward area including 24% more or less in action; they suffered 16.6 deaths per month and their strength ranged between 567 and 805. In 1916 the number of deaths per month remained constant despite spending 44 percent in the Front Line and 63 percent in the forward area. 1916 saw numbers range from 708 to 1072. Deaths in 1917 leapt to 25 per month although less time was being spent in the forward area and the overall numbers of men fighting was fewer, being between 644 and 976. In the final year of the War, deaths were at their highest at 29 per month while the time spent at the Front Line at 57 percent, was almost as much as in 1916, when the Battalion was committed the most. With their strength between a range of 694 and 988, this again signified fewer men involved and was also the most settled period for the Battalion as the fluctuation between high and low point was at its lowest.

The evidence shows that considerable effort was made to revitalise the Battalion after major losses in action and to maintain it as a unit. It was deployed in the Front Line with some regularity, implying that it had earned a degree of trust and reliability in the eyes of Army Command. As it gradually fought with fewer men but maintained success in battle, it demonstrated an increasing efficiency in action to go with its effectiveness. By the end of the War the Terriers of 7th King's showed that they were meeting the requirements of the tactical development the Army needed to achieve overall success.

Battles of the Somme 1916

The Battles of the Somme demonstrate a learning curve in 1/7th Battalion to the extent that by the end of September 1916 the Battalion understood that a successful attack relied upon preparation and all-arms coordination. The Brigadier General had already written to Marriott to congratulate him on his Battalion's efforts: 'They show that you fully realise, and, better still, put into practice, the cooperation of the various arms'.[22] Griffith, in his study of the development of the Army's tactics, outlined the key aspects to these lessons: close co-operation and the use of the creeping barrage; careful preparation and tactical analysis; and the creation of a new tactical unit based around platoons attacking as an 'army in miniature'.[23]

22 Marriott correspondence, 16 June 1916.
23 Griffith, *Battle Tactics on the Western Front,* pp. 65, 74–6 and 78.

One aspect of this preparation and tactical analysis continued to be raids in advance of major assaults. On 28 June a raid took place which represented the first significant action for the new 55th Division since its formation in January 1916. The raid consisted of 400 men from across a range of units in an area where they had been training and therefore knew well. It involved considerable integration and co-operation and produced important information for future attacks in terms of the amount of wire cut, the co-ordination of different units and the importance of direction. Men from 1/7th King's joined these comrades from other units in the Division. This, however, was only one of 70 raids conducted that day between Gommecourt and Ypres, as part of the plan to confuse the German defences.[24]

Raids could allow for precise action by a small unit such as a platoon or two carrying out a range of tasks, however a raid on this scale, with a bombardment and the use of gas proved a costly operation, so soon before the full assault of the Division in August. Many of the problems were caused by the time lapse between the wire being cut and the raid taking place, and the confusion which ensued when smoke and gas drifted onto friendly lines. Daylight, and the 'public advertisement of our intentions',[25] meant high casualties, with 1/7th King's losing fourteen men wounded and six men and two officers killed. In a Special Order to the troops concerned, Jeudwine congratulated the men because the raids secured important information about the enemy and inflicted 'great damage and loss' on them.[26] He referred especially to the 'discipline and soldierly spirit… which the most seasoned of troops could not have surpassed'.

The primary battles of the Somme involving 1/7th King's – Guillemont, Ginchy and Gueudecourt – represent a microcosm of the developing tactical success in the British Army. Guillemont had particular local significance for the Division as the battlefield was strewn with dead from Congreve's XIII Corps, who had been involved in trying to take Guillemont since 23 July.[27] The Corps included 30th and 35th Divisions battalions from the Lancashire Fusiliers and the Liverpool and Manchester Pals.[28] These were locally recognisable units, and potentially some of the casualties would have been personally known to the incoming Division, no doubt sapping their morale. In such conditions, battle success would be vital to maintain that morale. The continuing failure to take the village highlighted the need for proper preparation and communication before and during the battle. The attack at Ginchy followed a

24 Wyrall, *The History of the King's Regiment*, Vol. II, p. 252.

25 TNA: WO95/2899 55th Division War Diary Jeudwine report of raid to VI Corps, 3 July 1916.

26 TNA: WO95/2925 165th Brigade War Diary Special Order of the Day, Jeudwine, 29 June 1916.

27 Coop, *The Story of the 55th Division*, p. 30; Stedman, *Guillemont*, p. 70; Griffith referred to Congreve's Corps as now containing leading players in the 'premier league' of Divisions – 3rd, 9th, 18th and 55th: *Battle Tactics on the Western Front*, p. 82.

28 Maddocks, G., *The Liverpool Pals: 17th, 18th, 19th, and 20th Battalions the King's (Liverpool Regiment)*, (London: Leo Cooper, 1991), pp. 111–124.

period of recuperation and considerable training and produced mixed, though largely successful, results. The key attack on 25 September, at Gueudecourt, was part of an assault across the whole of the Fourth Army frontage. The importance of training and preparation appeared to bear fruit as most objectives were taken and held.

The failure to capture Guillemont sooner was due to two principal factors, according to Lieutenant-Colonel Cochrane, head of Jeudwine's General Staff and in command of 55th Division at Guillemont in Jeudwine's absence. Firstly, the German defensive positions and secondly the terrain over which the attack was made. A third factor, implicit in his correspondence, was the failure of Corps and Army Command to respect the local information of Brigades and Divisions and Cochrane wrote that this 'lack of touch with the front became more marked' as the War progressed.[29]

Guillemont village was bombarded throughout 7 August 1916 and until zero hour on 8th (4:20 a.m.), when 165th Brigade launched the attack.[30] By 5:20 a.m. it was reported that 1/8th King's were in Guillemont Station but the supporting Battalion on their flank, 1/4th Royal Lancasters, were cut down as they tried to get through uncut enemy wire. 2/5th Lancashire Fusiliers had high casualties from machine guns and enemy shells and a Battalion from 166th Brigade was rushed to replace them in the Reserve.[31] From the 2nd Division, 1st King's were also in Guillemont, and later suffered the same fate as the Territorials.[32] On the right, while 165th Brigade had succeeded in their objective and were consolidating, the problem lay between the two Brigades where there was no linkage at all.

Despite the casualties of the previous day, and against all the advice of local commanders, a renewed dawn attack for the same objectives was ordered for 9 August 1916, this time with 1/7th and 1/6th King's to the right and with 166th Brigade – Liverpool Scottish and 1/5th Loyals – to the left. Coop wrote that the Liverpool Scottish moved off at 4:20 a.m., following the barrage, but finding the wire uncut, could not get to the enemy trenches and after several attempts, returned to their original line.[33] The 1/5th Loyals could not get out of the trenches until 5:00 a.m. lost the artillery barrage support and failed to reach the German trenches. 165th Brigade had similar problems.[34]

The German machine guns were away from the trench systems so that the artillery bombardment on the enemy trenches ignored the threat from the flanks. Cochrane observed that every attack was held up by machine gun fire with heavy casualties.' Isolated attacks, preferred by Army Command, allowed the Germans to focus their

29 TNA: CAB45/132 Cochrane to Edmonds, 8 January [1934].

30 TNA: WO95/2900 55th Division War Diary, Narrative of Events, 25 July to 15 August 1916; Coop, *The Story of the 55th Division,* p. 31.

31 Coop, *The Story of the 55th Division,* p. 32.

32 Stedman, *Guillemont,* p. 76.

33 During this assault, Noel Chavasse, 1/10th Battalion King's Liverpool, won his first Victoria Cross.

34 Coop, *The Story of the 55th Division,* p. 35.

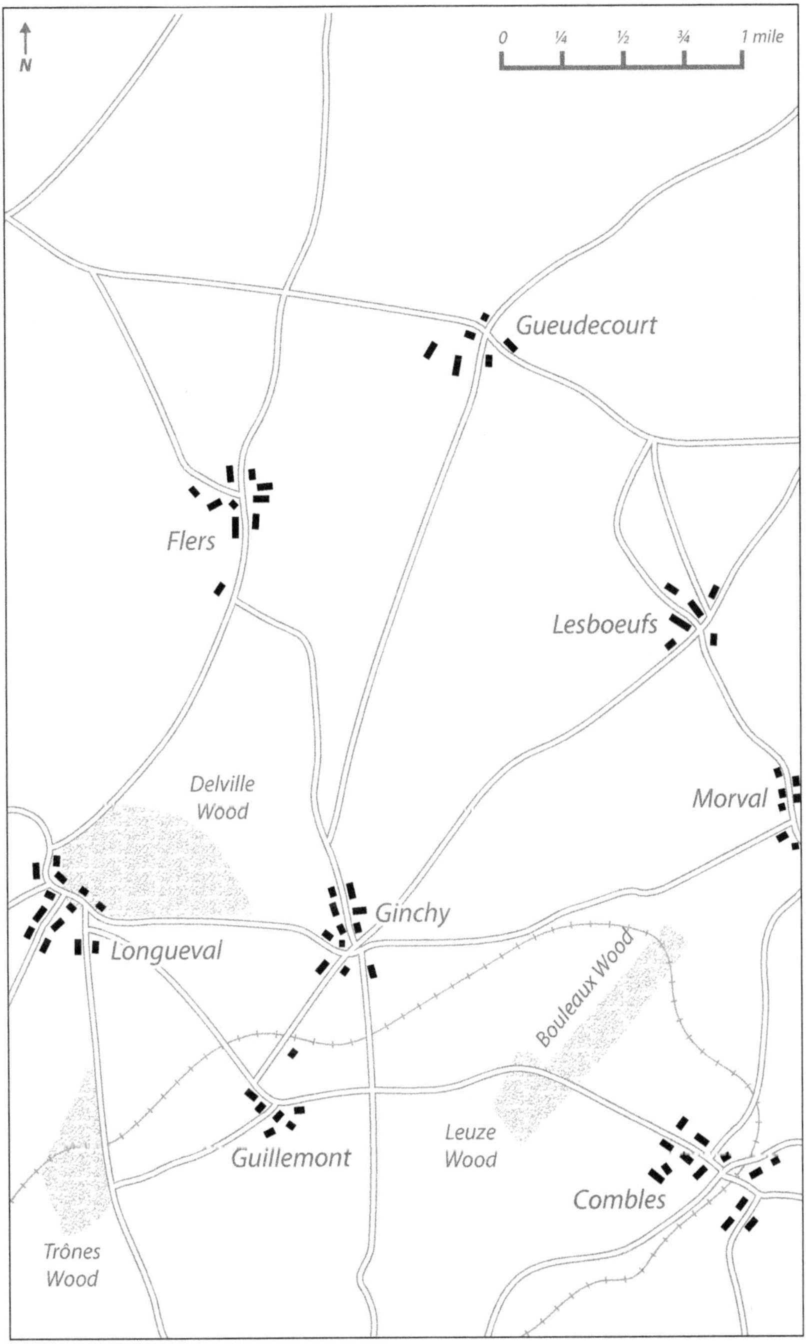

Map 2 The villages of Guillemont, Ginchy and Gueudecourt, 1916.

artillery on each particular sector to defend the village. These frequent calls to attack appeared confusing and Cochrane believed that subjecting the infantry to 'retaliatory bombardment in positions affording little protection was to expect the impossible.'[35]

The Divisional report stated that orders were received from XIII Corps for the relief of 1/5th King's but in the evening of 8 August further orders were received to renew attacks at 4:20 a.m. on 9th with the attack being forced by 165th and 166th Brigades. There had already been a preliminary order issued on 6 August for a further attack on 11th. The relief by 1/7th and a company of 1/6th King's Liverpools took place over unknown ground and in the face of the enemy barrage and machine gun fire on the night of 8th/9th. To the left, 166th Brigade had to move up to prepare for their attack at dawn. The consequence of this was crowded trenches, wounded coming one way, reliefs going another: limited room in communication trenches which had not been dug for such big numbers and activity.[36]

The night assault never happened. In his report, Colonel Shute, commanding 1/5th Battalion King's Liverpool Regiment, wrote that there was 'much confusion as to locality of troops of 166th Inf. Brigade. The CO's of 2 battalions and a representative of a third battalion all arrived at BHQ on ridge under the impression that these were their Batt.HQ.' He also observed:

> [C]ontinuous movement of troops of all kinds… many of whom clearly gave indecision as to direction and location. Confusion accentuated by the blocking of trenches by working parties, S. Bearer parties evacuating wounded, small parties of relieved troops and larger parties of 7th Liverpool going up to relieve or to old front line.[37]

Coop referred to the crowded conditions and the 'gallant assault', but not to the causes of this confusion.[38] Shute rang Brigade HQ to check the attack should still go ahead at 4:20 a.m. and unusually registered his view 'that the attack had not the slightest possibility of success'. In fact, Shute's Battalion should have been relieved, but at 5:00 a.m. the companies from 6th Liverpool's had still not done so, and by 9:00 p.m. 7th Battalion had still failed to relieve Shute's D Company.[39]

Cochrane's concerns were not just recorded with hindsight nearly twenty years later. On the day, he rang Lieutenant-General Congreve, XIII Corps Commander, to register concern at any renewed attack and insisted the decision be referred to the

35 TNA: CAB45/132 Cochrane to Edmonds, 8 January [1934].
36 TNA: WO95/2900 55th Division War Diary Narrative of events, 25 July to 15 August 1916.
37 TNA: WO95/2925 165th Brigade War Diary 1/5th King's Liverpool Battalion CO report, 22 August 1916.
38 Coop, *The Story of the 55th Division*, p. 35.
39 TNA: WO95/2925 165th Brigade War Diary 1/5th Liverpool Battalion CO report, 22 August 1916.

Army Command, but they were emphatic that it should go ahead.[40] Cochrane wrote to Jeudwine in 1933, recalling events: 'There was only one indifferent trench line so attacking troops were subject to intermittent artillery fire throughout. This caused considerable disorganisation and casualties. Control was difficult – such artillery can only be justified if there is adequate cover in allocating troops and the front line can be evacuated'.[41] This implication, that a lot of the damage being done to front line troops was by 'friendly' artillery, was clearer in his letter to Edmonds: [the artillery should have left] the front line to be held by a few outposts and thereby avoiding the terrible casualties.'[42]

Cochrane had said that there was no prospect of success and according to his response to Edmonds' draft of the *Official History* Jeudwine agreed:

> [T]roops had to come up a distance; crowded trenches, narrow trenches and men loaded with equipment, dark, no econnaissance opportunity and confusion following the unsuccessful attack during the day – hence only part of the attacking troops reached their jumping off point in time when the barrage lifted.[43]

In 1/7th King's official reports of the night of 8 August 1916 were no different. A Company was led by uncertain guides and at zero hour was in the open as the trench from which they were supposed to jump off did not exist as shown on the map. B Company had to cross open ground to reach their trench, again led by guides who did not know the way; they were out of touch with A Company and suffered heavy casualties. C Company were repulsed, owing to 'a lack of accurate knowledge of the ground'.[44] Marriott's report in the War Diary described the situation at noon on 9th as 'difficult'.

The issue of the terrain was crucial. Cochrane noted later that GHQ failed to appreciate that 'the sub-soil was chalk, and that it was impossible in a few hours to dig a trench with an entrenching tool'. This meant that men had no protection or concealment.[45] Difficulties in deployment 'were accentuated by the guides who, through no fault of 'FRED' did not know, and could not be made to understand the

40 TNA: CAB45/132 Cochrane to Edmonds, 8 January [1934]
41 LCRO: 356 FIF 56 Letter from Cochrane to Jeudwine, 1933, Jeudwine MSS.
42 TNA: CAB45/132 Cochrane to Edmonds, 8 January [1934].
43 LCRO: 356 FIF 56 Jeudwine's comments to Edmonds on the draft chapter on the Somme for the *Official History*, Jeudwine MSS.
44 TNA: WO95/2927 1/7th Battalion King's Liverpool Regiment War Diary report to 165th Brigade, 23 August 1916.
45 TNA: CAB45/132 Cochrane to Edmonds, 8 January [1934].

location required, and there are no landmarks to work on'.[46] Marriott had been more descriptive in a letter to his father when he stated:

> had a difficult task in walking across lines of devastated country to find our position … the difficulties of taking up a position for assault in the dark in an unknown country. There are no lamp posts and sometimes the direction of hostile artillery is the only indication you have.[47]

Marriott's report continued for 10 August, 2:00 a.m.: 'the Artillery (British) has caused us casualties'. He called for more fire to be turned on German lines.[48] This comment echoed that of Cochrane noted above and was not unusual. However, there appeared to be no evidence to substantiate MacDonald's assertion that 'the rumour began to spread that, in the mist and confusion, two British battalions had attacked each other'.[49]

The attack was renewed on 12 August at 5:15 p.m. having been postponed the previous day due to bad weather. 1/7th King's held their line of trenches while the rest of 165th Brigade cooperated with the French XX Corps.[50] XIV Corps Commander, the Earl of Cavan, expressed his admiration for the companies engaged in the fighting on 12 and 13 August.[51] Holding and consolidating these trenches by the Battalion continued to be difficult. B Company had been cut off for two days and was eventually reached, with the help of a photograph from an aeroplane which Marriott was able to interpret using a magnifying glass,[52] while the Battalion continued to be under bomb and machine gun fire. The trench was shallow, owing to the chalk land, and dead of both sides lay heavy on the ground.[53]

The German position was held strongly and no further ground was gained. The Division was relieved on 14/15 August.[54] In a line which almost word for word repeated one in Jeudwine's report, demonstrating that he had direct access to the War Diary immediately after the War, Coop wrote that: 'During this period from July 30 to August 16 our line was advanced 500 yards on the right and 300 yards on the left.

46 TNA: WO95/2927 1/7th Battalion King's Liverpool Regiment War Diary report by Lt. Col. Marriott, 17 August 1916. NB: 'FRED' was codename for 1/5th King's Battalion.
47 Marriott correspondence, 14 August 1916.
48 TNA: WO95/2927 1/7th Battalion King's Liverpool Regiment War Diary, Marriott report, 17 August 1916.
49 MacDonald, L., *Somme* (London: Michael Joseph, 1983), p. 210.
50 TNA: WO95/2900 55th Division War Diary Narrative of events, 25 July to 15 August 1916.
51 Coop, *The Story of the 55th Division,* p. 36.
52 Marriott letter to his father, 14 August 1916.
53 TNA: WO95/2927 1/7th Battalion King's Liverpool Regiment War Diary – Marriott's report, 17 August 1916.
54 TNA: WO95/2927 1/7th Battalion King's Liverpool Regiment War Diary, 15 August 1916.

13,000 yards of new trenches were dug by the Division during this time and over 3,000 yards were deepened and improved'.[55]

After their withdrawal on 15 August, the Division spent some time at rest and training before returning to the line on 4/5 September 1916.[56] Tilsley described a week spent training in the exhibition trenches at Bouzincourt, which were 'all beautifully sand-bagged and drained.' He described the training as much milder than the Bull Ring – the infamous training ground at Etaples – and much more instructive. Jeudwine's emphasis on training was beginning to show, as were his concerns about identification, communication and care for equipment with the Division being issued with new badges, PH gas helmets, breech covers and other equipment.[57]

After 165th Brigade, including 1/7th King's, and 166th Brigade went into the line between High Wood and Delville Wood, 164th Brigade followed into Ale Alley, south-east of Delville Wood on 7 September.[58] Artillery started shelling at 7:00 a.m. and the attack began at 4:45 p.m. on 9 September with the 55th Division moving forward between 16th Division on the right who were to capture Ginchy itself, and 1st Division (III Corps) to the left. The infantry advanced under the creeping barrage.[59] Tilsley described the 'sunshine attack' of the 'Cast-Iron Division' supporting the Irish Guards. Although his narrative referred to 164th Brigade, his comments about the attack on Ginchy are still relevant to other Brigades across the Front: 'Old hands stuffed sandbags and shovels up their backs between tunic and haversack. A few squashed Mills bombs into their breast pockets'. With machine guns raking the parapet, many got it in the head in the act of climbing out. 'He found himself on top and joined in the cramped walk of the irregularly formed line'. This was Tilsley's first attack and he soon found that 'he no longer wondered why men walked to attack, even in broad daylight… the ground was abominably loose and uneven. No real surface… a series of craters and holes'.[60]

The 164th Brigade attempts to attain their objectives failed, as did those of 166th Brigade, partly due to a previously unidentified trench – signalling another failure to map the terrain effectively – and a large garrison of machine guns in Hop Alley. However, 165th Brigade, employing 1/5th and 1/6th Liverpools, were more successful to the north. While they held Ginchy successfully, and consolidated, another attack two days later by 1/4th King's Own on Hop Alley and Ale Alley again failed, and the Division was briefly relieved on 10/12 September 1916.[61]

55 Coop, *The Story of the 55th Division,* p. 37.
56 Coop, *The Story of the 55th Division,* p. 37.
57 Tilsley, *Other Ranks*, pp. 24, 31.
58 Coop, *The Story of the 55th Division,* p. 37; Tilsley, *Other Ranks* p. 34; both sources are in agreement of the date 164th Brigade moved into the line.
59 Coop, *The Story of the 55th Division,* pp. 37–39.
60 Tilsley, *Other Ranks*, pp. 48, 51, 53.
61 Coop, *The Story of the 55th Division,* pp. 39–41.

This evidence demonstrates that there was considerable review of the results at Guillemont and that the conclusions of this analysis were put into practice firstly at Ginchy and more especially at Guedecourt. Jeudwine's after-action reports on the Guillemont battles indicated the areas which needed work to be more successful in the next attack. The headings in his memoranda, written on 21 and 24 August 1916, indicated the main problem areas quite clearly – his emphasis was on discipline, determination, care of arms, work in the trenches, patrolling, messages and reports, the organisation and supervision of trench work and the condemnation of any use of the word 'retire'.[62] All very general but more specifically, he highlighted the need for maps to be available down to NCO level, for trenches to be properly sited, for notice boards to be clear, for operational orders to be communicated down to NCO's and their Companies, the vital role of runners, the importance of communication and the need for adequate reconnaissance.[63] In short, Jeudwine wanted more communication and information to empower the troops at a more local level, despite the possible security risk which such steps involved.

All this pointed to the need for proper preparation before an attack and effective communication during it. Sheffield referred especially to the 'inadequate artillery support' as a key aspect to the failure to take Guillemont, in July and August.[64] There is also little answer to Cochrane's complaints that the attacks were contrary to routine policy. Writing later to Jeudwine, he recalled that 'GHQ instructions were definite – no attack other than minor operations, to take place without adequate preparation.'[65]

For his part, Cochrane was also scathing in criticism of senior officers:

> High Command plans were too frequently made after only a study of the map. Had they or their senior staff officers made a study of the ground with the local commanders many of these isolated and costly attacks would not have been ordered ... During the whole of my time on the Somme I never saw anyone from Army HQ above the rank of GSO3![66]

As an Army Commander, Rawlinson himself would not be expected to have been directly at the Front, but rather co-ordinating from Army HQ. It is also true that

62 TNA: WO95/2900 55th Division War Diary Notes on recent operations, 21 and 24 August 1916.

63 A further method of learning from the recent experience was provided for the men as they went into rest after Guillemont: in Tilsley's book, his narrator recorded that 'they returned to a farmhouse where a cinematograph picture of the Somme Battle was being shown in the yard on a white sheet hanging down one side of a barn ... the most unreal and outrageous attack that could be imagined, yet the film bore an official stamp': *Other ranks*, p. 13.

64 Sheffield, *The Somme*, p. 97.

65 LCRO: 356 FIF 56 Letter from Cochrane to Jeudwine, December 1933 Jeudwine MSS.

66 LCRO: 356 FIF 56 Letter from Cochrane to Jeudwine, December 1933 Jeudwine MSS.

Cochrane wrote after much hindsight and after many years of criticism of the Somme campaign. Nevertheless, his old commander appeared to share his frustration, sanctioning, and even endorsing, his views before they went to Edmonds. Another letter to Edmonds, vaguely quoted by Denis Winter but clearly from one of Congreve's Corps Staff, stated 'No-one in Corps or Divisional HQ understood why our attacks failed.'[67] A conference established that machine guns had been hidden so as to enfilade any reserve waves of troops. 'As soon as the first spark of originality was shown, Guillemont was taken. Success was simply due to avoidance of a completely frontal attack' – rather than the plan pursued over many weeks by Haig and his immediate Command.[68]

August's attack on Guillemont was a costly one for the Division and for 1/7th King's. It had proved largely ineffective as tactics and conditions had mitigated against success. It did, however, prove significant in terms of what was learnt and what developed as better practice in the Division over the following month, particularly in the assault on Gueudecourt in September.

On 25 September 1916 the Division's objectives were to take Gird Trench and Gird Support Trench, north of Gueudecourt, and this time 165th Brigade was much more successful in carrying out the attack.[69] This was the third piece of action for 165th Brigade in as many weeks. The 7th King's alone had already lost thirteen men killed, twenty-one were missing and 99 had been wounded by 20 September.

By 27 September, another forty-three had been killed, twenty-one more were missing, and a further 200 were wounded including three suffering from shell shock.[70] The identification of 'shell shock' as a medical condition, counting its sufferers amongst the casualties of battle, was still unusual in 1916. It implies a more liberal view of the issue in the Battalion and, indeed in the Division, since these statistics were reported to Jeudwine. The War Diary named Second Lieutenant Rawcliffe as being 'WOUNDED Shell Shock' but did not name the other two who could conceivably have been from the ranks. Oram noted that shell shock was usually seen as a disciplinary issue rather than a medical one, although even junior officers tended to receive more sympathy then the men.[71]

At 12:35 p.m. the assault began, with the first waves following the creeping barrage. Coop observed:

> [T]hey kept closer to the barrage than ever before, preferring to suffer some casualties from possible short shells from their own gunners, rather than to run

67 Winter D., *Haig's Command*, p. 64.
68 Winter, *Haig's Command*, p. 64.
69 Coop, *The Story of the 55th Division*, p. 41.
70 TNA: WO95/2927 1/7th Battalion King's Liverpool Regiment War Diary, 25 September 1916.
71 Oram, *Worthless Men*, pp. 85–9.

> the risk of allowing the barrage to get away from them and of being compelled to face the enemy's uninterrupted machine gun and rifle fire.[72]

A detailed account of the attack can be found in the draft reports prepared by Brigade and Divisional command. The Battalion War Diary showed that preparations went on from 23 September with C and D Companies in the Front Line. In the attack, on 25th, possession was gained of Goat and Gird Trench, Gird Support, the Sunken Road and Factory Corner at the expense of Second Lieutenants Lewis, Patterson and Turnbull, killed, and several injured officers, including Lieutenant Colonel Potter. He was wounded at about 2:10 p.m. and Captain J G Thompson MC went forward to take command of the Battalion.[73] After consolidating the next day, the Battalion moved back to Carlton and Savoy Trenches on 27th and away to billets at Buire on 28th.[74]

From the 165th Brigade report, it was clear that this was a successful attack.[75] The Field Artillery barrage commenced at zero hour and moved at 50 yards lifts every minute with the infantry following as closely as possible. The barrage for the second stage began at 2:41 p.m. from a point 150 yards in front of Gird Support. The New Zealand Brigade had already reported reaching their objective and 9th King's were at Factory Corner, although the two were not in touch. By 3:00 p.m. the second phase appeared to have been carried out and the enemy were seen in retreat. 6th King's held Gird Trench and Gird Support and part of the Sunken Road but were not in touch with 7th King's. Two Companies of 5th King's reinforced both 6th and 7th Battalions, and a company of 7th assisted a Leicester Battalion (21st Division) on the road.

In the early evening, 7th King's had a Company missing and another Company divided into Platoons along the Sunken Road, isolated but within sight of each other. By 10:00 p.m. the village was reported to be empty by an NCO of 7th who had walked through it. Through the night the situation was consolidated and connections made with the New Zealanders, although there was not direct touch between 7th King's and 110th Brigade, 21st Division. A brief German barrage began in the morning, but by afternoon the 21st Division was able to take Gueudecourt without opposition.

At 6:00 p.m. on 25th a wire was received from XV Corps preparing the Division for a renewed attack in the event of the situation remaining favourable and the cavalry going through on 26th, but this was postponed until 27th when the 164th Brigade took the remaining parts of Gird Trench and Gird Support to the north west of

72 Coop, *The Story of the 55th Division*, p. 42.

73 TNA: WO95/2900 55th Division War Diary 165th Brigade draft narrative of events, 23–27 September 1916 and Division Draft Narrative of operations, 17–28 September 1916.

74 TNA: WO95/2927 1/7th Battalion King's Liverpool Regiment War Diary, 27–29 September 1916.

75 TNA: WO95/2900 55th Division War Diary 165th Brigade Draft narrative of events, 23–27 September 1916.

Gueudecourt.[76] Although there was a counter-attack, this was repulsed and a number of prisoners were taken. The report concluded with the relief of the Division on the night of 28/29 September with all objectives secure.[77]

In relation to affairs a month previously, therefore, this was a much more successful operation for the Division and suggested that shortcomings at Guillemont might have been recognised and improved upon.[78] Jeudwine had made specific reference to discipline, communication to the lowest levels and full preparation. His lecture notes for training later in 1916 and into 1917 reiterated the point. The syllabus for the Divisional Training School listed discipline, preparation of work, trench warfare, topography and organisation of the unit amongst its main elements.[79] The combination of devolved leadership in the battle itself and the co-operation of the various arms appear to have helped deliver this success.

As early as January 1916, Jeudwine was pressing for more emphasis on small units becoming self-sufficient. He was keen on all ranks airing their opinions during training and insisted on Battalions making sure their own training was of a high order before any training and organisation began which covered a Brigade or Division.[80] Not only was this an effective way of ensuring high quality training, it also served to enhance levels of morale by involving the men in the process. Jeudwine's emphasis on the cooperation of the various arms at the lowest of levels – the platoon – was stressed through the training of late 1916 and 1917.[81] His view was summed up in a memorandum later in the year, 'The independent action of the platoon is the foundation of all battle training. The first thing to do is to teach the platoon how to act independently and on its own initiative'.[82] However, a more detailed appraisal was sent out from Divisional HQ in December 1916, pre-dating a similar memorandum from Kiggell at Army level, by some two months.[83] The reorganisation of platoons to contain specialist sections of Lewis gunners, rifle grenadiers, bombers and riflemen in early 1917 was in recognition of the need for an all-arms approach which Jeudwine, and other commanders, espoused. By involving the men and encouraging initiative, the Territorial *esprit de corps* could find some outlet despite the more Regular attention

76 Tilsley wrote that 'no horse [re. the Bengal Lancers] could gallop far enough ... over the shell bitten surface of no man's land – it's legs would snap'. See, *Other Ranks*, p. 74.
77 TNA: WO95/2900 55th Division War Diary 165th Brigade Draft narrative of events, 23–27 September 1916.
78 Tilsley wrote that the Lancashire's of the Cast Iron Division 'got mauled at Gueudecourt'. See, *Other Ranks*, p. 84.
79 LCRO: 356 FIF 13/2/651 55th Divisional School of Instruction Syllabus, 27 February 1917, Jeudwine MSS.
80 LCRO: 356 FIF 13 Various memoranda, 14–21 January 1916, Jeudwine MSS.
81 LCRO: 356 FIF 48 Jeudwine lecture notes Jeudwine MSS.
82 LCRO: 356 FIF 14 memorandum from Jeudwine, 27 August 1917, Jeudwine MSS.
83 LCRO: 356 FIF 13 memo from Jeudwine to Brigades, 8 December 1916; memo from Kiggell, Second Army GHQ, 7 February 1917, Jeudwine MSS.

to discipline. Initiative could assist men in feeling more than just a cog in the machine, thus addressing one factor affecting levels of morale.

Recent writers have recognised these significant developments: Griffith's analysis followed much the same route as Jeudwine: signposting, signalling and communication were important; preparation for attacks must include a full analysis of why the previous assault had failed; co-operation between Lewis gunners, rifle grenades, mortars and riflemen at a local level was vital; artillery support, and specifically the creeping barrage, was the key, leading the assault troops. Much of this became encompassed in the manual SS143, *Instructions for the Training of Platoons for Offensive Action*.[84] Sheffield, too, referred to the importance of the tactical learning curve and the operational success for the Fourth Army as crucial on 25 September.[85]

This learning process was also a costly one. Congreve's son had been killed earlier in the Summer and when he succumbed to dysentery, which was prevalent in his Staff, he had to relinquish command on 10 August 1916.[86] Consequently, in the middle of this lengthy assault on Guillemont, the Earl of Cavan took command and the XIV Corps took over the old XIII. Cavan himself succumbed to ill-health on 17 August, the day his full staff complement took over the Corps, to be replaced by Morland.[87] The stress proved too much for senior Battalion officers too. Marriott wrote to his father that: 'I shall be all right in a day or two, it is only a strain on the top of 18 months of it, practically always under fire. I sometimes think it is time I got a job somewhere else'.[88]

On 15 August he was called in by the General who 'evidently thinks I want a rest… one cannot go on interminable at that pressure'.[89] Marriott went home for several months before returning to the Western Front with the Manchester Regiment. His men were not so fortunate as to be given the choice: Tilsley wrote that 'old hands said the Divisional General had sworn to make the Somme either a Lancashire victory or a Lancashire graveyard'.[90] Jack Fearnhead was among 4,100 casualties in the Division in a few short weeks.[91] 1/7th King's suffered thirty-five killed, 113 wounded, ten missing and five shellshock cases in the five days from 8 to 13 August, in what the Battalion Diary called 'A small attack on German trenches'.[92] According to Wyrall, the King's Liverpool Regiment as a whole – Regulars, Territorials and Pals – lost close to 3,000 men during repeated assaults on Guillemont.[93]

84 Griffith, *Tactics of the Western Front*, pp. 74–8.
85 Sheffield, *The Somme*, pp. 126–7.
86 TNA: CAB45/132 Bald to Edmonds, 6 October 1934.
87 Stedman, *Guillemont*, pp. 80, 83.
88 Marriott letter to his father, 14 August 1916.
89 Marriott letter to his father, 16 August 1916.
90 Tilsley, *Other Ranks*, p. 90.
91 Stedman, *Guillemont*, p. 83.
92 TNA: WO95/2927 1/7th Battalion King's Liverpool Regiment War Diary, 9 August 1916.
93 Wyrall, *The History of the King's Regiment*, Vol II, p. 321.

The raid at Gouy at the end of June highlighted problems of inadequate preparation, confusion in the field, gas and coordination. Similar themes recurred through the battles of the Somme themselves, particularly at Guillemont where little ground was made against a strong German position. However, there was clear recognition, especially at Divisional level by Jeudwine and others, of what had gone wrong and attempts were made to learn and improve on the factors that they had control over. By the end of September, 7th King's do appear to have been acting with initiative and in co-ordination with the other arms of the assault. This short learning curve appeared to have produced greater effectiveness and success in the battle, and local commanders, such as Marriott, were recognised for their part in that development. In the process, however, the Battalion of volunteers from Bootle and Southport suffered another significant reduction in the ranks.

Third Battle of Ypres – 'Our finest hour'[94]

Further indication of the continued relationship between Home and Front and the Unit's combat effectiveness being fed by the morale inspired by that symbiotic relationship can be understood through a study of Third Ypres. This demonstrates that in spite of an apparent rise in discipline problems which could be an indication of a dip in morale, the links between Home and Battalion were maintained through newspapers and letters home. Third Ypres also demonstrates a further step in the tactical development of the Battalion in particular, and the Territorial Force in general.

As Southport prepared to celebrate the third anniversary of the Declaration of War, in August 1917, the editor of the *Southport Guardian* was forced to admit the enemy was 'still firmly entrenched' though in 'moral isolation'. Despite the hope that 1916 17 would be 'the year of restoration' he was enthusiastic in reporting that, having taken Vimy Ridge and the Messines Ridge, the Allies 'are now completing the capture of the Ypres salient'. In the same edition, on other pages, there were lists of the wounded being brought to Southport, fresh from the new assault on 31 July.[95] The community could read the words of encouragement but would be in no doubt of the sacrifice when they saw the flood of men to the local hospitals.

Having spent much of the spring of 1917, as Wyrall wryly noted, 'in trenches, usual routine',[96] 1/7th King's Liverpools were in action again at Ypres on 31 July. Later, despite fighting over much the same ground again in September, the Battalion achieved some tactical success. The wider strategy failed and lessons were learnt regarding still more flexibility in attack and reliance on local leadership decisions.

94 Critchley.
95 *Southport Guardian,* 4 August 1917, pp 4, 6.
96 Wyrall, *The History of the King's Regiment* Vol II, p. 425.

These factors formed key parts of the Divisional training in later 1917 and 1918, in both offence and defence.

The attack known later as Third Ypres, began at 3:50 a.m. 31 July, Zero Hour,[97] and 1/7th King's were in action until the Division was withdrawn early on 4 August. The 55th Division was now in XIX Corps, Fifth Army and attacked eastwards from Ypres, with 166th and 165th Brigades leading the assault. Their first objective was the enemy's front line trench system, or Blue Line, and then the rear battalions would leapfrog and capture the second line system, the Black Line (Stuzpunkt Line). Then 164th Brigade would pass through the lines to take the third line system, or Green Line (Gheluvelt – Langemarck Line).[98]

What actually happened on 31 July 1917, until it started to rain again, has been described as relatively successful by historians, and this appeared to be supported by evidence relating to 1/7th King's operations.[99]

The 165th Brigade captured the enemy's front line trench system.[100] Companies of 1/7th King's attacked and held Square Farm and Plum Farm; B Company secured Pommern Redoubt. Demonstrating local decision making, Captain Heaton of B Company also took command of A and D Companies as men came into the Pommern Redoubt to consolidate the position.[101]

Despite some advances as far as the Green Line, the Black Line was the farthest any Brigade held by the end of the day and XIX Corps were informed of the situation and 'the suggestion [was] made that supporting troops might be sent up'.[102] This was in response to Jeudwine's concerns for his position:

> Troops very much mixed up. Communicated this to BGGS [Brigadier-General] in case CC [Corps Commander] thought it advisable to bring a Bde up behind. Told him all my troops engaged, nothing in reserve, except 2 Bns in Blue line – but uncertain whether one of these had not been moved up. Told BGGS this on telephone at 5:35.[103]

Corps did indeed order a renewed attack but with the onset of rain Jeudwine and some of his staff visited the Brigade headquarters and at 11:00 p.m. he informed Corps that

97 TNA: WO95/2903 55th Division War Diary Report of operations, 29 July–4 August.
98 TNA: WO95/2903 55th Division War Diary Operations Order 23 July 1917.
99 Neillands, R., *The Great War Generals on the Western Front 1914–1918* (London: Robinson Publishing Ltd, 1999), p. 392; Lee, J., 'The British Divisions at Third Ypres', in *Passchendaele in Perspective*, pp. 216–7; Steel and Hart, *Passchendaele: The Sacrificial Ground*, pp. 135–6.
100 TNA: WO95/2925 165th Brigade War Diary, 31 July 1917.
101 Wyrall, *The History of the King's Regiment*, Vol. III, pp. 499–500 gives a considerable account.
102 TNA: WO95/2903 55th Division War Diary Report on Operations, July 29 to August 4 1917.
103 LCRO: 356 FIF 40 Jeudwine personal notebook [31 July 1917] Jeudwine MSS.

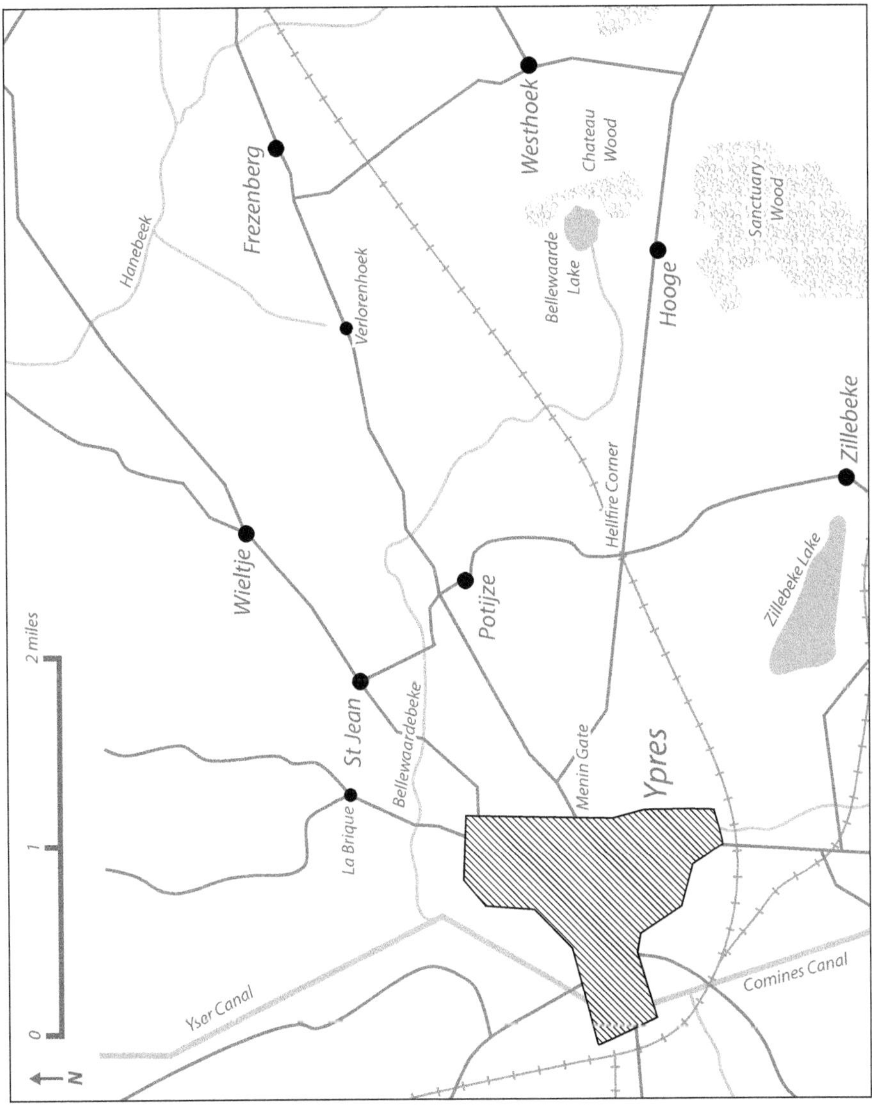

Map 3 Guillemont, Ginchy and Gueudecourt, Battle of the Somme 1916.

it would be impossible for the Division to attack again. He was so concerned at the state of his troops that he withdrew 164th Brigade entirely and demanded that trains were used to take the men away.[104]

The 165th Brigade War Diary entry for the following day is worth transcribing in full:

> Dawn found the Brigade holding tenaciously on to the dearly bought BLACK LINE. Throughout the whole night heavy rain had fallen and the terrain, already in a much churned up condition from the heavy shell fire, was now nothing but slush and mud. The men had spent the night standing in what were once trenches – now knee deep in mud and water – and although soaked through, tired out and hungry, they cheerfully stood the heavy enemy shelling.[105]

However, another day of being shelled under these conditions in the trenches made the situation untenable. A report at 8:50 a.m. on 2 August from 165th Brigade stated that 'the men were completely exhausted – some unable to stand.' The relief was delayed as another counter-attack was launched and it was not until 4:00 a.m. on 4 August that 36th Division took command of the sector and all Lancashire men and equipment had pulled back.

Critchley called 31 July the Battalion's 'finest hour',[106] and when the Brigadier-General's praise for the King's Battalions was published, the *Southport Guardian* heralded the 'Praise for Local Troops' which would be read with 'considerable pride and interest by Southport people'.[107] Letters home were more censored than they had been in 1915, omitting mention of the units and names of comrades, but they still gave the local community a graphic idea of the fighting. Private Baxendale wrote from hospital in Boulogne:

> One of my best pals has been wounded in the legs, and another one killed. I don't know how several other chums have fared. You will have read about the latest push, so it's no use telling you anything about it, except that I was there, I hope for the last time in that particular spot.[108]

Private Willie Miller was in the first wave and had 'cleared two lots of German trenches and we were going strong for the village of —— when I got shot in the left leg'.[109] Jack

104 TNA: WO95/2903 55th Division War Diary Report on Operations, July 29 to August 4 1917. Surprisingly, Tilsley barely mentions the operations on Pilckem Ridge.
105 TNA: WO95/2925 165th Brigade War Diary, 1 August 1917.
106 Critchley.
107 *Southport Guardian*, 1 September 1917, p. 6.
108 *Southport Guardian*, 18 August 1917, p. 6.
109 *Southport Visiter*, 25 August 1917, p. 8.

Farrington, promoted to Corporal but now acting Sergeant, won a Military Medal for his action on 31 July:

> We had 2,000 yards to go before we reached our objective. When we were half-way we had to halt on account of our barrage, and make the best cover we could get … [the officer had been killed] so I took charge of the platoon. Up to then we had six men missing. I got the remainder together, ready for the next advance, and I am glad to say we drove the Germans back and gained the position … I captured between 30 and 40 prisoners.[110]

It was estimated that thirty enemy officers and 600 men were captured by the Division, while it suffered 166 officer casualties and 3,384 men between 30 July and 4 August 1917.[111]

Casualties had been heavy from early on 31 July and reserve stretcher bearers had to be sent for. By 1 August over 400 men from other units were being used as stretcher bearers for the Division under terrible conditions:

> [Rain] rendered carrying a very difficult matter, for the trenches became impassable … and carrying in the open, which had in most cases to be resorted to, was slow by reason of the bearers having to pick their way between shell-holes. Towards the end it was found that 8 bearers had to be used for each stretcher.[112]

Miller described the conditions the wounded were left in: 'We were lying in shell holes on Wednesday night full of water and we had to cross a river after Fritz had blown up a bridge.'[113] Between midnight 30/31 July and midnight on 3/4 August, 1,150 stretcher cases were dealt with at the main Corps Dressing Station.[114]

The Divisional Report noted a number of specific areas where problems had arisen, not least because, 'as expected the Tanks were late'. Despite the heavy shelling, 'concrete dugouts were quite undamaged' and while communications had worked reasonably well, once damaged the reliance on runners was undermined by the rain which slowed that method of communication down. The Report noted that as 'the state of the ground rendered efficient work of Tanks impossible' it would have been

110 *Southport Guardian*, 5 September 1917 p. 4: Despite his promotion, Farrington was still as keen on souvenir-hunting as he had been at Festubert – 'they were very glad to give themselves up, they shook me by the hand … I was rather disappointed for they only gave me a couple of their caps for souvenirs.'
111 Coop, *The Story of the 55th Division*, p. 54.
112 TNA: WO95/2903 55th Division War Diary Report on Operations, July 29 to August 4 Section IX – Medical Service.
113 *Southport Visiter*, 25 August 1917, p. 8.
114 TNA: WO95/2903 55th Division War Diary Report on Operations, July 29 to August 4 Section IX – Medical Service.

better to use them to carry ammunition, wire and tools, thus potentially saving carrying parties and other casualties.[115]

In approaching the second phase of the battle, GHQ attempted to reinvigorate their tactics. Experience had shown the importance of following close on the barrage; the training on leapfrogging to bring in fresh battalions to relieve the attacking battalions and the need to prepare for defence against counter-attack as soon as an objective was secured were the main elements of what was a successful assault.[116] Also important were the multi-layered barrages and role of the gunners in dealing with any enemy counter-attack.

Still with Fifth Army, 55th Division found itself attacking virtually the same objectives on 20 September as it had on 31 July. Now in combination with Second Army, the attack was to secure Gheluvelt Plateau and the ridge from Zonnebeke to Gravenstafel.[117] The bombardment began at 3:00 a.m. on 20 September 1917, and at zero hour – another dawn assault at 5:40 a.m. – 1/7th Battalion, King's Liverpool, attacked from a line of shell holes and disused trenches. Casualties came from the start from enemy machine guns in Kaynorth, Iberian Farm and Hill 35, despite being close under the barrage as it crept forward. No Man's Land was, according to Wyrall, a mass of shell holes full of water and 'viscous mud which clung to the boots of the attackers'.[118] With assistance from the South African Brigade both Kaynorth and Iberian Farm – in effect a string of reinforced concrete dug-outs – were captured by 1/7th King's around 6:45 a.m. As the barrage had moved on, this was done without immediate artillery support.[119]

The positions were held and strong points constructed to prepare for the enemy's attack but despite heavy bombardment there was no counter-attack and the Battalion was relieved by 2/5th South Staffordshires at 1:30 a.m. on 23 September. Sixty-one men were killed, 166 were wounded, twelve had gone missing and three later died of wounds, while five Officers died and four were wounded.[120] Griffith referred to the attack as 'a convincing resumption of the assault' and noted particularly the lower figures of casualties.[121] The overall casualties in the Division were 127 officers and 2,603 men.[122]

When Private Baxendale had given scant details of the earlier battle because he assumed local people would have read about it already he was only partially correct.

115 TNA: WO95/2903 55th Division War Diary Report on Operations, July 29 to August 4 1917.
116 Lee, J., 'The British Divisions at Third Ypres' in *Passchendaele in Perspective*, p. 219.
117 Neillands, *The Great War Generals*, pp. 395–396.
118 Wyrall, *The History of the King's Regiment,* Vol. III, p. 515.
119 TNA: WO95/2900 55th Division War Diary Report on operations east of Ypres, 19–24 September 1917.
120 TNA: WO95/2927 1/7th King's Liverpool Regiment War Diary, 30 September 1917.
121 Griffith, *Battle Tactics of the Western Front,* p. 88.
122 Coop, *The Story of the 55th Division*, p. 64.

Those reports had been direct from GHQ and with little detail. However, this new attack was reported in much more depth in the local newspapers, using not only GHQ reports but also a number of letters from the Front. Official reports gave 'prominence to the West Lancashire troops, which in conjunction with London troops, repulsed the enemy's infantry with great loss.' Details, based on Press Association reports, were highlighted in the editorials, noting the capture of Iberian Farm, Gallipoli and the Pommern Redoubt by the local troops of the King's Liverpools.[123] The release of such detail indicated Haig's need to enthuse the Home civilian and political population with good news in the light of mounting casualties and the prolonged attack, both of which adversely affected the resources available to him.

More details were given by local troops, writing home about the Menin Road battle: 'the old regiment has won new laurels. The fighting was far above anything we have struck lately for fierceness'; 'We just sailed in with the bayonet and a nice selection of bombs'; 'Hottest of all … was the rush through the rough cart-track … named Scotland Road … shells were dropping by the dozen and mud went splashing up into the sky in showers'; 'The men fought splendidly … I have never seen greater steadiness under trying conditions. There were many deeds of heroism … In one instance a Liverpool docker rushed a German machine gun post on his own, killed the team and turned the gun on the enemy.'[124]

As at Festubert, the men were able to give a flavour of the battle for the home population, although the numbers of letters were fewer and details of the battle less so than in 1915. The newspapers continued to carry plenty of pictures of the dead and wounded with short biographies or letters from their company officer. Invariably these were printed alongside the reports of Military Tribunals in a deliberate juxtaposition of the community's commitment to the War.

The success in key aspects of the assault has been overshadowed by the subsequent deterioration of the Third Ypres campaign which has contradicted a positive analysis, and suggested that there had been a failure to learn from experience.[125] In contrast, Lee specifically pointed to the importance of Divisional and Brigade levels in pursuing new tactics in training, in preparation and in the troops' morale which was maintained through widespread loyalty to their unit, rather than a change at the top.[126] Troop morale was crucially important because these new tactics were not always as seamless or as successful as planned. Anything to enhance that morale was therefore important. Key elements such as more careful reconnaissance; the marking of platoon flanks by notice boards and tape to try and maintain better contact at ground level; and the three Infantry Brigade commanders in the Division being in a

123 *Southport Guardian*, 26 September 1917, pp 6 and 8.
124 *Southport Visiter*, 25 September, 1917 p. 6.
125 Griffith, *Battle Tactics of the Western Front,* pp. 88–9; Beckett, I.F.W., 'Operational Command: The Plans and the Conduct of Battle' in *Passchendaele in Perspective,* p. 111; Neillands, *The Great War Generals,* pp. 397–400.
126 Lee, 'British Divisions at Third Ypres' in *Passchendaele in Perspective*, pp. 223–6.

joint headquarters to ensure close liaison with artillery command, were deemed the most successful.[127]

Unfortunately 'liaison between Brigade Headquarters and the [artillery] Batteries was bad'. Communications were also a problem – visual, signal and running communications were better, when there was fine weather but all the wires which ran through Bridge House had been cut by shelling.[128] Jeudwine noted other difficulties such as rifle grenadiers having no grenades, officers without maps, men not knowing where their company or platoon headquarters were, lack of tools, flares, and sandbags.[129] These appeared to be earlier problems repeating themselves.

Following the Third Battle of Ypres, Second Army Headquarters issued detailed notes to Divisions to draw from their experiences at Ypres and to further develop the learning process begun on the Somme. They acknowledged that new tactics were required as objectives, such as definite lines of trenches, had disappeared. There needed to be new ways of providing flexibility in attack, in terms of attacking lines/waves and of increased local initiative and leadership. A key area was the liaison and junction between units. Rifle, Lewis gun and rifle grenades were becoming more important and it was argued bombing squads should be re-trained as riflemen. Some of this thinking was developed later in 1918 as platoons became the focus of attention for an all-arms attack.

All units had to be prepared for the inevitable counter-attack which had to be repulsed and followed up. Key to this was the need for training of junior commanders in developing the initiative to act in unexpected situations and in reorganising the men to prepare for counter-attacks. Training was also important in the use of a compass; in the value of using models and replicas; in enemy equipment, so that it could be turned on the Germans and used against them; in the particular problems of the Salient 'pill boxes'; and on more open warfare with junior NCOs and Privates needing to understand powers of leadership and initiative in the event of the loss of their officers.[130]

The significance of learning and adapting new tactics of attack would only become apparent the following summer. As 1917 turned to winter and the New Year, the important aspect of tactical development was to be one of defence.

127 TNA: WO95/2900 55th Division War Diary Report on recent operations East of Ypres, 19–24 September 1917.
128 TNA: WO95/2900 55th Division War Diary Report on recent operations East of Ypres, 19–24 September 1917.
129 LCRO: 356 FIF 40 HS Jeudwine personal notebook, [September 1917], Jeudwine MSS.
130 TNA: WO95/2901 55th Division War Diary Notes from experiences gained by the Second Army during the recent Ypres fighting [late 1917].

'Wipers'

Major Henry D'Armin Blumberg

Can yer 'ear the fellers singin' in Number One Platoon?
They're marchin' out o' Wipers – it ain't a day too soon.
Twelve months in the trenches, shelled, and gassed, and sniped and drowned,
With nothing else to stare at but them dismal swamps around.
Good-bye Wipers! Though I 'opes it is for good,
It 'urts me for to leave yer – I little thought it would.
When I gets back to Blighty, and all the fightin's done,
Mebbe the picters of the past will rise up one by one.
Like movies at the Cinema, they'll bob up in my brain,
The places that I knew so well, – I'll see them all again.
The battered-in Asylum; the Prison scorched and scarred;
And 'ole Salvation Corner with the guns a bellowin' 'ard.
The muddy, ruddy Ramparts; the mist upon the Moat;
The grey Canal between whose banks no barges ever float.
An' them Cathedral ruins – O Gawd the fearsome sight!
Like mutilated fingers they points up through the night.
Can yer 'ear the fellers singin' in Number One Platoon?
They're marchin' out o' Wipers – it ain't a day too soon.
The blighters what relieves us – we'll treat 'em fair an' kind,
They're welcome to the souveneers what we 'ave left be'ind.
Good-bye Wipers! Though I 'opes it is for good,
It 'urts for me to leave yer – I little thought it would.[131]

131 *Sub Rosa*, June 1918: Major Blumberg (pseudonym H. d'A.B) penned a number of other poems including one dedicated to Festubert (see *Southport Visiter*, 3 February 1921) as part of a local campaign to adopt Festubert. He also wrote 'Givenchy Field' about 9 April 1918. See *Stand To!*, op cit., December 1999.

6

1918: 'Backs to the wall'[1] and Final Advance

The year 1918 has been written about by several authors and from the outside it seems almost incomprehensible that Germany should move so quickly from a position of strength, launching wave after wave of attacks in the spring, to one of retreat and eventual demise, by the autumn. The reasons and consequences are documented elsewhere.[2] What is interesting however is to demonstrate how a unit which suffered greatly – 1/7th King's Liverpool – could end the War fighting effectively in the Final Advance. Key local reasons lay in part in Jeudwine's tactical planning at Givenchy, and in part, the April 1918 learning experience.

Battle of the Lys, April 1918

German attacks, known collectively as the Spring Offensive, began on 21 March 1918 with the opening of Operation Michael. This focused on the area south of Arras largely held by the British Fifth Army. Although inroads were made and casualties high, the offensive was halted. Secondly, Operation Mars was launched on 28 March, this time less successfully against the British Third Army. Finally, Ludendorff's attempt to break through British lines came further north, in Operation Georgette, beginning on 9 April.

The defensive action at Givenchy in the April 1918 was of strategic importance in stemming the German attack. It was also significant for it was founded on tactics developed and championed by Jeudwine and his Division which fell outside GHQ doctrine. It had particular significance for the men who fought it and for their local communities as it formed a significant part of the shared identity of the community which can be seen through the War and indeed after it. Its resonance will be seen in

1 Haig Special Order of the Day, 11 April 1918.
2 Palmer, A., *Victory 1918* (London: Wiedenfeld and Nicolson, 1998); Sheffield, *Forgotten Victory*.

the analysis of the postwar commitment to the area through charitable and memorable works.

The German attack, known by the British as the Battle of the Lys, has only recently been studied in depth. Known most for the alleged failings of the Portugese contingent, it has received little scrutiny, although the maintenance of the Line was seen at the time as being of crucial importance. This analysis of the role of the West Lancashire Territorials and particularly 1/7th King's in that defence, is preceded by an examination of Jeudwine's personal involvement in developing the defensive tactics of the BEF in advance of the German Offensive of spring 1918, demonstrating the Major-General's importance within the BEF and the consequent esteem in which the Division was held.

Festubert had been a formative experience for the 1/7th King's. It had been their first action undertaken when they were new to the real War, part of a Regular Division, and consisted of a strong local contingent. After almost exactly three years they were back in the Béthune sector in spring 1918, with Horne again in charge.[3] This time many of the local old guard had gone, but those who remained were now part of a Territorial Division which, as shown in chapter four, prided itself on its local identity. They had learned their lessons in attack since 1915, but had been castigated for the German breakthrough in the counter-attack after Cambrai in December 1917. As they had not seen any action since that attack, by April 1918 they were fresher than most of the other Divisions in the line, their 'physical and spiritual stamina was high'; but they had been reorganised and the numbers of Battalions reduced.[4] As has been seen, dilution meant reduced numbers of local men and a reliance on smaller optimum fighting strengths, though the sense of local identity still pervaded all that they did. The study of the 55th Division defence in this part of the chapter complements the appraisal of the whole Lys Battle carried out by Blades, and highlights the flaws in Samuels' analysis of the BEF defensive system.[5]

A court of enquiry into the German counter-attack at Cambrai on 30th November 1917 found that Jeudwine's Division – 166th Brigade and 2/5th South Lancashire Battalion in particular – had been surprised by the enemy, that warnings had gone unheeded, that there was a lack of both in depth defence and a strategy for a defensive battle.[6] Both Jeudwine and his Corps Commander, General Snow, argued that

3 Horne commanded Second Division in 1915 and First Army during 1916–18.
4 TNA: CAB45/123 Lt. Colonel R. Gardner MC, commander 1/4th King's Own, 164th Brigade, to Edmonds 8 August 1931; in January and February 1918 1/8th (164th Brigade) and 2/8th King's were amalgamated in 171st Brigade; 1/9th (165th Brigade) and 2/9th King's were amalgamated in 172nd Brigade; and 1/5th Loyal North Lancashires (166th Brigade) in 170th Brigade, 57th West Lancashire (Second Line) Division: Becke, *Order of Battle*, Part 2A, pp. 136–7.
5 Samuels, M., *Doctrine and Dogma: German and British Infantry Tactics in the First World War* (Westport Conn.: Greenwood Press, 1992).
6 LCRO: 356/FIF/50 Report of the Court of Enquiry, Jeudwine MSS.

the opinion of the Court was 'absurd and contrary not only to the truth but to the evidence'.[7] In correspondence throughout 1925 and 1926 they were very clear that it had been Ivor Maxse behind the Court's findings, referring to his 'personal advertisement' as 'very poisonous'.[8] Major-General Sir Ivor Maxse, erstwhile GOC of the 18th Division, was Commander of XVIII Corps. Neillands says that he set an example in tactical training and Griffith agreed that he was significant in developing tactics.[9] He was later Inspector General of Training. According to Griffith he was most keen on platoon organisation and an advocate of the 'blobs' system of defence, which was to fail in March 1918. However, his ideas were more successful in attack mode.[10] It is quite apparent that Jeudwine, as another leading advocate of training and tactics, was a rival, and this correspondence with General Snow suggests that the Court's findings were a personal attack by Maxse on Jeudwine's Division, while using it to promote his own opinions on tactics. Both Neillands' and Terraine's appraisals of the Cambrai attack support Snow's position,[11] the latter exonerating "all ranks of 55th Division of unpreparedness'.[12] By 1927, however, any damage to the morale of the men in the Front Line of the Division had already been done.

The Court's comments about a lack of defensive doctrine at Villers-Guislain were seriously undermined as within days of that German attack Jeudwine was heading a Committee of Generals to prepare new defensive procedures. Great merit was seen in the German systems and Jeudwine, Sir James Edmonds – then a staff officer in 4th Division – and Brigadier-General MacMullen of XIX Corps Staff were appointed by Haig to prepare some recommendations on how the British could develop a similar 'elastic' defence system.[13] There was considerable mystery about this Committee as it received scant attention in the *Official History*, despite Edmonds' involvement, and Blades noted that no copy of the report has survived.[14] The Committee's proposals represented an adaptation of the German defensive doctrines, gleaned from captured documents and experience. GHQ rejected the proposals and instead agreed a different adaptation of the German doctrine, apparently first propounded amongst Rawlinson's Second Army.[15]

7 LCRO: 356/FIF/50 and 356/FIF/51 Jeudwine and Snow correspondence, Jeudwine MSS.
8 LCRO: 356/FIF/50 and 356/FIF/51 Jeudwine to Snow, Jeudwine MSS.
9 Neillands, *The Great War Generals,* p. 310.
10 Griffith, *Battle Tactics of the Western Front,* pp. 95–100.
11 Neillands, *The Great War Generals*, pp. 432–437; Terraine, *Douglas Haig*.
12 LCRO: 356/FIF/49 Snow to Jeudwine, Jeudwine MSS.
13 Samuels, *Command or Control?,* p. 203. Curiously, there is no mention of the Committee or Edmonds' role in it in A.S. Green's study *Writing the Great War.*
14 *Official History* 1918, Vol. 1, fn. p. 42; Wynne, G.C., 'The Legacy', *Army Quarterly* Vol. XXXVII, No. 2, October 1939; Blades, 'The Battles of the Lys', p. 42. Even Samuels, who spent some time demolishing the Committee's credibility in *Doctrine and Dogma* only provided title and membership roster in his subsequent *Command or Control?*
15 Blades, 'The Battles of the Lys', p. 43.

The Jeudwine Committee's proposals were based on a recognition that the BEF could not adapt in full to the German doctrine of defence as quickly and as easily as was necessary. They therefore proposed an amended version that the outpost line be thinly held, but that it be a line. When the attack came, the attackers would be held up here, but defenders would then fall back to the main line of resistance.[16] By having a thin outpost line sufficient men were left further back to staunch the attack and to form counter-attacks. If possible, ordered and planned withdrawal to the main resistance line was a significant part of the defensive system.

Edmonds did later acknowledge that the German system should have been adopted but that not only were time and labour lacking in advance of 21 March, there was also no real understanding by GHQ of the principles involved in defence in depth.[17] Wynne and Samuels claimed that if this system had operated in March 1918 the Line would have broken.[18] That may have been true, but it was never tested on 21 March. When it was tested on 9 April against XI Corps the reverse proved true.[19]

The attack on 9 April 1918 was at the point where the BEF could least afford to give ground, threatening the rail and distribution centre at Hazebrouck, the coalfields, the road to Dunkirk and the channel ports.[20] This central part of the Line was held by a weakened IX Corps and XV Corps made up of re-formed or convalescing Divisions. The Portuguese 1st and 2nd Divisions sat to the north of the West Lancashire Division, with 51st (Highland) Division completing XI Corps.[21] While Jeudwine's men were comparatively fresh, not having been involved in the earlier offensive, it was Jeudwine's resolve in sticking to his rejected defensive doctrine that was to prove effective.[22] Sheffield referred to Jeudwne's new methods of defence training as paying off 'handsomely'.[23]

It is significant that Horne left the organisation of defence to his Corps commanders, noting only that without the strength to fight in depth they must concentrate the fight in the Forward Zone[24] – where the 'blobs' were. However, at a strategic conference the previous day, Haking, his divisional commanders, and Jeudwine, and his Brigade commanders, appear to have agreed a different defensive scheme, based on

16 Blades, 'The Battles of the Lys', p. 42.
17 Green, *Writing the Great War*, pp. 162–163.
18 Samuels, *Command or Control?*, p. 207.
19 Lieutenant-General de Lisle XIII Corps had followed the Committee's proposals and, coupled with the inherent strength of their Vimy Ridge position, the 56th Division defence against the German attack on 28 March was also successful. See De Lisle, Sir B., *Reminiscences of Sport and War* (London: Eyre & Spottiswoode, 1939), pp. 162–5.
20 Terraine, *Douglas Haig*, p. 431.
21 B Pitt, *1918: The Last Act* (London: Cassell, 1962), pp. 114–117.
22 Blades, 'The Battles of the Lys', p. 70.
23 Sheffield, *Forgotten Victory*, p 228–229.
24 TNA: WO95/175 First Army War Diary General Staff Corps Commanders Conference, 26 March 1918.

the Jeudwine Committee proposals.[25] One of Edmonds' later correspondents, General Green, cited Haking's 'strategical and tactical insight' as being crucial on 9 April 1918, as 'defensive measures were decided on, in place of the hitherto vague and uncertain policy'.[26] Correspondence between Jeudwine, Haking and Edmonds when compiling the *Official History* demonstrated that they 'had no truck' with the concept of a zonal defence in depth; in other words, neither the German system nor the GHQ version of it, but they used the version propounded by the Jeudwine Committee.[27]

The Conference agreed that, because of the limited number of troops available, emphasis should be put on defending Givenchy, in order to maintain the support flank across the La Bassée Canal to Cuinchy. It was agreed that the only objective for the front line troops was to defend the front system. Givenchy defences were to be strengthened, a counter-attack from the Village Line prepared, protection for the Village Line to be improved and the main line of defence to be made as strong as possible. The Village Line was to be made 'a continuous line so that troops can pass along it'.[28]

The southern sub-sector included a tunnel that had been constructed under Givenchy village with no forward line, thus the Line of Resistance for 164th Brigade was the Front Line – 'a definite line not zone composed of independent strongpoints'.[29] This gave no real depth to the defence, but the local environment did not allow for it. For 165th Brigade in front of Festubert, the marshy and boggy ground was unsuitable for fortified positions other than for delaying the attack, thus for 1/7th King's, their Line of Resistance was the Village Line, to which they could fall back from their outpost line.

Wynne and Samuels' critiques do not address the shortage of men available to implement the German defence doctrine in full. Corps Commanders were clear that the back line of defences had to be held by other units: 'If we have any idea of holding our front and holding our back system at the same time with our limited number of troops, we shall have insufficient to hold either and shall run the risk of being beaten piecemeal.'[30]

The forty-two Officers and 946 men of 1/7th King's Battalion had been in the trenches and outposts in front of Festubert since 31 March 1918.[31] Leave for the men

25 TNA: WO95/883 XI Corps War Diary Notes of Conference, 25 March 1918.
26 TNA: CAB45/123 Correspondence with Edmonds, 7 January 1931.
27 TNA: CAB45/123 Jeudwine copy letter to Edmonds, 21 August 1931; Haking letter to Edmonds, 25 August 1931. Given Jeudwine's shared involvement in the December Committee it is interesting that he made no reference to it to Edmonds in his correspondence on zonal defence.
28 TNA: WO95/883 XI Corps War Diary Notes of Conference, 25 March 1918.
29 TNA: CAB45/123 Jeudwine copy letter to Edmonds, 21 August 1918.
30 TNA: WO95/883 XI Corps War Diary Notes of Conference, 25 March 1918.
31 TNA: WO95/2927 1/7th Battalion King's Liverpool Regiment War Diary, 31 March–8 April 1918; WO95/2910 55th Division War Diary, 31 March–8 April 1918.

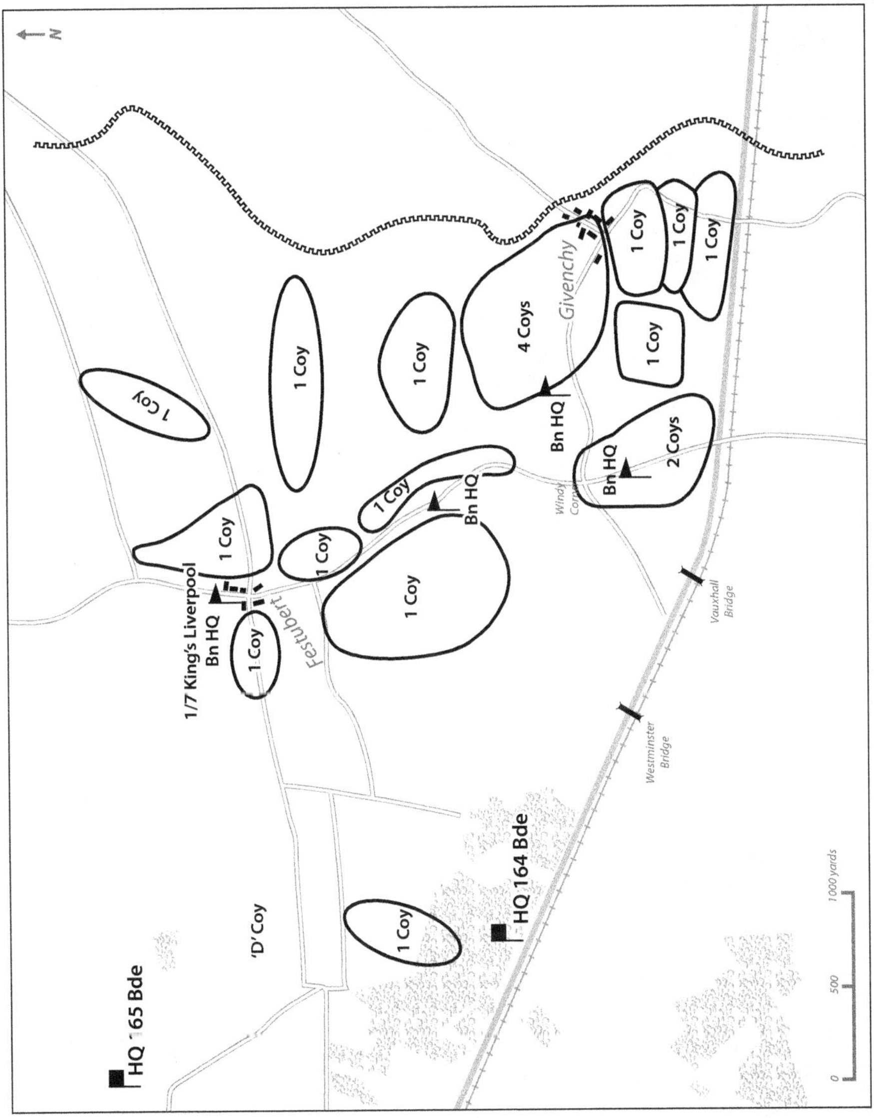

Map 4 Festubert and Givenchy, Battle of the Lys April 1918.

Men of 1/7th Battalion, King's Liverpool Regiment in the front line trenches, 15 March 1918. (IWM ref.Q10737)

Ration party of 1/7th Battalion, King's Liverpool Regiment in the front line trenches, 15 March 1918. (IWM ref. Q10743)

had been stopped for over a week though Private Erlam Greaves was still hopeful of getting back to Formby on Thursday 4 April[32] but on the morning of 9th he lay, with the rest of 1/7th King's, to the front of the central part of Festubert village. The 1/4th Loyals and 1/4th King's Own held the line in front of Givenchy to the canal.[33] Platoons were to hold the defended localities at all costs. They were wired for all-round defence, communication trenches were wired and wire ran in all directions to the Front to cramp the enemy's movement.[34] With this system of apron-fencing, tunnels and a mass of wire, extensive training in their own system was imperative in order to carry out any necessary counter-attacks. According to Colonel Crump, GOC 1/4th Loyals, it was this training policy which 'bore fruit – a remarkable example of the value of taking the British soldier into your confidence and making him understand 'why' he was being ordered to do something'.[35] Samuels describes this system as simply a return to the old 'Thin Red Line', but there was more flexibility than that and he is incorrect in calling the system 'entirely passive'.[36] All evidence points to Jeudwine constructing an 'offensive defence'.[37]

Jeudwine demanded battle narratives after each engagement down to the lowest level and these provide a clear description of events. At 4:15 a.m. on the cold and misty morning of 9 April 1918 the Germans attacked the Allied Line with a severe bombardment which lasted for over two hours. The infantry attack began around 8:00 a.m. with 1/5th King's being attacked shortly before 1/7th. At 9:51 a.m., Division reported the SOS in front of Festubert to Corps. By 10:30 a.m. the outpost line was lost.[38]

The thick mist or fog restricted visibility to about ten yards,[39] and when the assault came this added to the confusion. The front companies were overpowered, from the flank and the rear. However, 'the fierce and stubborn fighting of the platoons and companies in the front posts' had broken up and disorganised the attackers.[40] As the

32 Letter from Private Erlam Greaves, A Company 1/7th Battalion, King's Liverpool Regiment, to his father, 2 April 1918. His hope was in vain for he was killed in the German bombardment on the first day of the offensive: Coles, private collection.

33 Coop, *The Story of the 55th Division*, pp. 90–91.

34 TNA: WO95/883 XI Corps War Diary Notes on Recent Fighting No.7 German attack near Givenchy, issued 24 April 1918.

35 TNA: CAB45/122 Lieutenant Colonel Crump DSO to Edmonds, 30 December 1931.

36 Samuels, *Doctrine and Dogma*, p. 115.

37 LCRO: 356 FIF/14 Memoranda on training for defence, December 1917–February 1918, Jeudwine MSS.

38 TNA: WO95/883 XI Corps War Diary Brief Narrative of Events, 20 March to 30 April 1918.

39 TNA: WO95/2925 165th Brigade War Diary Narrative of Battle, 9–15 April 1918 – Lieutenant T.A. Lyon O.C. 9 Platoon C Company.

40 TNA: WO95/883 XI Corps War Diary Brief Narrative of Events, 20 March to 30 April 1918.

front posts were overpowered few men came back and the remainder were ordered by Company Commanders to fall back to the Village Line.[41]

Casualties in the battle were high, and came predominantly from the initial bombardment and subsequent attack.[42] A number of officers were taken out of the battle, leaving men to organise themselves. Initiative at a local level was quite prevalent and Brind referred to the defence by 'the men in the strongpoints whom General Judy had trained … to have confidence in themselves'.[43] The confidence to show initiative was crucial to holding the Division's frontage. In B Company, Critchley was surprised to see an officer – 'up to then an Officer was so scarce I don't know where he came from … Corporals and sergeants were the only persons in charge and made decisions.'[44] When it became necessary, the retirement was an orderly one:

> Officers NCOs and men began to retire down the CT [communication trench] in a very orderly manner, each in turn, whenever possible, taking up the position on the side of the CT and covering the retreat of others. This was done so well that again no casualties occurred … a further retreat was necessary, and again the CT was used where the retreat of the Company was done in a very magnificent manner, again each and all in turn covering each other … At the end of the CT a final stand was made by Lieut. Wolcock and a few NCOs and men.[45]

Strongholds changed hands often more than once but gradually the intiative was regained as Le Plantin, Windy Corner and others were recaptured.[46] During the battle all and sundry were being told off for fighting detail: 'Headquarters Details, including Cooks, spare Signallers, Pioneers, etc. had been ordered to take up a position…'.[47] Critchley said that once the Portuguese had retired and the enemy was behind them, 'every available man…transport, cooks and fellows that had soft jobs after being wounded' were called into the line.[48] Colonel Buckley, in describing the battle said 'the 7th Kings were doing heroic work…everybody was in it – RE's,

41 TNA: WO95/2927 1/7th Battalion King's Liverpool Regiment War Diary Report of Colonel Potter, 17 April 1918.

42 TNA: WO95/2910 55th Division War Diary, 9 April 1918.

43 TNA: CAB45/122 Correspondence in compiling the *Official History*, Major General J.S. Brind CB CMG DSO BGGS XI Corps to Edmonds, 3 January 1932.

44 Critchley.

45 TNA: WO95/2925 165th Brigade War Diary Narrative of battle, 9–15 April 1918 – Sergeant D. Lowes No.16 Platoon D Company.

46 Captain J.W. Cook MC won a bar to his Military Cross for leading the recapture of Le Plantin: Spalton private collection, citation in the *Times*, 19 September 1918.

47 TNA: WO95/2925 1/7th Battalion Kings Liverpool Regiment War Diary Report of Colonel Potter, 17 April 1918.

48 Critchley.

Pioneers, cooks, bottlewashers and all.'[49] Brind understood that, unusually, 'it was an order in the Division that every man, servants, clerks, cooks etc. had to fire so many rounds over the top every month' in which case at least they would know what to do.[50]

The following day was relatively quiet for 1/7th King's but attacks continued elsewhere and there was more heavy shelling on 11 April. The Battalion was relieved two days later, after fifteen days in the line. The Division pulled out on 16 April to great accolade.[51] The Division was relieved by 1st Division, whose 1st Battalion Black Watch could not hold the Givenchy ridge against another German attack.[52]

Jeudwine, perhaps naturally, reasoned that the success of the Division had been down to their adoption of his defensive scheme: 'the answer to the German tactics of infiltration, hitherto so successful, had been found'.[53] Much of the evidence supports this assertion. Blades believed that the training, encouragement of initiative and good communications were also vital elements of the Division's defence.[54] Sheffield called the defence 'stubborn'.[55] XI Corps' analysis was that the German failure was due to the stubborn defence by the local platoons and the prompt and skilful counter-attacks which were made to their flanks:

> [A]n enemy penetrating into gaps in our positions is very much at a disadvantage until he can widen the flanks of the gaps; if the defending troops strengthen the flanks of these gaps and hold on to their positions tenaciously, he is bound to be caught between two fires, and forced to surrender what he has gained.[56]

The importance of the line to Haig was shown by his Special Order of the day famously issued on April 11 1918 – 'Every position must be held to the last man: there must be no retirement. With our backs to the wall, and believing in the justice of our cause, each one of us must fight on to the end.'[57]

49 TNA: CAB45/179 Correspondence in compiling the *Official History*: Letter from Colonel Buckley 5th Battalion King's Liverpool Regiment to his brother, 20 April 1918 emphasising the precariousness of the situation by stating 'Don't on any account let any of it get into print'. The Official Historian duly obliged.
50 TNA: CAB45/122 Correspondence in compiling the *Official History*: Brind to Edmonds, 3 January 1932.
51 TNA: WO95/2927 1/7th Battalion King's Liverpool Regiment War Diary 165th Brigade, Report of Colonel Potter.
52 Wauchope, A., *A History of the Black Watch in the Great War 1914–18*, Vol. 2, (London: Medici Society, 1925–6), pp. 82–3.
53 Jeudwine, H.S., 'An Episode of the German Offensive of 1918 – The Lys Offensive of April 1918', *Royal United Services Institute Journal,* Vol. 73, No. 491, (1928), pp. 688–691.
54 Blades, 'The battles of the Lys', p. 73.
55 Sheffield, *Forgotten Victory,* p. 228.
56 TNA: WO95/883 XI Corps War Diary Notes on Recent Fighting No. 7, 30 April 1918.
57 Quoted in Terraine *Douglas Haig* p. 433.

Column of the 55th Division marching away from the fighting, 10 April 1918. (IWM ref. Q342)

The stand at Givenchy–Festubert was a crucial one for the profile of the Division. In Haig's General Despatch following the battle he referred to the 55th Division's 'success of this most gallant defence, the importance of which it would be hard to over-estimate,' which he said, in reference to units like 1/7th King's, 'was due in great measure to the courage and determination displayed by our advanced posts. These held out with the utmost resolution, though surrounded…'[58] The Special Order was not issued just to the 55th Division, though readers of Coop's history, or the special publication issued by the Division, could be forgiven for thinking that it was. However, it was a significant element in boosting morale in the Division and strengthening community identity.

In what seems like a unique idea by the Divisional Commander, all men of the Division were issued with a booklet which included comments and references praising the work of the Division during the battle. This was a healthy boost to morale and confidence. Congratulations came from the Army Commanders, Haig, Plumer, Horne and Haking, but the list of other individuals and organisations demonstrates the significance of the local community links. Led by Lord Derby, there were congratulations also from the mayors of Blackpool, Preston and Liverpool, from GOC's of 1st,

58 Coop, *The Story of the 55th Division,* p. 115.

42nd, 51st and 57th Divisions, the Liverpool Corn Trade Association, the Blackpool Branch of Discharged and Demobilised Soldiers and Sailors, Liverpool Branch of Comrades of the Great War, and many past and serving officers and commanders of 55th Divisional units.

Conan Doyle wrote 'it is the talk of England'; Lieutenant Colonel Duconge of 64th Infantry, French Army wrote: 'This Rose which met the Boche has made him feel its terrible thorns'. Despite the usual reporting not specifying which units were involved in particular battles, this local emphasis on 'Lancashire men' was repeated in the press reports, and these were quoted at length for the benefit of the men:

> It was the magnificent stand of the 55th Lancashire Division at Givenchy which prevented what might have been a rather serious disaster' (the *Times* 12 April); the magnificent fighting qualities shown by the Lancashire territorials (*Daily Mirror* 13 April); the Lancashires of the 55th Division made such a great and gallant stand (*Daily Chronicle* 19 April); Every one who has a relative in that Division must be proud today. It was the Manchesters who originally took Givenchy, and it is again Lancashire men who are holding what Lancashire won (*Manchester Guardian* 20 April).[59]

Both Formby and Litherland Councils made moves to have Haig's Order framed and hung in the Council offices. Nothing more was heard of this in Formby when the cost of framing – between £10 and £12 – was discovered.[60] Litherland agreed to hang the record in the Council Chamber and copies were sent out to local schools and organisations.[61] The success of the defence and the key role which the local Division, and particularly the local Battalion, had played in this test for the BEF would not be lost on the local community.

The stand at Givenchy was an important strategic success, built on the tactical nous of the Divisional General and the support and confidence shown in him by his Corps Commander. It was also built on the strengths and abilities of the men in this territorial unit, reaffirming the assertion that they were one of a limited number of more effective Divisions who could be relied upon in combat. Sheffield cited the importance of Jeudwine's training of the Division in the new methods of defence as paying off 'handsomely'. Sheffield, like Coop, referred specifically to the fighting of the outpost line, the counter-attacks and the initiative of local unit commanders down to platoon level.[62]

59 'Givenchy–Festubert 9–16 April 1918' booklet produced in the field (Imprimeries Reunies, Boulogne-sur-Mer, June 1918).
60 LRO: UDFo 2/4/4 Formby Urban District Council Minutes, 6 May and 2 July 1918.
61 CL: Litherland District Council Minute,s Vol. X, 6 May 1918.
62 Sheffield, *Forgotten Victory*, pp. 228–229.

This engagement also demonstrates, perhaps more than most, the importance of community links to enhancing and maintaining morale. The congratulations and desire to be linked with a successful action at the Front were equally key factors in motivating community support for the remaining months of the War. The action is a good demonstration of how morale and combat effectiveness are inextricably linked. The coincident significance of Givenchy and Festubert being neighbouring villages is explored in the next chapter.

Final Advance

Following the Spring Offensives, the BEF was further restructured and Battalions reorganised. Community identity had been firmly re-established at Home and in 1/7th King's, despite the reduction in the numbers of local men. Morale was boosted by Givenchy and the accolades which followed, although a handful of attempted desertions over the summer still indicated some problems. The Battle of Amiens, 8 August 1918, marked the turning point in the fortunes of the War, and was swiftly followed by attacks at Albert by Byng's Third Army, and by Rawlinson's 'new' Fourth to the south. At the end of August, Horne's First Army attacked around Arras.[63]

The leading role played by 55th Division in its sector of the Final Advance shows the reliance and confidence it had built in Army Command. Although not the main focus of attacks the central area was nonetheless a key link in the Allied Line. Under General Birdwood they were the most experienced and senior Division in the new Fifth Army,[64] joined in III Corps by the 74th Division, dismounted Yeomanry, recently returned from Palestine.[65]

During this final phase of the War, 55th Division were to advance 50 miles in the 80 days after they left the Givenchy–Festubert line.[66] The Division, and indeed the Allies as a whole, were able to do this by adapting a fuller understanding of what was required in terms of tactics. Bourne critically pointed out that none of these tactics were new.[67] This adoption of a weapons system, according to Sheffield, too, amounted to little more than using all available elements as part of an all-arms team.[68] Griffith showed that the use of the creeping artillery barrage, scouts, improved signals and tanks all contributed to this new-found effectiveness. Particularly important was the attack front which was carried out in the 'blob' formations designed to allow the platoon to switch direction and tactics, leading with any of the four sections, as

63 Sheffield, *Forgotten Victory*, pp. 242–243.
64 Becke, *Order of Battle*, Part 2A and Part 3A New Army Divisions.
65 Griffith, *Battle Tactics of the Western Front*, p. 218.
66 Coop, *The Story of the 55th Division*, p. 159.
67 Bourne, *Britain and the Great War*, p. 98.
68 Sheffield, *Forgotten Victory*, pp. 236–7.

demanded.[69] This more mobile attack front was considerably different to the more structured assaults of the middle years of the War but evidence of this platoon-focus has already been seen in 1/7th Battalion at Ypres and Givenchy.

The restructuring of the battalion focused increased firepower in platoons, reducing the official fighting strength to 900. However, 1/7th King's was always at the lower end of the permissible range, rarely going above 800 during the summer and, once the Advance was underway, facing a gradual reduction in men from 795 at the end of August to 694 at the Armistice. The significance of the new warfare developing can be seen in the Division's guidelines on battalion organisation where the post of 'scout' at platoon HQ has been added to the table in the War Diary by hand.[70] The strategy of following up the enemy withdrawal was reliant on maintaining the logistics of battle – supplies, transport, munitions[71] – and the local emphasis was on improved cooperation with RE [Royal Engineers]. Much better planning and involvement of platoon, company and battalion commanders were also needed in order to fully understand that 'in these days slinging mud about is a very necessary part of the fighting'.[72]

Further, by developing a relatively limited focus for each attack and switching the focus of attack from one Army to another, the Line was able to advance successfully.[73] Above all, the advance of the Line on all Fronts depended on the ability of each Army and each Division to adapt to these tactics. Griffith recognised this, referring specifically to the growing level of tactical skill amongst New Armies and Territorials, as essential for this success.[74]

On 3 September the enemy in front of 1/7th King's started to withdraw and over the next two days the line was advanced to Chapelle St Roch and Violaines.[75] As Sheffield notes, the relatively small scale operations by Fifth Army helped to force the Germans off the Lys battlefield by 6 September.[76] The progress was made by fighting patrols, co-ordinated by the three Brigades continually shifting from left, to right, to support, and no attempt was made to hold a continuous line.[77] Divisional instructions emphasised that obtaining information of the enemy's intentions should be done with 'the fewest number of men possible, and to follow up those with platoons acting boldly and with initiative.' It was further stressed to all ranks that: 'it is not necessary to advance in any definite line, but that each body of troops must push forward as far as

69 Griffith, *Battle Tactics of the Western Front,* pp. 95–8, 173.
70 TNA: WO95/2907 55th Division War Diary Notes on Organisation of an Infantry Battalion, c.October 1918.
71 Sheffield, *Forgotten Victory,* p. 247.
72 TNA: WO95/2907 55th Divison War Diary I Corps Notes on the Co-operation of Infantry and Engineers Nos. 468 (G) and 484 (G), 13 and 14 August 1918.
73 Sheffield, *Forgotten Victory,* p. 251.
74 Griffith, *Battle Tactics on the Western Front,* p. 196.
75 TNA: WO95/2927 1/7th Battalion King's Liverpool Regiment War Diary, 3–5 September 1918.
76 Sheffield, *Forgotten Victory,* p. 243.
77 Coop, *The Story of the 55th Division,* pp. 128–9.

it can … without waiting for neighbouring bodies which may have been temporarily held up.'[78]

These attacks met considerable enemy resistance, often in hand-to-hand fighting, and some trenches were held by both sides at the same time.[79] The capture of Canteleux Trench gave a clear view to the La Bassée–Fromelles Line and boosted the men's morale.[80] The Outpost Line was strengthened and the more indiscriminate establishment of advanced posts was ended. Between the Outpost Lines and the Main Line of Resistance, patrols were constantly on the watch for enemy movement.[81]

Across the Allied Front a co-ordinated series of attacks began in the south with a combined Franco-American offensive in the Argonne on 26 September 1918.[82] The attack was joined on Sunday 29th by 1/7th King's with platoons in light fighting order, without haversacks, to enable them to move quickly and quietly into action.[83] A hectic but successful day's fighting demonstrated the importance of the platoon as the focal point.[84] The Outpost Zone had now deepened so much that the Main Line of Resistance was only lightly garrisoned and these troops were to be ready to move forward to retake the Outpost Line should that be lost to a hostile counter attack.[85]

Sheffield acknowledges that the Germans were in a weakened position and that by late 1918, Allied numbers were overwhelming, but he maintains that it was the superior weapons system employed by the BEF that proved successful.[86] However, he does emphasise the significance of the psychological effects of the battles at the end of September and the crumbling of German morale.[87] Nonetheless, as the limited number of Divisions in Fifth Army could not sustain large-scale offensives against strongly held positions, III Corps advanced on a Front with 74th Division to the north and 55th to the south. Within 55th Division the advance would be in three groups – an all-arms Advanced Guard, a Main Body, and a Reserve. This was much the same as was already in place, with Outpost Battalions, the remainder of the two Brigades in the Line, and the Reserve Brigade. The key difference was to make the

78 TNA: WO95/2906 55th Division War Diary Instructions in the event of a withdrawal, 1 September 1918.
79 Coop, *The Story of the 55th Division,* p. 129.
80 Coop, *The Story of the 55th Division,* p. 131; TNA: WO95/2927 1/7th Battalion King's Liverpool Regiment War Diary, 18 September 1918.
81 Coop, *The Story of the 55th Division,* p. 133; WO95/2927 1/7th Battalion King's Liverpool Regiment War Diary, 20 September 1918.
82 Sheffield, *Forgotten Victory,* p. 248.
83 TNA: WO95/2927 1/7th Battalion King's Liverpool Regiment War Diary Operation Orders Lt.Col. Potter, 28 September 1918.
84 TNA: WO95/2927 1/7th Battalion King's Liverpool Regiment War Diary Narrative of Events 29.9.18 Lt. Col. Potter, 2 October 1918; Coop, *The Story of the 55th Division,* p. 257.
85 TNA: WO95/2907 55th Division War Diary Agenda for Conference at DHQ, 26 September 1918.
86 Sheffield, *Forgotten Victory,* p. 214.
87 Sheffield, *Forgotten Victory,* pp. 251, 259, 262.

Advanced Guard an all-arms affair and to this end the Division was reorganised so that, as well as the infantry, the Brigade commander in the Advanced Guard would command a troop of mounted divisional men, artillery, RE, machine guns and ambulance personnel.[88]

Decentralisation of command meant Divisional HQ now gave a Line as an objective for the Main Body to reach. Brigade commanders would decide how far the Advanced Guard should go in order to allow the Main Body to reach their objective. The Advanced Guard was to go beyond the Line which, when the Main Body reached it, would become the new Main Line of Resistance. In the case of 55th Division, astride the La Bassée Canal, the Advanced Guard had to operate in two Brigades. The main functions of the Advanced Guard were reconnaissance, exploration, engagement with the enemy, and protection of troops in the rear. Jeudwine's key emphasis was on the need for careful organisation of platoons and sections under their officers and NCOs.[89]

At first, the Advanced Guard with Battalions of 164th and 166th Brigades made good progress, covering five miles over 3 and 4 October 1918 and meeting little resistance except damaged or booby-trapped dug outs and cratered roadways. However, with the Division on one side of the Haute Deule Canal, and the Germans on the other, the advance halted for ten days. Artillery was ranged against the Division and hostile fire continued until attempts to cross the Canal were made from 13 to 15 October, finally enabling the Division to cross on 16 October.[90]

Instructions to the Advanced Guard stressed the need for commanders of Outpost Battalions to be able to see the commanders of his artillery, machine guns and mortar companies, as well as any reserve troops in the area. Company commanders were supposed to be able to maintain this contact and watch the action of platoons and, for the most effective adaptation to conditions, communications were vital.[91] A Fifth Army memo insisted that Corps commanders took a firmer grip on the situation and followed these principles. Army HQ was especially concerned that Battalion and Brigade commanders 'cannot command from headquarters and dug outs far in the rear'.[92] The message was re-emphasised by Jeudwine to his Brigadiers: 'a Battalion Commander whose troops are closely engaged with the enemy cannot possibly control the fight from behind a hill at 2,500 yards. He must be where he can see and give

88 TNA: WO95/2907 55th Division War Diary Agenda for Conference at DHQ, 26 September 1918; Coop, *The Story of the 55th Division,* pp. 136–137.
89 TNA: WO95/2907 55th Division War Diary Notes on the Situation G.S. 1565, 15 October 1918.
90 Coop, *The Story of the 55th Division,* pp. 140–144.
91 TNA: WO95/2907 55th Divison War Diary Notes on the Situation G.S. 1565, 15 October 1918.
92 TNA: WO95/2907 55th Division War Diary Fifth Army G.S. 436/39, 16 October 1918.

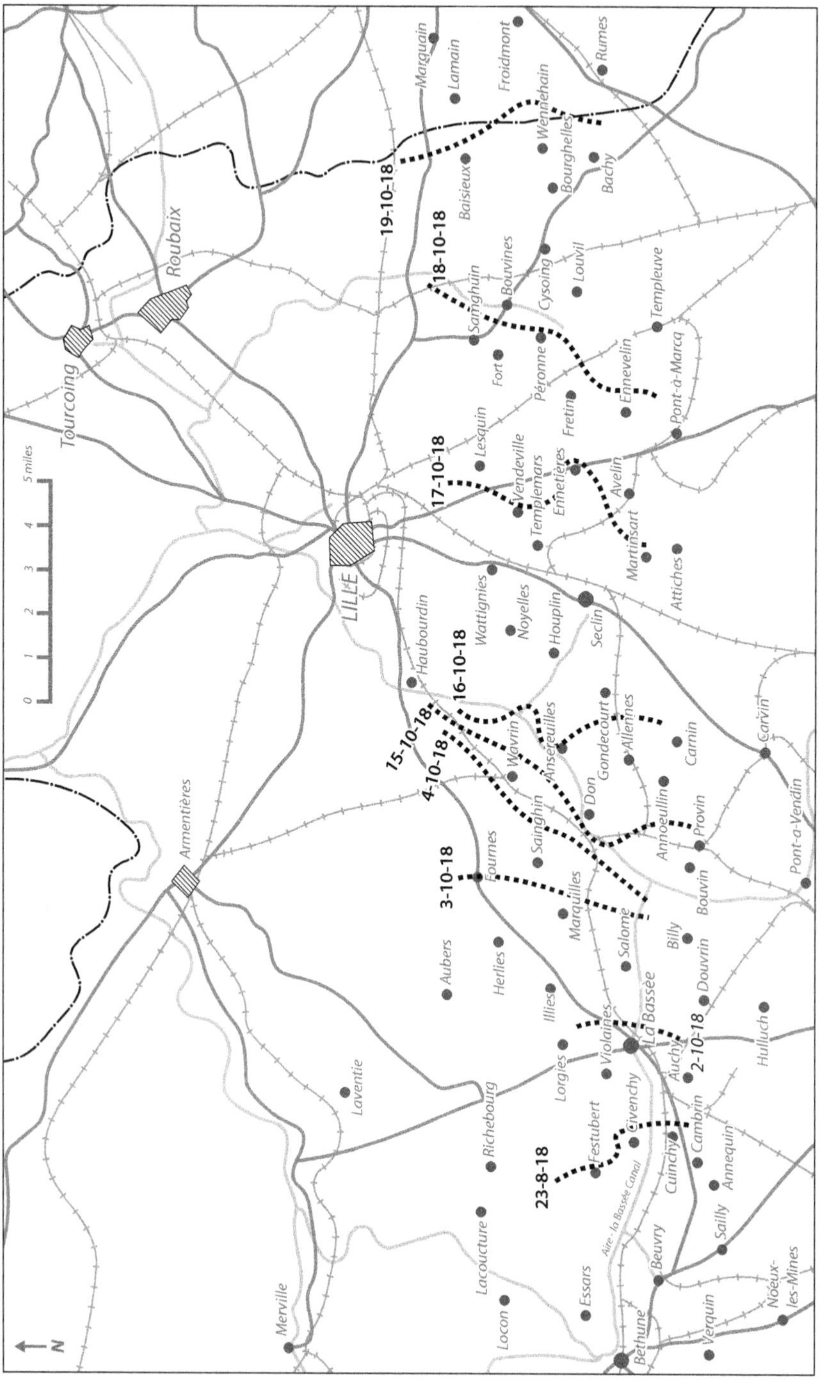

Map 5a Final Advance, 1918.

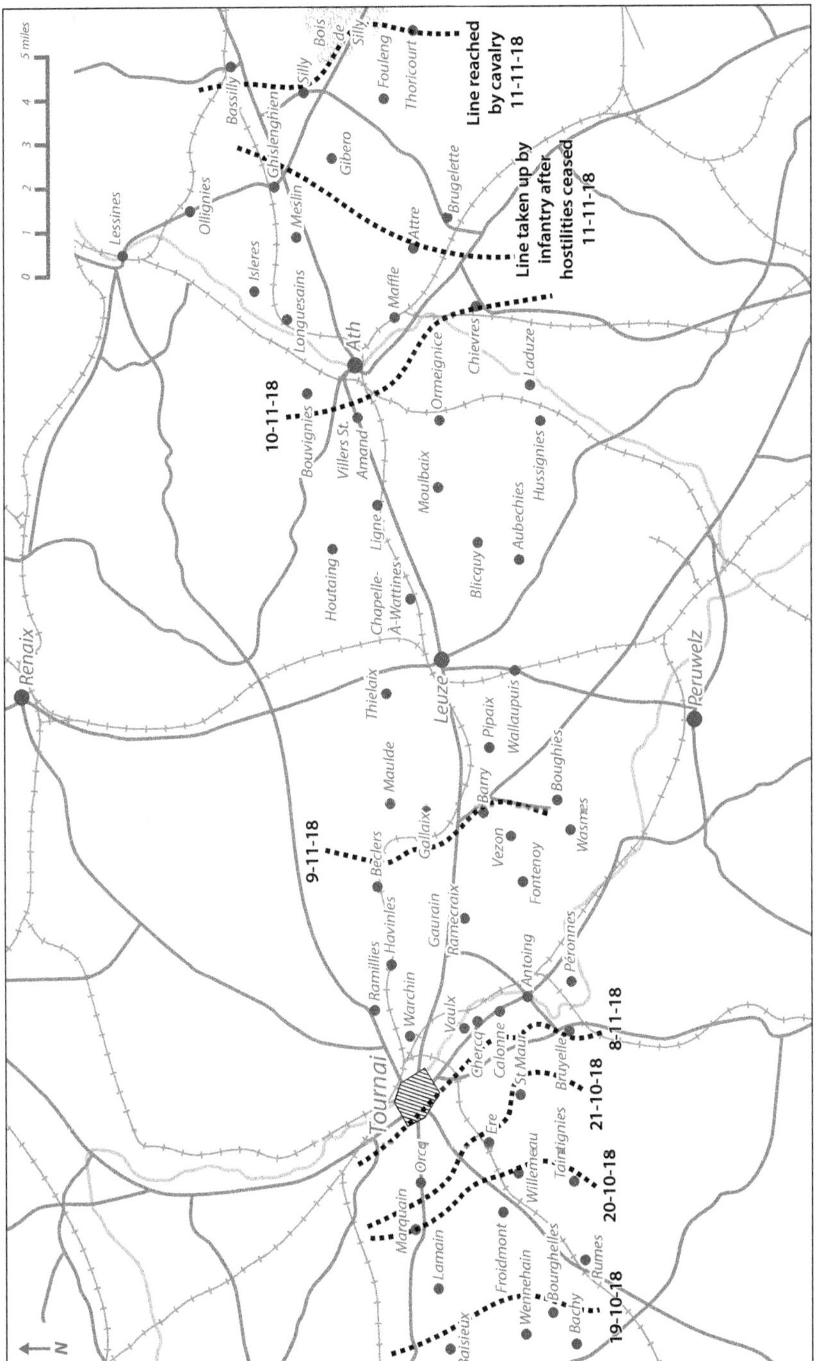

Map 5b Final Advance, 1918.

executive orders'. This was further demonstration of the decentralisation of command structures.[93]

A hastily typed addendum appeared on the War Diary carbon copy of this instruction: 'It is realized that the above remarks apply equally to Divisional Headquarters and it is for this reason that a forward Divisional Report centre is being established tomorrow.'[94] It is not clear whether this was a note only for the benefit of the official record, although other evidence of Jeudwine's command (his diary notebooks for example) would suggest that he would carry it out in reality.

Considerable distance was made over the 2 and 3 October 1918, and again between 16 and 20 October when 1/7th King's was the Advanced Guard.[95] The Battalion War Diary recorded that one battery of eighteen pounders and two howitzers, four machine gun sections, one field company RE and specialist REs were attached to the Battalion, demonstrating the level of all-arms co-operation down to Battalion level.[96] Seventh King's last significant engagement with the enemy occurred in a raid carried out on a wood west of Tournai, aimed at capturing prisoners to find out the enemy's intentions.[97]

The Corps advanced on a two-division front, with 74th Division following 55th Division and the all-arms support, cyclists, horse, artillery, transport and train divided in half. A daily move for Divisional Headquarters meant 'cutting down on office furniture, and other baggage'![98] On 9 November, the Escaut river was bridged and 1/7th King's, as Advanced Guard, pushed on east of Tournai to Beclers. By night on 10th the Battalion Outpost was at Ligne.[99] Orders for the immediate attack on Ath were issued for the 11th. The rest of 165th Brigade joined up with the Advanced Guard of the 1/7th King's in the morning of the 11 November. To the south the attack was made by 166th Brigade, while 165th Brigade took the north of the town. Lancashire Fusiliers reached the town by clearing the enemy from the bridge early in the morning. The attacking troops were in position to launch the assault. The news of the end of hostilities came incredibly late. A conference of Brigade commanders met at 9:00 a.m. to settle details but at 9:05 a.m. a telephone call from Divisional HQ informed the Conference that hostilities were to end at 11:00 a.m.[100] As Battalion

93 TNA: WO95/2907 55th Division War Diary G.S. 1571, 18 October 1918.
94 TNA: WO95/2907 55th Division War Diary G.S. 1571, 18 October 1918.
95 TNA: WO95/2907 55th Division War Diary Stages of Advance: maps.
96 TNA: WO95/2927 1/7th Battalion King's Liverpool Regiment War Diary, 18 October 1918.
97 Coop, *The Story of the 55th Division,* p. 150.
98 TNA: WO95/2907 55th Divison War Diary III Corps Memo G.O. 2654, 6 November 1918.
99 TNA: WO95/2927 1/7th Battalion King's Liverpool Regiment War Diary, 9–10 November 1918.
100 Coop, *The Story of the 55th Division,* pp. 157–8.

Commander, Colonel Potter was told shortly after 10:00 a.m. 'After 11.00 hours the Bn. moved off to billets in Lanquesaint.'[101]

Although Coop recorded that the Division travelled 50 miles in forty-four days he was referring to the furthest eastern point reached by the mobile force on the Bassilly–Thoricourt line.[102] Griffith compiled a graph showing the relative progress of the five Armies placing the Fifth Army at the bottom of the list, but still having travelled over 60 miles since the first week of August.[103] Regardless of the precise mileage, the 55th Division was undoubtedly the leading partner in III Corps' advance. The adaption of new tactics and changed circumstances came easily to Jeudwine and his troops were able to pursue the enemy effectively, reaching their objective of Ath on the very day that hostilities ceased.

Culmination of Jeudwine's Training Manual

The contribution made by 1/7th King's as Advanced Guard in the Final Advance demonstrate a reliability and combat effectiveness learned and honed over the preceding two to three years. The focus at platoon level, the all-arms ability and the mobility of unit and formation are evidence of a successful Territorial combat unit. This is a significant issue as the Battalion had been under considerable pressure from a variety of factors during 1917 and 1918. Casualties in 1916 and 1917 meant that the Battalion's fighting strength was low and the ranks were being filled by the drafts and conscripts sent under the Military Service legislation. Actual numbers of local men fell in the Battalion. After further casualties at Givenchy they were reorganised and refocused in what appeared to be a more efficient, leaner combat unit. As a divisional formation, there were difficulties associated with the counter-attack at Cambrai but Jeudwine appeared strengthened by that process and his determination to establish an 'offensive defence' won support from his immediate superiors even if not at GHQ. His tactics worked and the line held in April 1918 due to the training, tenacity and commitment of the troops. This effectiveness in combat was a clear indicator of high morale. Similarly, the disciplinary record of the Battalion indicated that there were few problems and that morale was good. Jeudwine's strictures on discipline do not seem to have resulted in large numbers of cases being tried in this Battalion.

The importance of good morale was never lost on Jeudwine, but it was the way it was engendered through establishing and maintaining the localness of the Division which demonstrates how significant the sense of belonging to that community was for the maintenance of high morale. A good example lies in the magazine, *Sub Rosa*

101 TNA: WO95/2927 1/7th Battalion King's Liverpool Regiment War Diary, 11 November 1918.
102 Coop, *The Story of the 55th Division*, p. 159.
103 Griffith, *Battle Tactics of the Western Front*, p. 94.

– 'under the rose'. Here, through cartoon, dialect and poetry the Lancashire soul of the Division was championed.

Finally, the defence of Givenchy provides a clear indication of how these different elements interacted. Givenchy was a triumph for training, tactics, commitment and luck. Its significance was crucial at the time, not least to boost the morale of other units who sat in wait for the next expected German attack. It demonstrated the true viability and flexibility of a Territorial division, which went on to take the lead role in III Corps' advance in the autumn. It was also significant in the attention it attracted from Home, almost all of which focused on the community identity of the unit. This was a victory for men of Lancashire, for the communities of Lancashire. That the area of the Lys was later to be the centre of attention for a number of the Lancashire towns who adopted French villages was not a coincidence. As will be seen in the final chapter, it held a significant place in the history of the Division, later marked by a war memorial.

The deployment of the 1/7th King's through the engagements described above demonstrated their effectiveness within the Division. Despite the pressures of the Front Line and the longevity of the War itself, morale remained high and their sense of belonging was reinforced by the successes. Their identification with Home may have been less evident until the reaction to the defence of Givenchy, but its obvious resurgence demonstrated that it was never far from the surface.

7

Reunions, Memorials & Anniversaries: How the War was Remembered in West Lancashire

Following the Armistice in November 1918, the return of servicemen to civilian life could take up to six months. There were difficulties and frustrations associated with the demobilisation of not only the men, but also of women and substitute labour, as those returning soldiers wanted their old jobs back – and generally got their wish. There was also the impact of the dead and wounded for families and communities to contend with. The fact of the death of a soldier was often only fully recognised by the family as life returned to normal for those around them. There were new hopes and expectations raised by legislation on housing and work, and the extension of the voting franchise to include women. There was also industrial conflict and a retrenchment by governments as economic pressures mounted. Above all, there was a period of readjustment to peace; but it was a return to normality marked by tension and a debate about creating a land fit for heroes.

The exhibition of remembrance in Southport and Bootle reinforced the local importance of the military unit. Armistice parades, reunions, erection of memorials, histories and links with the battlefields all formed crucial but competing elements. The organisation of Armistice and then the Peace celebrations gave a central role to the Battalion, although not all had returned from France and Flanders until April 1919. Some individual veterans remonstrated about their involvement or priorities but to the local communities the expression of a shared War experience was unquestioned. Tensions which did exist never reached the level seen in some other parts of the country. During the short but bitter police strike, both sides paraded veterans in support, demonstrating that there was a universal acceptance in having men, who had so recently made a valued and valued contribution in the War, associated with either side of the cause.

The Armistice, Peace Day and Socio-economic Challenges

The local activities around the Armistice, Peace Day and subsequent Remembrance Days indicate a commitment to recognise a shared War experience based on the local Battalion through a shared experience of commemoration for civilian and veteran. Local and regional pride was to the fore while the economic and social concerns of veterans were evident but not overwhelming. Faced with the police strike in Bootle, both sides claimed the allegiance of old soldiers and their links to their contribution made for the community on the War Front. The establishment and maintenance of ex-service organisations and particularly the Divisional Association demonstrated the desire for many veterans to perpetuate elements of their War experience in peace time but these retained the importance of local identity in their formation and activity.

The news of the Armistice was greeted with great local enthusiasm and this continued over the months leading to the official Peace celebrations in July 1919. Both Bootle and Southport put on mass events involving the local community and the local Battalion. The evidence shows that the news of the Armistice itself was greeted with huge excitement in Southport, captured evocatively in the local press –

> Boom! You heard that, and wondered if it was possible. And again: Boom! … Then one of the girls from downstairs [a domestic servant] rushed into the room,[1] face aglow and eyes shining with joy and excitement … You rose with a broad smile on your face, a foolishly inadequate expression … and bolted into the street … the sun was shining from a sky of crystal blue upon your face and upon the faces of all the other people … It was the faces of these people that struck you, each one bathed in sunshine and a set smile of breathless joy. [2]

The reporter continued in much the same vein, rehearsing the Mayor's speech from the Town Hall steps to a 'crowd so dense it was impossible to gain the … steps by frontal attack … but by a more strategic route.' The writer went on to comment knowingly in his own militaristic prose. The *Bootle Times* was more prosaic but no less enthusiastic in describing the bells from the Town Hall, chiming for the first time in four years. At least this reporter paused to reflect on the magnitude of the sacrifice:

> we thought of the hundreds of thousands of our dearest and best who would never return to share the blessing that their blood had purchased – and for a moment utterance was strangled. But now our pent emotions broke their barriers and we cheered, and cried, and sang, and cheered again without restraint and without shame. Indeed, why be shamefaced for our joy.[3]

1 An interesting comment on the social origins of the reporter himself.
2 *Southport Guardian*, 13 November 1918, p. 2.
3 *Bootle Times*, 15 November 1918, p. 5.

Bootle dockland stopped work as sirens and whistles blew, flags hung in every house and bunting in every street. The dock area filled with 'cheering, laughing crowds of workers' where 'there had evidently been a spontaneous cessation of work.'[4] The report referred to hundreds of people going to Liverpool, but thousands staying on the streets of Bootle to celebrate.

Thanksgiving services were held, including a civic one at Bootle Town Hall, where the Mayor, Councillor Pennington, whose son Lieutenant Stanley Pennington had just won the Military Cross, offered thanks for the success of the armed forces. Admiral Beatty spoke, followed by Brigadier-General Edwards, Officer commanding the Mersey Defences who praised the Regular Army, the Territorials, the Royal Defence Corps, the Examination Service and the Volunteer Service.[5] Similar events were held across the area, and almost everything was turned into a celebration – although these increasingly became more about thanks for deliverance than opportunities for rejoicing – a routine meeting of the Merchant Seaman's League became a thanksgiving meeting and a sale of work at Westminster Road Congregational Church, planned for some weeks, turned into a special occasion.[6]

The official Peace celebrations did not take place until July 1919, and in fact it had taken until April for the last group of 93 men and twenty-two officers to come home.[7] The Peace Day was an opportunity for rejoicing before everything else became a ritualised remembrance.[8] The celebrations were heralded in Bootle with a Victory march, children's festival, reception of widows and relatives of the fallen, and a gala.[9] The Victory procession in Bootle on 19 July 1919 had a range of bodies led by the police and the naval services, followed by 7th King's, the walking wounded and demobilised sailors and soldiers. There was a reluctance to parade the casualties of the War; equally, many were reluctant to be 'on display'. The 7th Battalion's contingent was split into four, consisting of pre-War Territorials under Marriot, and the three Line Battalions under the overall command of 'their popular commanding officer',[10] Colonel Hemelryk. Non-walking wounded had seats at the grandstand. This Victory procession, on Saturday 19 July 1919, was followed by events on Monday and Tuesday. The 'Peace Rejoicings' were widely and fully reported, with thousands witnessing the events – although the reports were anxious to refer also to the 'deeper note of gratitude' to those 'who have suffered so much and given so bravely'.[11]

4 *Bootle Times*, 15 November 1918, p. 5.
5 *Bootle Times*, 22 November 1918, p. 2.
6 *Bootle Times*, 15 November 1918, p. 7.
7 TNA: WO95/2910 55th Division War Diary A&Q Branch Returns of units fighting strengths, April 1919.
8 Bourne, *Britain and the Great War*, p. 242.
9 *Bootle Times*, 18 July 1919, p. 5.
10 *Bootle Times*, 25 July 1919, p. 5.
11 *Bootle Times*, 25 July 1919, p. 5.

There were less ostentatious events in Southport, where official celebrations were restricted to the old folks and children. The elderly were entertained at the Cambridge Hall with a band and vocal performances. Nearly 9,000 children taking part in a demonstration in the municipal gardens. The editorial of the *Southport Guardian* referred obliquely to 'the circumstances which necessitated' a more restricted programme. This was a reference to the bigger parade in Bootle taking the limelight. [12] The focus on old people and children somewhat excluded the ex-servicemen. Gregory commented that: 'If ex-servicemen retained a place in the popular perception of what 11 November was about...it was a subordinate place'.[13] This unfortunate fact was noted by the *Southport Guardian*, although much more time was spent reporting all the events in the various churches of the Borough, including the children's festival and especially the 'Joy Procession' in Churchtown and Marshside. It was this event which had most attention with photographs of fancy dress competitions and the procession. There were also aerial stunts from Avro, fireworks, and celebrations at Formby, Birkdale and Litherland.[14] Absent from any local Victory procession, however, were the colours of 1/7th King's – they had been invited to represent Lancashire in the Victory Parade in London, and were carried by Captain Roper and Lieutenant Nesbitt. The colours of 2/7th were paraded in Bootle.[15]

In granting the Freedom of the Borough to Sir Douglas Haig, Southport reaffirmed its allegiance to the War effort and the significance it had for the local community. He responded by confirming the importance of the local community's sacrifice and specifically referred to the 55th Division and the Liverpool Regiment at Givenchy. [16] He had witnessed a Divisional march past in Liverpool the previous week although 7th King's had withdrawn from that as only thirty-six men had registered to take part. Hemelryk recognised that the main source of local pride was not Liverpool but the local communities: 'after all, the Battalion is not recruited in Liverpool, but between Bootle and Southport'.[17]

There was some confusion and concern about the position in the community of ex-servicemen which went on for some time. This was demonstrated by the creation of a range of comrades associations, some of whom took different stances on the role of veterans in the Peace celebrations. In relation to the debate about whether the anniversary of the Armistice should be marked as a celebration or a time of reflection, Gregory has suggested that for the more secure and affluent, the first five years after the War were marked by veterans' festivities, citing the Leeds Rifles as an example.[18]

12 *Southport Guardian*, 19 July 1919, pp. 4 and 5.
13 Gregory, A., *The Silence of Memory: Armistice Day 1918–1946* (Oxford: Berg Publishers, 1994), p. 51.
14 *Southport Guardian*, 23 July 1919, pp. 7–10; *Bootle Times*, 25 July 1919, p. 6.
15 *Bootle Times*, 18 July 1919, p. 5.
16 *Southport Guardian*, 9 July 1919, p. 7.
17 *Southport Guardian*, 5 July 1919, p. 2.
18 Gregory, *The Silence of Memory*, p. 66.

For others, however, such revelry was either unseemly or mocking of the poverty of the majority of ex-servicemen. It was no surprise, then, that there appeared to be some confusion in the minds of ex-servicemen about their involvement in the Peace celebrations. A procession of veterans, including several wounded, walking and in bath chairs, marched in their own recognition of Peace Day, but they were equally met by crowds of well-wishers and supporters. Representatives of the Discharged and Demobilised Sailors and Soldiers attended the numerous church services in Southport over the weekend.[19]

Officially, the National Federation of Discharged and Demobilised Sailors and Soldiers took no part in the Peace Celebrations and the Bootle organisation was adamant in its support for that national position. They had refused to take part in the Mayoral Thanksgiving Service, enumerating various grievances in their reply to the invitation – unemployment, inadequate pensions and allowances, delays in processing claims and a lack of housing.[20] One veteran letter writer from Bootle commented that they should not be forgotten and that six months after the Armistice 'there are still ex-soldiers parading the streets in search of employment; the pensions awarded disabled men and the widows and dependants of those who have fallen are still woefully inadequate; the treatment meted out to the returned soldier is still unfair and unjust'.[21]

The economy became a focal point in Southport at the annual Armistice Day, or Remembrance Day as it quickly became. For example, after the Mayor, Miss Hartley, and the officials had left the gardens following the 1921 Act of Remembrance, the unemployed took over the Bandstand and made speeches to a rally of local people.[22] The *Southport Guardian* used the occasion the following year to warn of the 'spectre of economic anarchy', and raised a fundamental question for the national conscience – 'They won the war. What have we done to win the Peace?'.[23] This unsubtle piece of electioneering, criticising Lloyd George's Coalition, came only days before the General Election confirmed a Government under Bonar Law with a slim Conservative majority.[24] Similar sentiments were expressed in Bootle where the claims of the men who returned had been ignored. How extreme the thoughts of one mother were, however, is unclear: 'God knows I'd rather have my boy at peace than see him tramping the streets looking for work'.[25] In 1923, the Mayor of Southport dedicated his year to a hope that the twenty-three disabled ex-servicemen in the Borough would gain employment.[26]

It was these signs of discontent which Gregory noted as the roots of the transformation of local bands of unemployed ex-servicemen into more active local associations at

19 *Southport Guardian*, 23 July 1919, p. 10.
20 *Bootle Times*, 11 July 1919, p. 4.
21 *Bootle Times*, 25 July 1919, p. 4.
22 *Southport Guardian*, 12 November 1921, p. 5.
23 *Southport Guardian*, 11 November 1922, p. 5.
24 C.L. Mowat, *Britain Between the Wars 1918–1940* (London: Methuen 1968), p. 145.
25 *Bootle Times*, 17 November 1922, p. 9.
26 *Southport Guardian*, 14 November, 1923 p. 6.

the end of 1920.[27] Initially, these associations, primarily of the 'other ranks', were variously attached to one of three centrally organised bodies of the National Association of Discharged Sailors and Soldiers, the National Federation of Discharged and Demobilised Sailors and Soldiers, and the Comrades of the Great War. Given that the latter was formed by the Conservative Party and heavily promoted by Lord Derby amongst Lord Lieutenants and the Territorial Associations,[28] it is significant that despite the amalgamation into the apolitical, conservative and traditionally low membership organisation of the British Legion by 1923,[29] a 'Comrades of the Great War' club survives in both Ormskirk and Waterloo.

In addition to these ex-servicemen's organisations and social clubs, specific Divisional and Regimental Associations were also being established. The 55th Divisional Association, formed under General Jeudwine's presidency in Belgium in December 1918, underlined the importance of loyalty and identity within the Divisional structure.[30] By the time of its first Annual Meeting – significantly on 10 April 1920 – the Association claimed 12,075 members.[31] Even with the 'election' of a committee, Jeudwine's endorsement reinforced the organisation as one designed to replicate the hierarchy of the Army. The intent of this may have been to make the members feel comfortable and secure in an organisation now that they were cut adrift in society; or it may have been about the control and direction of the organisation.

The Association was primarily set up as an unemployment bureau for discharged servicemen. The secretary, CQMS Mercer, reported that there had been 673 requests for assistance to the Divisional Aid Fund, which had already been set up while in France. There are many requests for testimonials and introductions from officers now unemployed amongst General Jeudwine's papers and also amongst Lord Derby's papers.[32]

By 1924, the Association had around 600 registered members of whom 530 were officers. Their work in running an unemployment register continued, as did the Aid Fund for widows and orphans of Divisional men, but the discounts offered to members at the various clockmakers, tailors, furniture stores, china and jewellery dealers were probably of little interest to any rankers who may have joined for welfare purposes. A War Graves Fund was also established which allowed assistance for relatives to visit the war graves, all marked by metal cocardes placed in 1919 and 1920. Scarves, handkerchiefs, badges, copies of *Sub Rosa* and the Givenchy Battle report, and postcards

27 Gregory, *The Silence of Memory*, p. 56.
28 King, A., *Memorials of the Great War in Britain: The Symbolism and Politics of Remembrance* (Oxford: Berg Publishers, 1998), p. 79.
29 De Groot, *Blighty*, pp. 268–270.
30 TNA: WO95/2907 55th Division War Diary, 2 December 1918.
31 *Southport Visiter*, 13 April 1920, p. 6.
32 IWM Ref. 72/82/2 Jeudwine MSS; LCRO: 920 DER (17) 21/3–5 Derby MSS.

Major-General Jeudwine at 55th Division review with King Albert of Belgium 3 January 1919, the third anniversary of the division's formation. (Private collection)

of the Front were all available to those who wanted to continue their military connections into civilian life. [33]

The Association had merged with the Second Line (57th) Division and had their Annual Dinner at the Midland Adelphi Hotel in Liverpool in 1921.[34] After a pause between 1932 and 1935 due to the economic depression, Association Dinners restarted in 1935, but a separate Divisional Dinner Club was also established, meeting in London as so many of the attendees (including Marriott and Major Heaton from 7th King's) lived there.[35] Lord Derby's involvement had initially been craved. When he was unable to attend the 1929 Dinner, the organisers had moved it to suit him, although only fifteen tickets were then sold.[36] By 1936, in an indication that the

33 IWM Ref. 72/82/2: *55th Divisional Association Year Book*, 1924 Jeudwine MSS.
34 LCRO: 356 WES 8/1 WLTAF: 55th and 57th Divisional Dinner Committee Minutes, 1924–39.
35 IWM Ref. 72/82/2: Menu card, Second Annual Dinner, 4 April 1936, Jeudwine MSS.
36 LCRO: 356 WES 8/1 WLTAF 55th and 57th Divisional Dinner Committee Minutes, 25 March 1929.

influence of the landed gentry had waned still further, the Dinner was not moved, even though it clashed with Derby's own 71st birthday. The guest list indicated that, perhaps inevitably, the organisation was by now restricted to serving or retired officers.[37] The twentieth anniversary of Givenchy was marked by the Dinner Club on 13 April 1938 in London, presided over by Jeudwine. As principal guest, Derby recalled his involvement in the evolution of the Territorial Force thirty years previously and spoke of the 55th's inspiring wartime record.[38] The following year over 230, including Lord Derby, attended the 20th Annual Dinner of the Association on 15 April 1939 at the Exchange Station Hotel, Liverpool.[39] The survival of the Association through the interwar years is an indication of the strength of the cameraderie and regional identity which was built up by Jeudwine during the War itself.

The continuity of structures and values which Jeudwine was keen to preserve through the Divisional Association can also be seen within the civilian community. A good example occurred during the Bootle police strike which showed that the handling of an industrial dispute was largely along the same lines as those before the War. The additional factor was the involvement of veterans, providing support to both sides.

The (last) national police strike broke out in London, on 31 July 1919, soon spreading to Liverpool and Birmingham. Support was sparse except in Liverpool where 932 out of 1,860 were on strike, and in Bootle, where 63 of the 77-man force came out.[40] The editorial in the *Bootle Times* the following week called it 'indefensible' and 'a mutiny'.[41] The newspaper praised the community for the maintenance of law and order during the strike although there were disturbances and looting of shops and property, particularly in Marsh Lane.[42] The damage was reminiscent of the looting during the *Lusitania* strikes in 1915 and direct references were made although the newspaper appeared to have forgotten its ambivalent stand on the so-called 'patriotism' of that time, talking now of the 'undesirable hooligan-class' which 'infests all large centres of population'.[43]

As the strikers were sacked and a new force reconstituted the *Bootle Times* reported that some of these recruits were ex-servicemen, with one still in khaki, reinforcing the uprightness and respectability of soldiers serving within the community, as opposed to the mutineers amongst the police ranks.[44] This emphasis on community solidarity against the strikers was contrasted by reports of support, in the form of meetings

37 LCRO: 356 WES 8/1 WLTAF 55th and 57th Divisional Dinner Committee Minutes, 3 April 1936.

38 *Southport Guardian*, 13 April 1939, p. 4.

39 LCRO: 356 WES 8/1 WLTAF 55th and 57th Divisional Dinner Committee Minutes 1924–39. Photographs are included with the Minutes of later Annual Dinners.

40 Waller, *Democracy and Sectarianism*, p. 284.

41 *Bootle Times*, 8 August 1919, p. 4.

42 *Bootle Times*, 8 August 1919, p. 5; CL: Bootle Borough Watch Sub-Committee Minutes, 19 August 1919.

43 *Bootle Times*, 8 August 1919, pp. 4–5.

44 *Bootle Times*, 22 August 1919, p. 5.

and correspondence. The War record of the strikers was reported, with 48 of the 63 Bootle strikers having seen active service. Both sides claimed the respectability of having War service, including one of the speakers at a rally of supporters for the strike, ex-Sergeant Major Hands DCM, of the Liverpool Police.[45]

In a further characterisation of the continuity of pre-War social divisions between the two communities of Bootle and Southport, Mr. MacLeod, Secretary of the Bootle Trades Council, attacked the Borough Council 'half of whom should be in bath chairs at Southport – elderly gentlemen who were too effete to efficiently look after the affairs of the Borough'.[46] In one short sentence MacLeod highlighted the differences between the old guard and the new Labour politicians as well as the differences between the two Boroughs. Despite several public meetings organised by the Bootle Trades and Labour Council, sometimes comprising several thousand according to one report, which 'unanimously' passed resolutions against reconstitution of the force and for the reinstatement of the strikers, the campaign dissipated.

The local communities' identification with the local Battalion continued into the peacetime commemorations and activities with organisers keen to involve veterans, if they were not too badly wounded, and their families. The veterans themselves were largely compliant in this process, reintegrating in their community while proudly displaying their 7th Battalion heritage.

Local and Divisional War Memorials

The concept, design and subscription of War memorials, in Britain and France, and the associated commemorative events, are significant in terms of their number, size and publicity as they demonstrate fully the effort and contribution of the whole of the local community in the War. War memorials proliferated after the First World War for several reasons. There was a wish to memorialise the dead, as with any deceased. There was a need to commemorate the dead because they were not buried locally. There was also a spiritual need – religious or civic – to communicate the loss, sacrifice and recognition of the gap left in the local community. In Bootle and Southport there was a shared sense of community ownership and a wish to commemorate the sacrifice with permanence. It was important for the local community to have a constant reminder of the sacrifice which they had made. Three memorials serve to typify this response: Southport for its size, solidarity with the local Battalion and its utilitarian attributes; Bootle, again for its links with the Battalion and ex-servicemen; and the Divisional memorial in Givenchy, France, for its significance to continued regional community identity. The micro-politics of how the memorials were developed and opened also demonstrates the reintegration of veterans within local society.

45 *Bootle Times*, 15 August 1919, p. 6.
46 *Bootle Times*, 15 August 1919, p. 6.

The reasons for the flourishing of memorials after the Great War were mixed. Moriarty has said that their primary purpose was to console the bereaved, particularly important due to the lack of a body to grieve over.[47] Dyer recognised their function as giving shape to the past.[48] Memorials could praise the dead and their sacrifice, their heroism. They could weep for the dead and the loss. They could mark respect for the dead and make a statement that said it should never happen again. The Divisional memorial's emphasis was on the first function; Bootle's the second; and Southport's aim was the last, although there are elements of each function in all three.

There is no missing the memorial in Southport. There are few like it around the country, in terms of size and central position. It was built so that everyone would pass it and have to think about it and what it meant. This was what the War Memorial Committee wanted when they said it had to be 'lofty and well set-up, visible from a distance'.[49] A huge obelisk stands in the middle of London Square on Lord Street, the attractive and elegant Edwardian shopping centre of the town. On either side are colonnades of names of the fallen listed in alphabetical order. Emphasising the importance of the local Regiment, the King's Liverpool men are listed first, and then those from other regiments and units. The Committee calculated that c.10,000 of Southport's men and women had served in the War, from a total population of 72,500.[50] The memorial had been expected to contain 800–1000 names, and when it was opened in 1923, actually listed 1,133. A further 150 were added the following year.[51]

The Southport War Memorial Committee appeared to be egalitarian and pertinent, including four representatives of the Soldiers and Sailors Fund, two from the Comrades of the Great War Association and three serving officers. They were clearly anxious to involve and commit the veterans in the process, however arguments over the inscriptions to be used betrayed more interest in highbrow civic pride. This memorial was always going to be a major statement about the commitment and sacrifice shown by the local community and it needed to be sufficiently imposing to emphasise the scale of Southport's contribution to the War. The design competition was judged by Sir Reginald Blomfield RA.[52] Public involvement was guaranteed firstly through the subscriptions which were required to fund the project – £17,474 had been raised by

47 Moriarty, C., 'Christian iconography and First World War memorials', *Imperial War Museum Review* (1992), p. 63.

48 Dyer, G., *The Missing of the Somme* (London: Hamish Hamilton, 1994), p. 65.

49 SAL: Southport Borough Council War Memorial Committee Minutes, 25 July 1919.

50 *Southport Guardian*, 21 November 1923.

51 SAL: Southport Borough Council War Memorial Winding-Up Sub Committee Minutes, 4 January 1924.

52 The design competition was judged by Sir Reginald Blomfield RA who had designed the 'Cross of Sacrifice'. Blomfield, Herbert Baker and Edwin Lutyens were the three principal architects chosen by the War Graves Commission to design the war cemeteries: Longworth, P., *The Unending Vigil: A History of the Commonwealth War Graves Commission 1917–1984* (London: Secker and Warburg, 1967), pp. 36–7.

War memorial, Lord Street, Southport. (Private Collection)

November 1919 [53] – and secondly by requesting names to be sent in to be included on the list. Liverpool sculptor, G H Tyson Smith, was chosen to implement the Grayson and Barnish design.[54]

The opening on Armistice Day 1923 was a grand affair.[55] The involvement of Battalion, Regiment and Division emphasised the importance of all elements of the War establishment to just one of the local community memorials. Lord Derby was invited to open it, stressing his local significance. The procession was led by the 55th Divisional band, standard bearers came from the King's Liverpool Regiment and the Divisional RASC Train, and official invitees included the 7th Battalion's Festubert Association and 320 children who had been orphaned in the War. Two admission tickets were sent to the relatives of all those listed on the memorial, though they did not have reserved places. Priority at the front of the site was given to the subscribers to the Fund,[56] demonstrating a prevailing deference to the local establishment. Ex-servicemen were encouraged to take part in the procession, although tickets

53 SAL: Southport Borough Council War Memorial Committee, 3 November 1919.

54 Boorman, D., *At the Going Down of the Sun: British First World War Memorials* (York: Sessions, 1988), p. 142. Boorman also identified Tyson Smith as the sculptor of Accrington's memorial: p. 141.

55 The north east end of the cenotaph was still uncompleted at the unveiling. See *Southport Guardian*, 17 November 1923, p. 5.

56 SAL: Southport Borough Council War Memorial Committee Minutes 26 September, 20 October, 5 November, 9 November 1923; War Memorial Opening Committee Minutes 2 October, 8 October 1923.

for the enclosure were restricted.[57] Reportedly, 2,000 people walked in the procession and 30,000 lined the streets.[58]

The significance of the occasion cannot be overstated. The *Southport Guardian* was not unusual in devoting several pages to reports and photographs, and to a full list of the names on the cenotaph. Ironically, this edition of the newspaper itself has become a memorial. The paper emphasised in particular the 320 'Hero' children who took part, listing them all with their ages and addresses. Aged between five and fourteen, they laid wreaths for their dead fathers, many of them with their medals pinned to their coats. One inscription was reported 'In remembrance of the daddies who did not come back, from one whose daddy did come back'.[59] In a separate report a veteran who walked in the procession wrote that there were reckoned to be over 1,000 ex-servicemen on parade. If accurate, that would mean around half of the procession was made up of local veterans. Maintaining the class and status afforded military officers during the War, the newspaper published a long list of officers in full.[60]

The unveiling of the memorial was an opportunity to re-emphasise the role of the whole local community in the War. It was estimated that 10,000 people had been with the forces, and in addition there were the VAD hospitals, troop billets, the Red Cross and the voluntary and charitable organisations all contributing to the War effort. The stress laid on the children reflected not only the sacrifice of their fathers, but also the continuing community and the hope for the future.

The memorial which can best be compared to that in Southport is the one unveiled a year earlier in King's Gardens, Stanley Road, Bootle. The two major centres of the area and bases for the Battalion had very different memorials. Southport opted for a large, sprawling secular monolith. The Bootle War Memorial Committee [61] went for a more figurative, though still secular, approach with an imposing set of figures, identifying with the people who had fought – soldier, sailor, airman – and who they had fought for – a woman and her child.

Work began to clear the site in late May 1922 and by October of that year the memorial was ready for unveiling. The ceremony was widely covered in the newspaper, with photographs and a full list of the names of the dead from Bootle, listed on the memorial.[62] Local Councillors and dignitaries were present, but few from the military establishment. In fact, although 7th King's – 'Bootle's Own' – formed a guard of honour, Colonel Hemelryk OC was unable to be present. The choice of Major

57 *Southport Guardian*, 14 November 1923, p. 4.

58 *Southport Guardian*, 21 November 1923, p. 6.

59 *Southport Guardian*, 21 November 1923, p. 7.

60 *Southport Guardian*, 21 November 1923, p. 6.

61 Consisting of Alderman Mack J.P., who had sat on the Military Tribunal and whose son had been killed, Councillors King and Rafter, Mr J.W. Doodson, Mr James Rogerson, Mr Hugh McQuaker, Mrs W.A. Jones, Mrs Annie Malcolm and Mrs MH Hazlewood.

62 *Bootle Times*, 20 October 1922, p. 5. A further 300 names were collected over the following months and added later. See *BootleTimes*, 25 May 1923, p. 5.

Airman sculpture, Bootle war memorial. (Author)

Burnie to unveil the memorial was an interesting one, given that other candidates may have included Haig, Lord Derby or possibly Jeudwine. Burnie had ended the War commanding 2/7th Battalion, still a local Bootle man, who also happened to be the Parliamentary candidate for the Liberal Party in the forthcoming elections. He spoke movingly as he unveiled the memorial. 'He had known so many of those whose names were there; like them he was not a professional soldier; he had gone out and suffered with them, but he was spared to return. "What words can I use to express the thoughts that come from my heart when I think of these my comrades, playfellows at school, comrades of my youth?"' He went on to make a rather more controversial plea:

> I am fit. I am strong, and many like me returned fit, but many others returned maimed in body, ruined in health, and weakened in mind. To those who have this world's goods I say give of them freely; to those who have less, give sympathy. They have passed through hell. I say it is our right and our duty to help them.[63]

This closing appeal – which emphasised the veterans who returned in a way apparently not reflected in Southport – was picked on by Alderman Turner at a meeting during the following week when he accused Burnie of using the occasion to make a political speech. Letters to the paper, however, were more critical of the Conservative Alderman – 'how many men of a military age in the Conservative Party in the Bootle Town Council went and did their bit for King and Country?'[64] Another wrote: '[Dr. Turner's sarcastic remarks] are uncalled for and ill become a man of his position.'

A number of correspondents emphasised Burnie's credentials as a local man, and said they would vote for him even though they were usually Conservative. Burnie's War record was clearly an important factor in this decision:

> He is an old Volunteer and territorial, just a private until war came, when he immediately gave up home life and business and was given a commission in 7th King's. He trained hundreds, perhaps thousands of men at Blackpool and Canterbury, and then went out himself. Thus he rose from the ranks to be temporary Lieutenant-Colonel, and was demobilised with the rank of Major. How he won his MC is a very fine example of coolness and devotion to duty under heavy fire.

The same writer concluded, 'there is no real Conservative to vote for here, so I shall vote for the next best thing'.[65]

63 *Bootle Times*, 20 October 1922, p. 5.
64 *Bootle Times*, 10 November 1922, p. 2.
65 *Bootle Times*, 10 November 1922, p. 2. The general election on 15 November 1922 had been caused by the prolonged collapse of Lloyd George's post-war coalition. Bonar Law's new Cabinet, which included Lord Derby, was confirmed as the sole party for government. However, there was division within the Conservatives as some had wanted to remain in

Two more ordinary complaints were also made. A veteran, Edward Cox, complained that he was debarred entry to the ceremony as he had no ticket 'beyond my 1914–15 medal. I thought that was quite enough', and was then forcibly ejected by the police. The editor thought it necessary to point out that there was limited space in the gardens and that if it had been practicable, room would have been made for all the ex-servicemen to honour their dead comrades.[66] Another letter writer, a bereaved mother, was upset that her son's name had been almost permanently obscured by flowers and wreaths laid against the names on the memorial, rather than on the steps.[67]

The memorialisation process continued throughout 1920 and 1921 as the fruition of the establishment across the area of local war memorial committees. There is evidence of a desire to create something which would be an organic memorial, relevant and useful to the living but established in the names of the dead. A very limited example of this was at Ince Blundell where their main civic memorial was a drinking fountain, 'Erected by public subscription to remember the men of Ince Blundell who served in the Great European War AD 1914 to AD 1918'.

Litherland Council agreed to set up a memorial committee before the Armistice was signed to erect a permanent war memorial.[68] Unusually, the War Memorial Committee had all Council members invited, as well as local religious ministers, employers and representatives from ex-servicemen. Additionally, there were representatives from the Dockers' Union, Merchant Service Guild, Allotment Holders Association, Oddfellows, Friendly Societies, Tramway Workers Union, schoolteachers and chairmen of political clubs. Even after such a range, the question of representatives from workmen of local firms was deferred.[69]

However, in May 1923, a War Memorial Committee was re-established to look at endowing beds in a local hospital as a suitable memorial. The Chairman of the Council wrote that 'Cenotaphs do not appeal, as they are painful reminders. I would prefer some form of recognition to benefit the living, whilst at the same time being a memorial to the dead… Such a memorial would be a true commemoration'.[70] His words echoed the nature of a debate, common by 1923, which balanced remembrance of the War with the economic crisis. In the end, Litherland erected a Doric style column outside the Town Hall. It included the words: 'Erected to the Glory of God in Fond memory of the men of Litherland who made the Supreme sacrifice for God, King and Country in the Great War 1914–1919' – a strangely religious tone for such a secular beginning.

Coalition with the Liberals, to keep the socialists out. The Liberals had been split between Asquith and Lloyd George's followers, since midway through the War. A vote for Burnie would be a vote for the Coalition which had won the War – but had, arguably, lost the Peace.

66 *Bootle Times*, 20 October 1922, p. 2.
67 *Bootle Times*, 17 November 1922, p. 2.
68 CL: Litherland UDC Minutes Vol. X, 4 November 1918.
69 CL: Litherland UDC War Memorial Committee Minutes, 21 January 1919.
70 *Bootle Times*, 11 May 1923, p. 5.

The memorialisation in Southport was not just the stone edifice. Original costs for the London Square Memorial were not to exceed £14,000, but the total cost of the memorial to the fallen of Southport was not to exceed £30,000. As well as the monument, the War Memorial Committee wanted to balance that spending with an ongoing benefit for the local community. In this vein, a victory scholarship was established for children of men or women who had been killed, and also an additional wing to the Southport infirmary, costing around £12,000, was envisaged.[71] The annex was opened by Lord Derby following the unveiling of the main memorial in London Square.[72] The first applications for the Victory Scholarship Fund were agreed in October 1924 and applications continued to be approved up until 1935.

The majority of stone memorials however, mixed the quasi-religious with public duty. A Celtic cross was an understated religous motif, found at Formby, Ainsdale and even Crossens, where it stands within a churchyard. Ainsdale's tribute, which has one of the few women commemorated – Sister Stella Blandy – was also 'Erected by the residents as a mark of respect and affection 1914–1919'. At Crossens, where it stood within St. John's churchyard, the memorial was also 'Erected by the people of Crossens to the Immortal memory of [names] who gave their lives for their country in the Great War 1914–1918'. Great Crosby provided a civic and secular memorial while Hightown and Waterloo had angels, weeping and triumphant respectively. These last two, not far apart, demonstrate the different attitudes, the one stressing grief and sacrifice, the latter, the 'Five Lamps' of Waterloo, concerned with victory and glory.

The 55th Divisional memorial was established in Givenchy further reinforcing General Jeudwine's continued emphasis on the importance of loyalty and identity in the Division and its constituent units after the War. This emphasis can also be seen in reunions and Divisional dinners, the writing of a Divisional History and Jeudwine's own 'conversion' to the usefulness of the Territorial Force. Jeudwine's concern for Divisonal identity – and identity in Lancashire – went further, to include those who had died. He had already insisted that the dead were treated with honour and respect during and after battle. In his final order to the Division, he observed:

> Many, I am glad to say, who saw the formation of the Division are with us now, but very many more … are not. There are some still suffering from wounds, and some whose graves we have left on hard-fought fields and behind grim trench lines, where they faced the enemy with such splendid courage and determination. They are not forgotten.[73]

71 Southport Borough Council War Memorial Committee Minutes, 17 and 25 March; 25 July 1919.
72 *Southport Guardian*, 14 November 1923, p. 4.
73 Jeudwine Special Order of the Day 3 January 1919 quoted in Coop, *The Story of the 55th Division*, pp. 161–3.

Waterloo (Merseyside) war memorial 'Five Lamps'. (Author)

Jeudwine had been keen to mark the graves of all his troops as memorials. In instigating grave markers for his Divisional heroes Jeudwine was unique, and combined the loyalty of the Division with the importance of respect for the dead. Canon Coop led two expeditions to place Divisional 'cocardes' on graves of men from the West Lancashire Division, in February and October 1919. While a further visit in 1920 was also planned it is not known if this went ahead. The visits were with the full co-operation of the Graves Identification Committee and travel was provided, at a reasonable fee, by Thomas Cook and Son.[74] According to Coop, they were the only Division to do something like this. The cocarde was a metal roundel with the Lancashire rose in the centre and around the edge the Divisional motto: 'They win or die who wear the rose of Lancaster'.[75]

Grave marker or *Cocarde*, instituted by Jeudwine. (Author)

The cocardes had first been planned by Jeudwine in the summer of 1918. In a memo to staff he had expressed concern about the treatment of the dead, desiring more reverence to be paid. While he acknowledged the difficulties of the times, and the tendency of war to make its participants appear callous, he believed that honour and reputation demanded more thoughtful treatment. This would be achieved by railing off the area, keeping them tidy and well maintained wherever possible. Additionally, he wrote: 'Arrangements are being made to procure a supply of metal divisional badges, similar to the 'Cocarde' placed by the French on every soldier's grave … placing one over the grave of every soldier of the 55th Division who has fallen in France or Flanders'.[76] The £800 which these memorial tablets cost was raised through public subscription.[77] While Coop took 3,000 markers in October they only used half that number, largely because there were so many unknown soldiers buried. Coop was particularly upset at

74 D.W. Lloyd has emphasised the commercial significance of Battlefield Tourism to such agents as Thomas Cook. See Lloyd, David W., *Battlefield Tourism: Pilgrimage and the Commemoration of the Great War in Britain, Australia and Canada 1919–1939* (Oxford: Berg Publishers, 1998), pp. 28–31.

75 Daglish correspondence in *Stand To! The Journal of the Western Front Association*, No. 61, April 2001, pp. 44–5.

76 LCRO: 356 FIF 15 Memo from Jeudwine 28 June 1918 Jeudwine MSS.

77 *Bootle Times*, 2 August 1918, p. 2.

this 'appalling' feature, though he noted that it mainly occurred on the Somme, when the men were still casual about wearing identity discs.[78]

At this stage, the graves all had wooden crosses and it would have been easy to nail on the cocarde.[79] It was equally easy to remove them and Coop found that many placed at Gorre in February 1919 had later been removed for souvenirs. Coop also expressed concern at the practice of the Graves Commission in bringing in men from smaller cemeteries into large, new cemeteries – he saw it as the only sensible answer, but it meant that men they had buried in a known spot were now difficult to find, such as the twenty Liverpool Regiment men killed between January and May 1915, reburied in February 1920 from King's Claire cemetery in Cuinchy – also known as King's Liverpool Graveyard[80] – at the Woburn Abbey Cemetery.[81]

In erecting a memorial in France, the Division followed the pattern of many other army units.[82] The memorial to the men of the 55th Division stands in Givenchy at the edge of the village. To see it now, not too prominent at the edge of the village, one could concur with the sentiment of a tourist in the 1930s who said 'why did they put it here of all places, right off the beaten track?', perhaps not realising that it was sited to commemorate their stand in April 1918.[83] Initially, the 55th Divisional Association had wanted the memorial to be on the mound where Givenchy church had stood, or at Windy Corner but the Mairie 'begged us to have it in Givenchy'.[84] It was unveiled by Marshal Joffre at a ceremony on Whit Sunday 1921.[85] Visiting arrangements for

78 *Bootle Times*, 2 August 1918, p. 2; IWM Ref. 72/82/1. Coop to Jeudwine, 16 October 1919, Jeudwine MSS.

79 Gravestones did not start to arrive in France until 1920. See Longworth, *The Unending Vigil*, p. 72.

80 There are seventeen Liverpool's buried at Woburn Abbey Cemetery, killed between January and October 1915. Eleven were from the 1/5th Battalion and three from 1/7th. Although Woburn Abbey expanded as a result of reburials from a number of local smaller cemeteries, only the five mentioned above are known to have come from 'King's Claire'. See *War Graves of the British Empire*, Vol. 24, Imperial War Graves Commission (1929) and research corrrespondence. Note also references to Kingsclere being used as a Battalion Headquarters for the Royal Sussex Regiment in 1916: Blunden, E., *Undertones of War* (London: Penguin, 2000, first published 1928), p. 26.

81 The Graves Commission's practice is well documented by Longworth in *The Unending Vigil*. For the Somme area, Martin and Mary Middlebrook's guide provides brief analysis of the differences beween battlefield, communal and concentrated cemetery sites. It also gives details of the history of each cemetery in the sector; Middlebrook M. and M., *The Somme Battlefields: A Comprehensive Guide from Crecy to the Two World Wars* (London: Penguin, 1994).

82 For an earlier war, there is the King's Liverpool Regiment memorial to the dead of the South African wars in St. John's Gardens, Liverpool.

83 Lloyd, *Battlefield Tourism*, p. 42 quoting from 'The Loos Battlefield Revisited' in Swinton, E. (ed.), *Twenty Years After: The Battlefields of 1914–18 Then and Now*, Vol. 1, (London: Amalgamated Press, 1936–1937), p. 531.

84 IWM Ref.72/82/1 Revd. Coop to Jeudwine, 19 August 1920, Jeudwine MSS.

85 *Southport Guardian*, 9 April 1921, p. 4.

members of the Divisional Association to attend were made by Thomas Cook's, third class travel for the weekend costing £8–10s-0d.[86] Liverpool later adopted the village, under a scheme addressed below, and built a memorial hall close by the Divisional cross, opened by Liverpool's Lord Mayor on 28 September 1924.[87] This was followed by a later gift from the Divisional Comrades Association of stained glass windows and a peal of bells.[88] In 1929, the memorial was officially handed over to the care of the Imperial War Graves Commission at a ceremony attended by various units of the Division. Twenty-six oak saplings were planted at the same time.[89]

The location of the memorial was a deliberate reference to the action which firmly established the combat effectiveness of the Division and confirmed the significance of its Lancastrian identity, both of which Jeudwine was so keen to rely upon and develop. Givenchy was as important to the Division as a whole as Festubert was to Southport in establishing and maintaining that sense of community identity.

Festubert: Association & Adoption

Both Givenchy and Festubert were significant places for the 1/7th King's Battalion and 55th Division, marked by memorials and associations. At its most obvious level, the Divisional Comrades Association had their first Annual Meeting on 10 April and the Festubert Association held its annual events around 15 May, the dates of the battles. In pursuing the adoption of the villages by Liverpool and Southport, the link with the community identity which had grown during the War was firmly maintained. In fact, only a new conflict in 1939 stepped in the way.

Other battalions had a claim to the connection with Festubert – 5th King's, for example, were also in the battle in 1915, and the Berkshires had also been in the first attack – but Southport's 7th Battalion reunions were called the 'Festubert Association' from the start. The Battalion had held reunions on Armistice night since 1920,[90] but prior to that a social club had already been established. Colonel Hemeryk advertised in the *Bootle Times* for comrades of all three units of 7th Battalion – perhaps as he had ended up as the Colonel of the Third Line – to gather together for 'social intercourse and reminiscence under pleasant conditions'. His aim, according to the item, was to resume the Territorial Force connection, to promote welfare, and not lose the comradeship built up on the battlefield. The newspaper went on to report that Park Street

86 IWM Ref. 72/82/4 Invitation and visit details, Jeudwine MSS.
87 *The Times*, 29 September 1924 in IWM Ref. 72/82/1 Jeudwine MSS.
88 *Liverpool Daily Post* and *Mercury*, 7 September 1931 – in IWM Ref. 72/82/1 Jeudwine MSS.
89 *Liverpool Courier*, 22 May 1929, p. 7; *Daily Sketch*, 20 May 1929, p. 10; programme of the Blessing of the Trees, Whit Sunday 1929; Invitation and visit itinerary – IWM Ref. 72/82/2 Jeudwine MSS.
90 *Southport Visiter*, 6 November 1920, p. 6; 13 November 1920, p. 7.

The 55th Divisional war memorial at Givenchy. (Author)

Headquarters already had facilities which were being used by Battalion veterans. The social divide remained, however: the Sergeant's Mess was 'very well furnished' while the men's room was 'more plainly furnished', though of course 'not less comfortable'.[91] In Southport the Soldiers' Club, under the presidency of Miss Willett, had taken similar steps to be open as a free social centre for demobbed veterans.[92]

In 1922, again it was a group of officers of the Battalion who decided to establish the Association on a more formal footing. This automatically made it less attractive to the other ranks. The Association's aim was to hold a celebration of survivors of Festubert, open to those who had fought there, and those who would have done if they had not been out of the line for some reason at that time. One suggestion was to hold a re-enactment of the battle at the war memorial. This suggestion was not pursued.[93]

The Festubert Association established a committee, still dominated by officers, with Captain Hodge as President, Major Blumberg, Captains Paton, Patterson and Pittendrigh as Vice-presidents, Captain Taylor as Secretary, Mr. (Lieutenant)

91 *Bootle Times*, 4 April 1919, p. 5.
92 *Southport Guardian*, 15 March 1919, p. 4.
93 *Southport Guardian*, 8 April 1922, p. 7.

Wainwright as Assistant Secretary, Mr. (Lieutenant) Hodson as Treasuer, and Messrs. Sharrocks, Arthur Butterworth, Walters and Cash on the Committee. The chief aim of the Association was to hold a hot-pot supper to bring together as many local veterans of the battle as possible on or near the anniversary of Festubert.[94] There appears not to have been the welfare role concerning the men to which the Divisional Association at least aspired. The first event, held in May 1922, was attended by over 100 people, with guests in Lieutenant Colonel White, MP, Colonel Formby, Lieutenant Colonel P.H. Hemelryk and the Deputy Mayor.[95] The Deputy Mayor, Councillor Potts, was largely responsible for driving the adoption of Festubert by Southport and a worthy guest in his own right who continued to be invited as years went on, but it can have been no coincidence that it was he as deputy, rather than the Mayor herself, who attended the inaugural reunion. The Mayor, Miss Hartley, would have been the only woman in attendance.

The reunion continued in much the same vein each year. There were guests and toasts, and a speech about regimental tradition which reinforced the military aspect to what had become a very social affair. The Kings' regimental tradition was of more importance here than the 55th Divisional one, although undoubtedly many members were common to both Associations. This reaffirmation of the significance of morale and discipline was followed by a reply, usually given by the Mayor, about the town's involvement in the War. This was a suitable balance to the event, demonstrating the continued shared identity between soldier and civilian. The evening was considered so relevant to the community that the newspapers reported proceedings verbatim. The fayre rarely strayed from hot-pot, but after several years at the Queen's Hotel, they moved to the Imperial Hotel in 1925.[96] There were close links and interest with the progress on the adoption of Festubert and the building of the Memorial Hall. The Association was also a key invitee to lay a wreath on Armistice Day. However, they also agreed to lay a wreath at the memorial on the anniversary of the Festubert Battle, but it was decided that it should be on the nearest Sunday as there would be conflict between the laying of the wreath and getting to the dinner on time.[97] It was unanimously agreed that Sergeant Hines, crippled at Festubert and confined to a wheelchair, would lay that first wreath the next day.[98]

The onset of high unemployment may have accounted for the low – 60 – attendance in 1924, but the outside world rarely seems to have played any part in the celebrations. That was not the case at the inaugural first dinner when the Deputy Mayor was speaking. Councillor Potts was explaining that the building of the War Memorial had been delayed due to costs of wages to the workers, when a heckler shouted that the

94 *Southport Guardian*, 8 April 1922, p. 7.
95 *Southport Guardian*, 17 May 1922, p. 6.
96 *Southport Guardian*, 16 May 1925, p. 4.
97 *Southport Visiter*, 17 May 1924, p. 6.
98 *Southport Visiter*, 20 May 1924, p. 7.

wages were poor. A shouting match clearly ensued, which Potts was able to win.[99] The aim of the Festubert Association continued to be to get together with old comrades, reinforcing the importance and links with the battle and the place for Southport, and as Major Blumberg said in his presidential address in 1925, the laying of a wreath was 'not a passing phase, but a perpetual pilgrimage'.[100]

And so it proved, as reunions continued on the anniversary of the battle. The eighteenth Annual Reunion on 13 May 1939 marked the twenty-fourth anniversary. The dinner was chaired by Major Eckes and apologies included those from Major Thompson and Captain Marriott. The following day the Association held a service at St. Andrew's church, a procession through Southport, and the laying of wreaths at the cenotaph.[101] The importance of Festubert to the local community was only overshadowed in subsequent years by the new conflict.

The establishment of an identification between 1/7th King's Liverpool Battalion and Festubert, in May 1915, was immortalised by the whole community in Southport's choice of Festubert as its 'god-child' under the adoption scheme organised by the charity, the British League of Help for Devastated Areas of France.[102] The League of Help launched a national appeal in June 1920, writing to all municipal mayors inviting them to adopt a town in order to raise money, goods and assistance to help them recover from the War. The League's publicity stressed that these towns in north east France and Belgium had been prepared to inundate the area if the need had arisen during the German Spring Offensive in 1918. Many of the towns had been destroyed by British shelling, not just German bombardment.[103] The reference to the Spring Offensive may have had a particular resonance in Southport, but the Mayor was more concerned in his re-election campaign to promote any activity regarding such a scheme.[104]

The British League of Help was only one of a number of charities and organisations working to complement the Reparations. It was established by Lady Lilias Bathurst,

99 *Southport Guardian*, 17 May 1922, p. 6.
100 *Southport Guardian*, 16 May 1925, p. 4.
101 *Southport Guardian*, 17 May 1939, p. 7.
102 For an initial study of the activities of the League of Help see: Gregson, A., 'The British League of Help for Devastated Areas of France: A forgotten memorial of the Great War', *Stand To! The Journal of the Western Front Association* No. 66 (January 2003), pp. 23–27 and Lewis, B.F., 'Adoptive Kinship and the British League of Help: Commemoration of the Great War through the Adoption of French Communities', PhD thesis (Reading University, 2006).
103 British League of Help Publicity Appeal brochure, Common Council papers 1921 – Corporation of London Record Office.
104 *Southport Visiter*, 28 October 1920. p. 6. Unionist Councillor Robert Wright was so busy he was barely able to send out his election address. While the *Visiter* did not stint from hounding Wright on this matter, it was equally indignant that he should have had to fight an election at all in his mayoral year. (30 October 1921, p. 6).

owner of the *Morning Post*, and run by her editor there, H A Gwynne.[105] Amongst the patrons and committee members were a number of influential figures including Viscount Burnham, owner of the *Daily Telegraph*, Major General Seely MP and the Roman Catholic Archbishop of Westminster, Cardinal Bourne.[106] A key individual, however, was Lord Derby, who presided over the London Commitee (which adopted Verdun) but had input to a number of other adoptions, notably those in the north west.[107]

The way the League operated lends further weight to the main point of this thesis. The League emphasised the importance of choosing a town to adopt where there was some connection and identity, where the local Battalion had fought and where local men were buried or commemorated. As part of the adoption process, the League supplied lists of towns who would be a suitable 'God child' and also historical information about the war record of appropriate battalions.[108] The list of adoptions demonstrated how effective this was in securing links between towns in Britain and France.[109]

Correspondence in the Derby papers reveals the extent of Lord Derby's 'facilitation 'of the process. The towns of Festubert, Merville, Armentiéres, Etricourt, Estaires and Givenchy were being actively promoted by the League for adoption at the end of 1920. The *Southport Visiter* campaigned for Merville.[110] In the face of some frustration from the League's secretary, Gilmer argued that a place like Southport 'untouched by the War', should commit to help. Derby stepped in and placated the organisers. He understood that 'these Lancashire people are funny to deal with' and rewrote Gilmer's draft.[111] As Liverpool was developing its adoption of Givenchy, Gorre and Essars, Derby proposed that Southport should adopt one of the other local villages with which it had direct links – Festubert.[112]

Gilmer had wanted Windsor, as the home of the Guards, to adopt Festubert – the Guards Cemetery at Windy Corner standing in the village.[113] Turton, near Bolton,

105 Gwynne's correspondence with his proprietor has been edited and published in Wilson, K. (ed.), *The Rasp of War: The Letters of H.A. Gwynne to the Countess Bathurst 1914–1918* (London: Sidgwick & Jackson, 1988). This correspondence provides a background to his motivation in running the League of Help, and Wilson makes interesting comment on him and his connections, referring to his anti-Semitism and anti-libertarian perspective, and said he was 'never far from paranoia', (p. 322, p. 329 and p. 321).

106 IWM Ref. K33309, First Annual Report British League of Help.

107 LCRO: 920 DER (17) 38/4 correspondence on British League of Help Derby MSS.

108 Brotherton Library, Leeds University (BLLU) MS deposit 1990/1 Ref. 2031 Bathurst Collection Letter, 27th September 1920.

109 BLLU: Ref. 2040 Bathurst Collection Second Annual Report of the British League of Help.

110 *Southport Visiter*, 16 October 1920, p. 5.

111 LCRO: 920 DER (17) 38/4 Correspondence with Gilmer, 5 and 6 January 1921, Derby MSS.

112 LCRO: 920 DER (17) 38/4 correspondence, 27 January 1921, Derby MSS.

113 A number of 7th Battalion men are buried in the Guards Cemetery at Windy Corner, Cuinchy. Some were killed in the 1918 attack, but mainly they are from the 1915 Battle of

had also been interested in adopting Festubert at the time Southport was making its decision. As both towns agreed the adoption on consecutive nights, unbeknown to each other, Turton bowed in favour of Southport as the wealthier of the two places and therefore more able to contribute effectively to its recovery.[114] Bootle, Litherland and Great Crosby dallied with the scheme, but only Southport went through with it.[115] The emphasis on local identification with the adopted town was mirrored across west Lancashire. While Liverpool, the heart of the King's Regiment and headquarters of the Division, adopted Givenchy, Preston had adopted La Bassée, and Blackpool, Neuve Chapelle, both towns in the Lys where Lancashire men had fought in 1915 and 1918.[116]

The League had been concerned to see Southport take on a bigger task and as Festubert had barely 400 inhabitants in 1920, compared to 1,347 in 1914, and Merville had over 4,000 returning people, the need in the larger town was greater.[117] As the mayor was 'indisposed', having less interest in the scheme than in his own re-election, the League's campaign was largely run by the *Southport Visiter*. An initial meeting was held at the end of November[118] and another public meeting addressed by Lord Derby in February 1921 agreed adoption of Festubert.[119] This gave an opportunity for the *Southport Guardian* to re-emphasise the appropriateness of the adoption and to reprint Private Carl Purser's account of the battle from 1915.[120]

The nature of the help provided came by way of raising money through public subscription to build a memorial hall in the village. Subscription lists were printed in the newspapers and letters from the Mairie reproduced, thanking the people of Southport and explaining what state Festubert was in following the War.[121] By May, the public fund had reached £938 5s 6d.[122] There was considerable delay in building the hall, to the frustration of the Southport Council who, in wanting to secure the recognition in everyone's minds, revealed another ulterior motive.[123]

More importantly for League aims than a community hall were the links between the two towns. The Second Annual Report referred to the links between the young people of Britain and France as being the 'most valuable propoganda for the friendship

Festubert including Lieutenants Kingston Adams, Gamble and McClelland and Captain Tweedale. See *Index of Cemeteries*, Commonwealth War Graves Commission.

114 *Southport Guardian*, 12 February 1921, p. 5.

115 Bootle held a lantern lecture in aid of the Fund for the War Devastated Villages of France in November 1921, a separate organisation to the League, but one with similar aims and Approaches. See *Bootle Times*, 11 November 1921, p. 5.

116 IWM Ref. K33309 First Annual Report of the British League of Help, 1921.

117 *Southport Visiter*, 7 October 1920, p. 6.

118 *Southport Visister*, 27 November 1920, p. 5 and 8.

119 *Southport Visiter*, 5 February 1921, p. 6; *Southport Guardian* 5 February 1921 p. 7.

120 *Southport Guardian*, 12 February 1921, p. 8.

121 *Southport Visiter*, 19 February 1921, p. 4.

122 *Southport Visiter*, 7 May 1921, p. 2.

123 *Southport Guardian*, 17 May 1924, p. 7.

The community hall, opposite the Divisional memorial at Givenchy. (Author's private collection)

Plaque on the community hall, Givenchy citing Liverpool's gift. (Author's private collection)

Community Hall, Festubert. (Author)

of the two nations'.[124] To further these links for the future, a party of schoolchildren from across the country was taken over to France in 1923. Originally Gilmer had planned to take 1,000 children for a fortnight,[125] but this was modified considerably to 350. The children were to be between thirteen and sixteen and whose fathers had been killed in the War. There were so many applications that the names were drawn from a hat.[126] Ten children from Southport went on this first visit over the Whit weekend, receiving a mayoral send-off at the Town Hall.[127] The boys were: Cyril Ardron, James Ainscough, Cuthbert Corcoran, Luke Woodward, R. Leadbetter, Leonard Smith, George Benson, L. Oldfield, James Howard and Albert Long.[128] In an item commemorating the 50th anniversary of the War, the *Southport Visiter* described the links with Festubert and recorded that these trips continued every year up to the Second World War. In an item commerorating the 50th Anniversary, the *Southport Visiter* noted the important link with Festubert.[129] As well as visiting various battlefield sites and

124 BLLU: Ref. 2040 Second Annual Report of the British League of Help, Bathurst Collection.
125 LCRO: 920 DER (17) 38/4 Correspondence with Gilmer, 28 May 1923, Derby MSS.
126 *Southport Visiter*, 12 May 1923, p. 6.
127 *Southport Visiter*, 17 May 1923, p. 2.
128 *Southport Visiter*, 26 May 1923, p. 7.
129 *Southport Visiter*, 11 July 1964, p. 7.

Local street in Festubert named after Southport. (Author's private collection)

Festubert itself, the boys laid wreaths at the graves of two local teachers from Holy Trinity School who served in 7th King's – Sergeant Knowles at the Guards cemetery, and Sergeant Loveridge in Béthune.[130]

The adoption of Festubert and subsequent activity can be seen as a key aspect to the identification with the War Front by the local community. The notion of this 'community', however, was expanded to include the people of Festubert itself. These school visits developed into an exchange programme and children from Festubert came to stay in Southport the following August.[131] Such a development should be seen as the successful culmination of the work of the charity, tapping into the community need for wider demonstrations of its role in the war itself.

Festubert Recherche

In returning to France, one of the more privileged veterans, Colonel Marriott, emphasised the significance of Festubert for the men who survived. It had been their first taste of real action and the Battalion suffered great losses in that one event.

130 *Southport Visiter*, 26 May 1923, p. 7.
131 *Southport Guardian*, 10 May 1924, p. 5.

Pilgrims, tourists and visitors in the years since have had a variety of motivations. For the bereaved it was often a part of the grieving process, an attempt to get close to where their loved ones had last been. Lloyd suggested that while the visits were multi-faceted, they had something in common – they were an attempt by the individual to relate the tangible place to their own remembered experience of the War, be it Home or War Front.[132]

Marriott revisited with a variety of motives but one of them seems to have been guilt at his own survival.[133] He mourned the loss of his friends and comrades in the attack, for many of whom he felt responsible. When he returned there in December 1918 he wrote two letters home, one to his wife Cicely – sister of Kingston Adams – and a less censored version to his brother Tom:

> I found Kingston's grave, by a destroyed German pillbox. Lieutenant Gamble is there too and 4 of the King's lead company. The Germans had a little graveyard in the same field. I retraced all the events of 16–19 May. I found several other graves including Major Hughes and Captains Tweedale, McLelland, Hannon. I went 'over the top' where I led the Company over. Then turned south and walked for hours through an unmaginable country of trenches shell holes and all the debris of battle: skulls, skeletons, equipment right on to Givenchy. Here I inspected the mine craters, dozens of them some nearly 100 yards across, and then on to the La Bassee Canal and on to … Brick Stacks at Cuinchy. Could not locate the old Headquarters and with difficulty located old front line between the brick-stacks … of 1915 are still there. The line had remained stationary there since the beginning until the last retreat, and the back areas are simply dotted with huge cemeteries. I could not find the grave of Captain Chisholm in Festubert. I did find many of the earlier graves of 1914 and 1915. I made my way back through le Plantin and Gorre to Béthune, walking all the way. There is not a single house standing either in Gorre or Essars, places we knew so well in 1915.[134]

While Cicely was given a clear picture of the physical devastation, Tom also learnt of the grim reality:

> [T]he old ground is desolate beyond description, not a soul for miles, and the place strewn with upturned skeletons, heads and boots with feet in them. I was glad to come away. I actually found the old trench bay I was lying in when a runner crept up with an order to 'go over the top' and I went over.[135]

132 Lloyd, *Battlefield Tourism*, pp. 217–8.
133 This was a not uncommon experience: Gregory, *The silence of memory*, p. 19; Lloyd, *Battlefield Tourism*, p. 133; van Emden, R. and Humphries, S., *Veterans: The Last Survivors of the Great War* (London: Leo Cooper, 1998), p. 10.
134 Marriott letter to wife, Cicely, 10 and 11 December 1918.
135 Marriott letter to brother, Tom Marriott, 12 December 1918.

Through letters like these from Colonel Marriott, the Home Front got to hear from soldiers directly about the War they were fighting, from beginning to beyond the end. At the same time, Marriott's correspondence appears to indicate that the soldiers themselves survived much of the experience by being able to tell their families and friends and feel part of that wider community.

Conclusion

The declaration of the Armistice was felt in Bootle and Southport, as across the country, as a bitter-sweet experience; relief and rejoicing mixed with the trauma of the bereaved and disabled. The key aspect in marking it, with the Peace Day and in subsequent anniversaries, was the continued connection these gave the community with the experience of the War. They provided further opportunities for the community to single out the 1/7th Battalion as the important element in the formal events. This extended beyond the formality of the unit to individual soldiers, although the extent to which attention was paid to the veterans and especially to War casualties, was mixed. Nonetheless, the erection of momuments to the dead and the number of charitable ventures for the living indicated that the locality was committed to mark and respect the men who had fought and died.

The limited amount of opposition to these processes, even in the context of an increasingly failing economy, strengthens the significance of that commitment. Even on opposite sides of an industrial dispute, such as the Bootle police strike of 1919, claims and links to servicemen were blatant. Opposition by veterans to demonstrations of remembrance was limited, but it appears that any high level involvement by veterans in the organisation or development of memorialisation was restricted mainly to the officers. Even the association into, albeit smaller, comrade groups had limited common appeal, except perhaps for the creation of social club premises. Nonetheless, those Associations did maintain the loyalties and traditions forged in the trenches by linking themselves to key battle honours. These links were also continued and reinforced by the local communities who took part in the adoptions scheme of French villages, the links with Festubert proving to be one of the most enduring in Great Britain today.

Grave of 202768 Rifleman Harry Hulm, 5th Battalion, King's Liverpool Regiment, killed 20 September 1917, Tyne Cot Cemetery. The gravestone bears the 55th Division motto 'They win or die who wear the rose of Lancashire'. (Author)

Bibliography

PRIMARY SOURCES

The National Archives (Kew)

CAB44	Draft Official History
CAB45/120–121	Correspondence in compiling the Official History: Loos
CAB45/122–125	Correspondence in compiling the Official History: Lys
CAB45/132–138	Correspondence in compiling the Official History: Somme
CAB45/179	Correspondence in compiling the Official History:165th Brigade, Givenchy
CAB45/180	Correspondence in compiling the Official History: 166th Brigade, Givenchy
CAB45/182	Correspondence in compiling the Official History: Jeudwine
MUN3; MUN4; MUN8	Ministry of Munitions correspondence
WO154/6	V Corps Assistant Provost Marshal War Diary
WO154/8	IX Corps Assistant Provost Marshal War Diary
WO162/7	Embarkation records
WO213/3–26	Field General Courts Martial Registers
WO329	Great War Medal Roll
WO363–364	Soldiers Service records
WO374	Army Officers Service Records (TA)
WO86/65–87	District Courts Martial
WO90/6–8	General Courts Martial (Abroad) Registers
WO92/3–4	General Courts Martial (Home) Registers
WO95/1284–1288	2nd Division General Staff War Diary
WO95/1306	2nd Division Adjutant and Quarter Master General War Diary

WO95/1343	5th Brigade War Diary
WO95/1352–3	6th Brigade War Diary
WO95/1360	1/7th Battalion King's Liverpool Regiment War Diary
WO95/154–155	First Army War Diary
WO95/1630	7th Division General Staff War Diary
WO95/1636	7th Division Adjutant General War Diary
WO95/1660	22nd Brigade War Diary
WO95/185	First Army Adjutant and Quarter Master General War Diary
WO95/24	British Army of the Rhine General Staff War Diary
WO95/2899–2910	55th Division War Diary
WO95/2918	2/1 West Lancashire Field Ambulance War Diary
WO95/2918	1/3 West Lancashire Field Ambulance War Diary
WO95/2925	165th Brigade War Diary
WO95/2926	1/5th Battalion King's Liverpool Regiment War Diary
WO95/2927	1/7th Battalion King's Liverpool Regiment War Diary
WO95/2964–2975	57th Division War Diary
WO95/2980–2981	171st Brigade War Diary
WO95/2982	2/7th Battalion King's Liverpool Regiment War Diary
WO95/367	Third Army Adjutant and Quarter Master General War Diary
WO95/378	Third Army Adjutant and Quarter Master General War Diary
WO95/525–526	Fifth Army Adjutant and Quarter Master General War Diary
WO95/590–592	I Corps War Diary
WO95/754	V Corps Adjutant and Quarter Master General War Diary
WO95/760	V Corps Assistant Provost Marshal War Diary
WO95/844	IX Corps Assistant Provost Marshal War Diary
WO95/883	XI Corps General Staff War Diary
WO95/887	XI Corps Adjutant and Quarter Master General War Diary
WO95/963	XIX Corps Adjutant and Quarter Master General War Diary

Liverpool City Local Studies Library and Record Office

Liverpool Echo

356COU	Council of County Territorial Associations Minutes
356FIF	55th Division papers deposited by Jeudwine

356WES	West Lancashire Territorial and Auxiliary Force Association
920DER(17)	Papers 17th Earl Derby

Southport (Atkinson) Library, Sefton Borough Council

Southport Visiter
Southport Guardian
Formby Times
Southport Borough Council Minutes
Southport Borough Council National Aid Committee
Southport BC Recruiting Appeal Committee
Southport BC Local Food Control Committee
Southport BC Profiteering Committee
Southport BC War Memorial Committee
Southport BC War Memorial Scholarships Trustees Committee
Southport BC Watch Committee
Southport BC Medical Officer of Health reports

Crosby Library, Sefton Borough Council

Bootle Times
Waterloo and Crosby Herald and *Formby, Bootle* and *Seaforth Gazette*
Bootle Borough Council Minutes

B/MO4–8	Bootle BC Medical Officer of Health Reports
CCG/3	Christchurch Girls School logbook, Waterloo
CCW/4	Christchurch Primary School logbook, Waterloo
GC53–54	Little Crosby Local Board and Urban District Council Minutes
GC61	Great Crosby Township Overseers Minutes
LRH 1	Litherland UDC Roll of Honour Fund General Committee
LUD7	Litherland Urban District Council Minutes
SLH/2	Great Crosby Endowed Infants School logbook
SLH/5	Great Crosby Halsall Girls School logbook
STS1/4–1/17	St. Thomas School, Seaforth
WL601–602	Ince Blundell Parish Council Minutes
WL603–604	Lunt Parish Council Minutes
WL606–610	Sefton Parish Council Minutes
WS21	Waterloo UDC Tribunals Committee
WS22	Waterloo UDC Profiteering Committee
WS65	Seaforth Overseers Minutes

Lancashire Record Office

1911 Census, Lancashire
1921 Census, Lancashire
UDFo 2/4/3 and 4 Formby Urban District Council Minutes

Merseyside Record Office (Since transferred to Liverpool Record Office)
Bootle Borough Council Minutes
Litherland Urban District Council Minutes

Imperial War Museum (IWM)

72/82/1–4	HS Jeudwine papers
86/48/1	JT Lawton memoir 1/5th Battalion King's Liverpool Regiment
92/36/1	JS Handley papers 1/6th Battalion King's Liverpool Regiment
MS/E/S 851	Sub Rosa: trench magazine of the 55th Division

Liverpool University Archives

B4/44–50	Cunard Archive: Executive Committee Minutes
PR5/1	Cunard Archive: Cunard magazine Vols. 1–11
D42/C1/28	Cunard Archive: Directors' correspondence

Brotherton Library, Leeds University

G.S. – Marriott, SC	Liddle Collection
MS deposit 1990/1	Papers of Countess Bathurst

King's Regiment Collection, Museum of Liverpool Life, National Museums and Galleries on Merseyside

1982.250	Interview transcript of Arthur Critchley
1984.321	Sydney Marriott Diary

House of Lords Record Office

Vol.2 Nos. 35–83	Bonar Law Correspondence Papers

Private Collections

Cook letters	D. Spalton
Fearnhead	P. Hall
Greaves	Coles, Gregson

SECONDARY SOURCES

Place of publication is London unless otherwise stated

Anon *Record of 11th Battalion of the King's (Liverpool) Regiment, August 1914–March 1919* (Liverpool: RE Thomas & Co., 1920)

—— *History of the Ministry of Munitions Volumes I-XII* (Hassocks: Harvester Press, 1976)

—— *Manual of Military Law* (War Office, HMSO, 1914)

—— *Soldiers Died in the Great War 1914–19: Part 13 – The King's (Liverpool Regiment)* Polstead, Suffolk: J.B. Hayward & Son, 1989)

—— *The Year Illustrated: A Record of Notable Achievements and Events* (Headley Brothers, 1914, 1915, 1916, 1917, 1918

——*Votes for Women: The Events on Merseyside 1870–1928* (National Museums and Galleries on Merseyside Liverpool, 1992)

—— *War History of the 1/4th Battalion the Royal North Lancashire Regiment now the Loyal Regiment 1914–18* (Preston: George Toulmin and Sons Ltd, 1921#)

Andrews, W.L., *Haunting Years: The Commentaries of a War Territorial* (Hutchinson, 1930)

Arthur, M., *Forgotten Voices of the Great War* (Ebury Press/IWM, 2002)

Ashworth, T., *Trench Warfare 1914–18: The Live and Let Live System* (Macmillan, 1980)

Aspin, C., *The Frst Industrial Society: Lancashire* (Preston: Carnegie Publishing, 1985)

Babington, A., *For the Sake of Example: Capital Courts-Martial 1914–18 –The Truth* (Leo Cooper, 1993)

Bannister, V., (compiler) *Southport's Splendid Hearts: A Tribute to the Men of Southport Who Gave Their Lives in the Great War* (Southport: Watkinson and Bond, 2002)

Barrett, D., *Men of Letters* (Basingstoke: AA Publishing, 2014)

Baynes, J., *Morale: A Study of Men and Courage: The Second Scottish Rifles at the Battle of Neuve Chapelle 1915* (Leo Cooper, 1987)

Becke, A.F., *History of the Great War: Order of Battle of Divisions* (HMSO Part 1, 1936, Part 2A, 1936 and Part 3A, 1938)

Beckett, I.F.W., *The Great War 1914–1918* (Pearson Education Ltd, 2001)

Beckett, I.F.W. and Simpson, K. (eds.), *A Nation in Arms: A Social Study of the British Army in the First World War* (Tom Donovan Publishing, 1990)

Belchem, J., (ed.) *Popular Politics, Riot and Labour: Essays in Liverpool history 1790–1949* (Liverpool: Liverpool University Press, 1992)

Bet-El, I.R., *Conscripts: Lost Legions of the Great War* (Stroud: Sutton Publishing, 1999)

Blunden, E., *Undertones of War* (Penguin, 1982 (1928))

Bond, B. (ed.), *The First World War and British Military History*, (Oxford: Oxford University Press, 1991)

Boorman, D. *At the Going Down of the Sun: British First World War Memorials* (York: Sessions, 1988)

Bourne, J.M., *Britain and the Great War 1914–1918* (Hodder Arnold, 1989)

Braham, M., *Southport Liberal Association – The First 100 years* (Southport: M. Braham, 1985)

Braybon, G., *Women workers in the First World War* (Oxford: Routledge, 1989)

Brogden, M., *On the Mersey Beat: Policing Liverpool Between the Wars* (Oxford: Oxford University Press, 1991)

Brown, M., *The Imperial War Museum Book of the Western Front* (Sidgwick and Jackson, 1993)

Burk, K.M. (ed.), *War and the State: The Transformation of British Government 1914–1919* (London, 1979)
Burke-Gaffney M.C., Lt.Col. J.J. *The Story of the King's Regiment 1914–48* (Liverpool: Sharpe & Kellett, 1954)
Cannadine, D. (ed.), *Patricians, Power and Politics in Nineteenth Century Towns* (Palgrave Macmillan, 1982)
Cecil, H. and Liddle, P.H. (ed.), *Facing Armageddon: The First World War Experienced* (Leo Cooper, 1996)
——*At the Eleventh Hour: Reflections, Hopes and Anxieties at the Closing of the Great War, 1918* (Leo Cooper, 1998)
Chandler, G., *Liverpool Shipping: A Short History* (Liverpool: Phoenix House, 1960)
Clark, A., *The Donkeys* (Pimlico, 1991, first published 1965)
Coetzee, F. and Shevin-Coetzee, M. (ed.), *Authority, Identity and the Social History of the Great War* (Oxford: Bergahn Books, 1995)
Conan Doyle, A., *The British Campaign in France and Flanders 1915* (Hodder and Stoughton, 1917)
Connerty, I., Gilbert, M., Hart, P., MacDonald, L. and Steel, N., *At the Going Down of the Sun: 365 soldiers from the Great War* (Belgium: Lannoo, 2001)
Constantine, S., Kirby, M.W. and Rose, M.B. (ed.), *The First World War in British History* (Hodder Arnold, 1995)
Coombs, R.E.B., *Before Endeavours Fade* (Battle of Britain Prints International Ltd, 1994)
Coop, Rev. J.O., *The Story of the 55th (West Lancashire) Division 1916–1919* (Liverpool: *Liverpool Daily Post*, 1919)
Corns, C. & Hughes-Wilson, J., *Blindfold and Alone: British Military Executions in the Great War* (Cassell & Co, 2001)
Crosby, A., *A History of Lancashire* (Chichester: Phillimore & Co, 1998)
Cuttell, B., *148 Days on the Somme: 2nd July to 26th November 1916* (Peterborough: GMS Enterprises, 2000)
Dalton, J.W., *Conscription and Conscience: A History* (Allen & Unwin, 1922)
Davies, A.J., *To Build a New Jerusalem: The Labour Movement from the 1880s to the 1990s* (Michael Joseph, 1992)
De Groot, G., *Douglas Haig, 1861–1928* (London, 1988)
—— *Blighty: British Society in the Era of the Great War* (Longman, 1996)
—— *The First World War* (Palgrave, 2001)
De Lisle, Sir B., *Reminiscences of Sport and War* (Eyre and Spottiswoode, 1939)
Dewey, P., *War and Progress: Britain 1914–1945* (Longman, 1997)
Dyer, G., *The Missing of the Somme* (Hamish Hamilton, 1994)
Edmonds, J.E. (Gen. ed.), *History of the Great War: Military Operations, France and Belgium (ie Official History)* (Macmillan, 1922–1949)
Evans, M.M., *1918: The Year of Victories* (Leicester: Arcturus Publishing, 2002)
Farrar, M.J., *News from the Front: War Correspondents on the Western Front 1914–18* (Stroud: Sutton Publishing, 1998)

Ferguson, A.P., *Royal Air Force Woodvale: The First Fifty years* (Reading: Airfield Publications, 1991)

Ferguson, N., *The Pity of War* (Allen Lane, 1998)

Fox, J., *Forgotten Divisions: The First World War from Both Sides of No Man's Land* (Wilmslow: Sigma Leisure, 1994)

Frederick, J.B.M., (compiler), *Lineage Book of British Land Forces 1660–1978* (Wakefield: Microform Academic Publishers, 1984)

French, D., *British Strategy and War Aims 1914–1916* (Allen and Unwin, 1986)

Fridenson, P. (ed.), *The French Home Front 1914–18* (Penguin, 1977)

Fuller, J.G., *Popular Culture and Troop Morale in the British and Dominion Forces 1914–1918* (Oxford: Clarendon Press, 1990)

Fussell, P., *The Great War and Modern Memory* (Oxford: Oxford University Press, 1975)

Giblin, H., *Bravest of Hearts: The Biography of a Battalion – the Liverpool Scottish in the Great War* (Liverpool: Winordie publications, 2000)

Gilbert, M., *First World War* (Weidenfeld and Nicolson, 1994)

Graves, R., *Goodbye to All That* (Penguin, 1960, first published 1929)

Grayzel, S.R., *Women's Identities at War: Gender, Motherhood and Politics in Britain and France during the First World War* (Chapel Hill, NC: University of North Carolina Press, 1999)

Green, A.S., *Writing the Great War: Sir James Edmonds and the Official Histories 1915–1948* (Frank Cass, 2002)

Gregory, A., *The Silence of Memory: Armistice Day 1919–1946* (Oxford: Berg Publishers, 1994)

Grieves, K., *The Politics of Manpower 1914–18* (Manchester: Manchester University Press, 1988)

Griffith, P., *Battle Tactics of the Western Front: The British Army's art of attack 1916–18* (New Haven: Yale University Press, 1994)

Griffith, P. (ed.), *British Fighting Methods in the Great War* (Frank Cass, 1996)

Hardach, G., *The First World War 1914–18* (Penguin, 1977)

Hart, P., *The Somme* (Weidenfeld and Nicolson, 2005)

Haste, C., *Keep the Home Fires Burning: Propaganda in the First World War* (Allen Lane, 1977)

Hodgkinson, Capt. A., *The King's Own Territorial Forces – Being a record of the 1/5th Battalion of the King's Own (Royal Lancaster) Regiment in the European War 1914–18* (Manchester: Lewis Press, 1921)

Holmes, R., *Fatal Avenue* (Pimlico Press, 1993)

—— *Army Battlefield Guide* (HMSO, 1995)

—— *Riding the Retreat* (Jonathan Cape, 1995)

—— *War Walks* (BBC Books, 1996)

—— *The Western Front* (BBC Books, 1999)

Holt, T. and V., *Battlefields of the First World War* (Pavilion Books Ltd, 1993)

Hope, T.S., *The Winding Road Unfolds* (Putnam, 1937)

Horn, P., *Rural life in England in the First World War* (Dublin, 1984)

Hurd, A., *A Merchant Fleet at War* (Cassell and Co, 1920)

Hyde, F.E., *Liverpool and the Mersey: The Development of a Port 1700–1970* (Newton Abbot, 1971)

Hynes, S., *A War Imagined: The First World War and English Culture* (New York: Bodley Head, 1990)

James, Brig. E.A. (ed.), *Historical Records of British Infantry Regiments in the Great War 1914 – 1918* (Samson Books, 1978)

Jones, N.H., *The War Walk: A Journey Along the Western Front* (Robert Hale, 1983)

Jones, S., (ed.) *Courage Without Glory: the British Army on the Western Front 1915* (Solihull: Helion and Company, 2015)

Joyce, P., *Visions of the People* Cambridge: Cambridge University Press, 1991)

Kearsey, Lt. Col. A., *1915 Campaign in France: The Battles of Aubers Ridge, Festubert and Loos Considered in Relation to the Field Service Regulations* (Naval and Military Press (reprint), 1929)

King, A., *Memorials of the Great War in Britain: The Symbolism and Politics of Remembrance* (Oxford: Berg Publishers, 1998)

Kingsley Ward, G., *Courage Remembered: A History of the Commonwealth War Graves Commission* (HMSO, 1989)

Knightley, P., *The First Casualty: The War Correspondent as Hero, Propagandist and Mythmaker from the Crimea to Vietnam* (Andre Deutsch, 1975)

Laffin, J., *Butchers and Bunglers of World War I* (Stroud: Alan Sutton Publishing, 1988)

Latter, Maj.-Gen. J.C., *A History of the Lancashire Fusiliers 1914–18* (Aldershot: Gale and Polden, 1949)

Leed, E., *No Man's Land: Combat and Identity in World War I* (Cambridge: Cambridge University Press, 1979)

Lewis, B.F., *The British League of Help: How British Communities Helped in the Reconstruction of Devastated French Villages after the Great War* (Great Britain: direct-pod.com, 2014)

Lewis, D. (ed.), *Remembrances of Hell: The Great War Diary of Writer, Broadcaster and Naturalist – Norman Ellison* (Shrewsbury: Airlife Publishing, 1997)

Liddle, P.H., *The 1916 Battle of the Somme: A Reappraisal* (Leo Cooper, 1992)

—— *The Worst Ordeal: Britons at Home and Abroad 1914 – 1918* (Leo Cooper, 1994_

—— (ed.), *Passchendaele in Perspective: The Third Battle of Ypres* (Leo Cooper, 1997)

Lloyd, D.W., *Battlefield Tourism: Pilgrimage and the Commemoration of the Great War in Britain, Australia and Canada, 1919–1939* (Oxford: Berg Publishers, 1998)

Lloyd, N., *Loos 1915* (Stroud: Tempus Publishing, 2006)

Lloyd, N., *A Hundred Days: The end of the Great War* (Viking, 2013)

Lomas, Col. A.D. (ed.), *Territorial Force – West Lancashire Division* (Southport: The Southport Visiter, c.1910)

Longworth, P., *The Unending Vigil: A History of the Commonwealth War Graves Commission 1917–1984* (Secker & Warburg, 1967)

MacDonald, L., *They Called it Passchendaele: The Story of the Third battle of Ypres and the Men Who Fought It* (Michael Joseph, 1978)
—— *The Roses of No-Man's Land* (Michael Joseph, 1980)
—— *Somme* (Michael Joseph, 1983)
—— *1914* (Michael Joseph, 1987)
—— *1915: The Death of Innocence* (Headline Book Publishing, 1993)
Maddocks, G., *The Liverpool Pals: 17th, 18th, 19th and 20th Battalions the King's (Liverpool Regiment)* (Leo Cooper, 1991)
Marriner, S., *The Economic and Social Development of Merseyside* (Liverpool: Croom Helm, 1982)
Marriott, W.F., *The War Letters of Colonel Sidney Charles Marriott the Great War 1914-1918* (Christchurch, New Zealand: Blurb Inc., 2012)
Marwick, A., *The Deluge: British Society and the First World War* (Macmillan, 1991, first published 1965)
McCartney, H., *Citizen Soldiers: The Liverpool Territorials in the First World War* (Cambridge: Cambridge University Press, 2005)
McGilchrist, A.M, *The Liverpool Scottish 1900–1919 (1/10th and 2/10th King's)* (Liverpool: Henry Young, 1930)
McIntyre, C., *Monuments of War: How to Read a War Memorial* (Robert Hale, 1990)
Messenger, C., *Terriers in the Trenches: The Post Office Rifles at War 1914–1918* (Chippenham: Picton, 1982)
Middlebrook, M., *The Kaiser's Battle – 21st March 1918: The First Day of the German Spring Offensive* (Penguin, 1983)
—— *The First Day of the Somme, 1 July 1916* (Penguin, 1984, first published 1971)
Middlebrook, M. and M., *The Somme Battlefields: A Comprehensive Guide from Crecy to the Two World Wars* (Penguin, 1994)
Mileham, P., *'Difficulties be damned': The King's Regiment 8th, 63rd, 96th – A history of the City Regiment of Manchester and Liverpool* (Knutsford: Fleur de Lys Publishing, 2000)
Mitchinson, K.W., *Gentlemen and Officers: The Impact and Experience of War on a Territorial Regiment (London Rifles)* (Imperial War Museum, 1995)
—— *Pioneer Battalions of the Great War: Organised and Intelligent Labour* (Leo Cooper, 1997)
Moorhouse, G., *Hell's Foundations: A Town, its Myths and Gallipoli* (Dunton Green: Sceptre, 1993)
Morton, A.L., *A People's History of England* (Lawrence & Wishart, 1964)
Mottram, R.H., *The Spanish Farm Trilogy 1914–1918* (Penguin, 1979, first published 1927)
Mowat, C.L., *Britain Between the Wars 1918–1940* (Methuen, 1968)
Neal, F., *Sectarian Violence: The Liverpool experience 1819–1914. An Aspect of Anglo-Irish History* (Manchester: Manchester University Press, 1988)
Neillands, R., *The Great War Generals on the Western Front 1914–1918* (Robinson Publishing Ltd, 1999)

O'Shea, S., *Back to the Front: An Accidental Historian Walks the Trenches of World War I* (Robson Books, 1997)
Oram, G., *Death Sentences Passed by Military Courts of the British Army 1914–1924* (Francis Boutle, 1998)
—— *Worthless Men: Race, Eugenics and the Death Penalty in the British Army during the First World War* (Francis Boutle, 1998)
Palmer, A., *Victory 1918* (Wiedenfeld & Nicolson, 1998)
Panayi, P., *The Enemy in Our Midst: Germans in Britain during the First World War* (Oxford: Berg Publishers, 1991)
Passingham, I., *Pillars of Fire: The Battle of Messines Ridge June 1917* (Stroud: Sutton, 1998)
Pelling, H., *A History of British Trade Unionism* (Penguin, 1963)
Phillips, C.B. & Smith, J.H., *Lancashire and Cheshire from AD1540* (Longman, 1994)
Pidegon, T., *Somme – Flers and Gueudecourt: Battleground Europe Series* (Leo Cooper, 2002)
Pitt, B., *1918 The last act* (Papermac, 1984, first published 1962)
Preston, D., *Wilful Murder: The Sinking of the Lusitania* (Corgi, 2002)
Prior, R. and Wilson, T., *Command on the Western Front* (Oxford: Blackwell, 1992)
—— *Passchendaele: The Untold Story* (New Haven: Yale University Press, 1996)
Putkowski, J. *British Army Mutineers 1914–1922* (Francis Boutle, 1998)
Putkowski, J. & Sykes, J., *Shot at Dawn: Executions in World War One by Authority of the British Army Act* (Barnsley: Wharncliffe Publishing, 1989)
Rae, J., *Conscience and Politics: The British Government and the Conscientious Objector to Military Service 1916–1919* (Oxford: Oxford University Press, 1970)
Reader, W.J., *'At duty's call': A Study in Obsolete Patriotism* (Manchester: Manchester University Press, 1988)
Richards, W., *His Majesty's Territorial Army: A Descriptive Account of the Yeomanry, Artillery, Engineers and Infantry with the Army Service and Medical Corps Comprising 'The King's Imperial Army of the Second Line'* Vol.II (Virtue and Co, c.1910)
Roberts, E.H.G., *The Study of the 9th King's in France* (Northern, Liverpool, 1922)
Rogerson, S., *The Last of the Ebb* (York: Arthur Barker, 1937)
Royle, T., *The Kitchener Enigma* (Michael Joseph, 1985)
Samuel, R., *Theatres of Memory: Vol. I – Past and Present in Contemporary Culture* (Verso, 1994)
Samuels, M., *Command or Control? Command, Training and Tactics in the British and German Armies, 1888–1918* (Frank Cass, 1995)
—— *Doctrine and Dogma: German and British Infantry Tactics in the First World War* (Westport Conn: Greenwood Press, 1992)
Sanders, M.L., & Taylor, P.M., *British Propaganda During the First World War 1914–18* (Macmillan, 1982)
Sassoon, S., *The Complete Memoirs of George Sherston* (Faber and Faber, 1972, first published 1937)

Sheffield, G., *Leadership in the Trenches: Officer-man Relations, Morale and Discipline in the British Army in the Era of the First World War* (Macmillan, 2000)

—— *Forgotten Victory – The First World War: Myths and realities* (Headline Book Publishing, 2001)

—— *The Somme* (Cassell, 2003)

Sheffield, G. & Bourne, J., *The Haig Diaries: The diaries of Field Marshal Sir Douglas Haig* (Weidenfeld and Nicolson, 2005)

Simkins, P., *Kitchener's Army: The Raising of the New Armies 1914–16* (Manchester: Manchester University Press, 1988)

Simpson, C., *Lusitania* (Wirral: Avid Publications, 1996)

Smith, C.H., *Rising Above the Ruins in France: An Account of the Progress Made Since the Armistice in the Devastated Regions in Re-establishing Industrial Activities and the Normal Life of the People* (New York: GP Puttnam's & Sons, 1920)

Smith, H.L., *The British Women's Suffrage Campaign 1866–1928* (Longman, 1998)

Smithers, A.J., *This Fighting Nation: Lord Kitchener and His Armies* (Leo Cooper, 1994)

Stanley, Brig.-Gen. F.C., *History of the 89th Brigade 1914–18* (Liverpool: *Liverpool Daily Post*, 1919)

Stedman, M., *Somme – Guillemont* (Leo Cooper, 1998)

Steel, N. and Hart, P., *Passchendaele: The Sacrificial Ground* (Cassell & Co, 2000)

Stevenson, D., *With Our Backs to the Wall: Victory and Defeat in 1918* (Allen Lane, 2011)

Strachan, H., *The First World War: A New Illustrated History* (Simon and Schuster, 2003)

Swinton, E., (ed.), *Twenty Years After: The Battlefields of 1914-18 Then and Now* Vol. 1 (London: Amalgamated Press 1936-1937)

Taplin, E., *Near to Revolution: The Liverpool General Transport Strike of 1911* (Liverpool: Bluecoat Press, 1994)

Taylor, A.J.P., *The First World War* (Penguin, 1963)

—— *English History 1914–1945* (Oxford: Clarendon Press, 1965

Terraine, J., *The Smoke and the Fire* (Sidgwick and Jackson, 1980)

—— *Douglas Haig: The Educated Soldier* (Cassell and Co, 1963)

—— *To Win a War: 1918 the Year of Victory* (Cassell and Co, 1978)

Thom, D., *Nice Girls and Rude Girls: Women Workers in World War I* (I.B.Tauris, 1998)

Threlfall, T.R., *The Story of the King's (Liverpool) Regiment, Formerly the 8th Foot* (*Country Life*, 1916)

Tilsley, W.V., *Other Ranks* (Cobden Sanderson, 1931)

Travers, T., *How the War Was Won: Command and Technology in the British Army on the Western Front 1917–18* (Oxford: Routledge, 1992)

—— *The Killing Ground: The British Army, the Western Front and the Emergence of Modern Warfare 1900–1918* (Oxford: Routledge, 1993)

Van Emden, R., *Boy Soldiers of the Great War* (Headline, 2005)

Van Emden, R. and Humphries, S., *All Quiet on the Western Front: An Oral History of Life in Britain During the First World War* (Headline, 2003)

Van Emden, R. and Humphries, S., *Veterans: The Last Survivors of the Great War* (London: Leo Cooper, 1998)
Wadham, Lt. Col. W.F.A. and Crossley, Capt. J., *The Fourth Battalion The King's Own (Royal Lancaster) Regiment and the Great War* (Crowther and Goodman, 1935)
Waites, B., *A Class Society at War: England 1914–18* (Leamington Spa: Berg, 1987)
Waller, P.J., *Democracy and Sectarianism: A Political and Social history of Liverpool 1868–1939* (Liverpool: Liverpool University Press, 1981)
Walton, J., *Lancashire: A Social History 1558–1939* (Manchester: Manchester University Press, 1987)
—— *The English Seaside Resort: A Social History 1750–1914* (Leicester, 1983)
Wauchope, A., *A History of the Black Watch in the Great War 1914–18* Vol. II (Medici Society, 1925–6)
Wilson, K. (ed.), *The Rasp of War: The Letters of HA Gwynne to the Countess Bathurst 1914–1918* (Sidgwick and Jackson, 1988)
Wilson, T., *The Myriad Faces of War* (Cambridge: Cambridge University Press, 1988)
Winter, D., *Haig's Command: A Reassessment* (Penguin, 1991)
—— *Death's Men: Soldiers of the Great War* (Penguin, 1978)
Winter, J.M., *Socialism and the challenge of War: Ideas and Politics in Britain 1912–1918* (Routledge, 1974)
—— *Sites of Memory, Sites of Mourning: The Great War in European Cultural History* (Cambridge: Cambridge University Press, 1996)
—— *The Great War and the British people* (Macmillan, 1985)
Wolff, L., *In Flanders Fields: Passchendaele 1917* (Penguin, 1958)
Woollacott, A., *On Her Their Lives Depend: Munitions Workers in the Great War* (Berkeley: University of California Press, 1994)
Wrigley, C.J. (ed.), *A History of British Industrial Relations 1914–39* Vol. II (Hasocks: Harvester Press, 1987)
Wurtzburg, Capt. C.E., *The History of the 2/6th (Rifle) Battalion, the King's (Liverpool) Regiment 1914–19* (Aldershot: Gale & Polden, 1920)
Wylly, Col. H.C., *The Loyal (North Lancashire) Regiment* (Royal United Services Institute, 1932)
—— *The History of the Manchester Regiment (Late 63rd and 96th Foot)* (2 Vols.) (Forster, Groom & Co, 1923–5)
—— *The York and Lancaster Regiment 1758– 919* (2 Vols.) (Richmond: Butler & Tanner Ltd, 1930)
—— *The Green Howards in the Great War 1914–19* (Richmond: Butler & Tanner Ltd, 1926_
—— *The History of the 1st and 2nd Battalions the Leicestershire Regiment in the Great War* (Aldershot: Gale & Polden, 1928_
Wylly, Col. HC & Bond, R.C., *History of the King's Own Yorkshire Light Infantry* (3 Vols) (Bradford: Percy Lund, Humphries & Co, 1930)
Wyrall, E., *The History of the King's Regiment (Liverpool) 1914–19* (3 Vols.) (Edward Arnold, 1935)

—— *The West Yorkshire Regiment in the War 1914–18* (2 Vols.) (The Bodley Head, 1924–7)
—— *The East Yorkshire Regiment in the Great War 1914–18* (Harrison, 1928)
—— *The History of the Duke of Cornwall's Light Infantry 1914–19* (Methuen, 1932)
—— *The History of the 2nd Division 1914–18* (Thomas Nelson, 1921)
—— *The Gloucestershire Regiment in the War 1914–18* (Methuen, 1931)
—— *The Die-Hards in the Great War: a History of the Duke of Cambridge's Own (Middlesex Regiment) 1914–19* (2 Vols.) (Harrison & Sons, 1926–30)
—— *The History of the Somerset Light Infantry (Prince Albert's) 1914–19* (Methuen, 1927)

Articles, Periodicals, Theses & Journals

Anon, "Givenchy–Festubert April 9th–16th 1918" *Imprimeries Reunies, Boulogne-sur-Mer,* June 1918
Adams, A.J., "Working class organisation, industrial; relations and the labour unrest 1914–21" Unpublished PhD, Leicester, 1988
Bean, R., "Custom, job regulation and dock labour in Liverpool 1911 – 39" *The International Review of Social History,* 1982
—— "Police unrest, unionisation and the1919 strike in Liverpool", *Journal of Contemporary History,* Vol. 15, 1980
Bigwood, G., *The Lancashire Fighting Territorials, Country Life*, 1916
Blades, G.D, "The Battles of the Lys: The British Army on the Defensive in April 1918" M.Phil thesis King's College London, 1999
Brown, J., "Recording War Memorials in Northumberland" *The Local Historian,* November, 1996
Brown, J.H., "The King's Regiment (Liverpool) – 1.Liverpool's Volunteers and Territorials and their Shako, Helmet and Cap Badges" *The Bulletin of the Military Historical Society* Vol. IV, No.14, November 1953, pp. 23–7
Cocroft, W.D. & Leith, I., "Cunard's shellworks, Liverpool" *Archive: The Quarterly Journal for British Industrial and Transport History,* Issue 11
Englander, D., "Troops and Trade Unions, 1919" *History Today* Vol. 37, March 1987
—— "The National Union of Ex-Servicemen and the Labour Movement 1918–1920" *History*, Vol. 76, No. 246, February 1991
Finn, M., 'The Realities of War', *History Today*, Vol. 52, No. 8, August 2002
Foster, M., "Landownership and residential differentiation: a Southport case study" Unpublished BA dissertation University of Sheffield, 1987
Gardner, N., "The King's Own Royal Lancaster Regiment, 1/5th battalion, Territorial Force, and Volunteers of 1914 and 1915 during the Great War in France and Flanders 1914–1918" *Lancashire History Quarterly* Vol. 8 Issues 2 and 3, 2004
Green, A.S., "Sir James Edmonds and the Official Histories of the Great War 1915 1948" Unpublished PhD thesis University of Leeds, 1999

Gregson, A.S., "The British League of Help for devastated Areas of France: A forgotten memorial of the Great War" *Stand To! The Journal of the Western Front Association* No.66, January 2003

Grieves, K., "The Liverpool Dock Battalion: Military intervention in the Mersey Docks 1915–1918" *Transactions of the Historical Society of Lancashire and Cheshire* Vol. 131, 1982

——" 'There are times when we would all prefer the factory life': letters from the trenches to the Shippam Works in Chichester during the First World War" *Family and Community History* Journal of the Family and Community Historical research Society, Vol. 6, No. 1, May 1993

——"Military Tribunal papers: the case of Leek Local Tribunal in the First World War" *Archives: the Journal of the British Records Association* Vol. xvi, No. 70, October 1983

Humphrys, B.P., "Experiences of and attitudes towards working class women in Liverpool and its surrounding areas during the First World War" Unpublished MA dissertation University of Lancaster, 1984

Hussey, J., "A contemporary record or post-war fabrication? The authenticity of the Haig diaries for 1914" *Stand To! The Journal of the Western Front association* No. 42, January 1995

Inglis, K.S., "The Homecoming: the War Memorial movement in Cambridgeshire, England" *Journal of Contemporary History,* Vol. 27, No. 4, 1992

Jeudwine, H.S.J., "An Episode of the German Offensive of 1918 – the Lys Offensive of April 1918" *Royal United Services Institute Journal,* Vol. 73, No. 498, 1928

Joyce, P., "The end of Social History?" *Social History,* Vol. 20, No. 1

Kavanagh, G., "Museum as Memorial: The Origins of the Imperial War Museum" *Journal of Contemporary History,* Vol. 23 No. 1, 1988

Levine, P., " 'Walking the streets in a way no decent women should': Women police in World War One" *Journal of Modern History,* Vol. 66, No. 1, 1994

Lewis, B.F., Adoptive Kinship and the British League of Help: Commemoration of the Great War through the Adoption of French Communities, Unpublished PhD thesis, Reading University, 2006

McCartney, H The 1/6th and 1/10th Battalions of the King's (Liverpool) Regiment in the period of the First World War Unpublished PhD thesis, Cambridge, 2001

Moore, Lt. Col. A.J., "The Territorial Battalions of the King's" *Stand To!: The Journal of the Western Front Association,* No. 49, April 1997

Mor – O'Brien, A., "A community in Wartime: Aberdare and the First World War" Unpublished PhD thesis University College, Swansea, 1986

Moriarty, C., "Christian iconography and First World War Memorials" *Imperial War Museum Review,* 1992

Morris, P., "Leeds and the Amateur Military Tradition: The Leeds Rifles and their Antecedents, 1859–1918" Unpublished PhD, Leeds University, 1983

Mutch, A., "Rural Society in Lancashire 1840–1914" Unpublished PhD thesis, University of Manchester, 1980

Orr, NG., "Keep the home fires burning: Peace Day in Luton 1919" *Family and Community History*, Vol. 2/1, May 1999
Osborne, J.M., "The Voluntary Recruiting Movement in Britain 1914–16" *Modern British History*, Vol. 5, 1982
Panayi, P., "The Lancashire ant-German riots of May 1915" *Manchester Region History*, Vol. 2, 1988, pp. 3–11
Pandrich, B.F.J., "Dundee's Flodden – the Battle of loos: a sociological study through the written word" Unpublished PhD thesis, Dundee University, 1988
Sheffield, G.D., "Officer-men Relations, Morale and Discipline in the British Army 19902 – 1922" Unpublished PhD thesis, King's College, London, 1994 (later published as *'Leadership in the Trenches'* op cit.)
Slocombe, I., "Recruitment into the armed forces during the First World War: the work of the Military Tribunals in Wiltshire, 1915–1918" *The Local Historian,* Vol. 30, No. 2, February 2000
Spinks, P., "'The War Courts': the Stratford-upon-Avon Borough Tribunal 1916–18" *The Local Historian*, Vol. 32, No. 4, November 2000
Stephens, A.P., "Dock Labour in the Port of Liverpool 1890–1914" Unpublished MSocSc thesis, University of Birmingham, 1981
West, J., "A book of Remembrance" *Local History,* January/February 1998
Wilton, D., "'Their name liveth': Analysing the Approaches to First World War Remembrance using records in Liverpool and Worcester" Unpublished MARM thesis, Liverpool University, 1998
Woodeson, A., "The First Women Police: A Force for Equality or Infringement?" *Women's History Review,* Vol. 2, No. 2
Woollacott, A., " 'Khaki fever' and its Control: Gender, Class, Age and Sexual Morality on the British Homefront in the First World War "*Journal of Contemporary History,* Vol. 29, 1994
Wynne, G.C., "The Legacy" *Army Quarterly,* Vol. XXXVII, No. 2, October 1939

Index

INDEX OF PEOPLE

INDEX OF PLACES

INDEX OF MILITARY UNITS & FORMATIONS

INDEX OF GENERAL & MISCELLANEOUS TERMS

CPSIA information can be obtained
at www.ICGtesting.com
Printed in the USA
BVHW04*1528100818
523878BV00007B/53/P

9 781911 512165